love & courage

MY STORY OF FAMILY, RESILIENCE, AND OVERCOMING THE UNEXPECTED

A MEMOIR

Jagmeet Singh

Published by Simon & Schuster

New York   London   Toronto   Sydney   New Delhi

SIMON &
SCHUSTER
CANADA

Simon & Schuster Canada
A Division of Simon & Schuster, Inc.
166 King Street East, Suite 300
Toronto, Ontario M5A 1J3

This Simon & Schuster Canada edition April 2019

SIMON & SCHUSTER CANADA and colophon are trademarks of Simon & Schuster, Inc.

For information about special discounts for bulk purchases, please contact Simon & Schuster Special Sales at 1-800-268-3216 or CustomerService@simonandschuster.ca.

Interior Design by Carly Loman

Library and Archives Canada Cataloguing in Publication

Title: Love & courage : my story of family, resilience, and overcoming the
    unexpected / by Jagmeet Singh. Other titles: Love and courage
Names: Singh, Jagmeet, 1979– author.
Identifiers: Canadiana (print) 20190074191 | Canadiana (ebook) 20190074272
    | ISBN 9781982105396 (softcover) | SBN 9781982105402 (ebook)
Subjects: LCSH: Singh, Jagmeet, 1979– | LCSH: Lawyers—Canada—Biography. |
    LCSH: Politicians—Canada— Biography. | LCSH: Sikhs—Canada—Biography.
    | LCSH: South Asians—Canada—Biography. | CSH: Sikh Canadians—Biography |
    South Asian Canadians—Biography
Classification: LCC FC656.S56 A3 2019 | DDC 971.07/4092—dc23

Manufactured in the United States of America

10 9 8 7 6 5 4 3 2 1

ISBN 978-1-9821-0539-6
ISBN 978-1-9821-0540-2 (ebook)

To my family

Contents

love & courage

Prologue

LOVE & COURAGE

Four months had passed since I'd made one of the biggest decisions of my life. I was running to become the eighth leader of one of Canada's largest political parties, the New Democratic Party. From the moment I announced my candidacy, I had been riding a wave of life-changing events, and on that particular day in September, there was another one in store for me.

It was a beautiful day—the kind when summer hasn't lost its hold and the weather seems to ignore that fall is just around the corner. I was heading to an event at Professor's Lake Recreation Centre in Brampton, Ontario. As I drove through the surrounding neighbourhoods, I looked out my window and took in the buildings where I'd held countless community events over the years, each one bringing together hundreds of constituents who made up one of Canada's most diverse communities. This was the riding I had represented for the past six years in the

Legislative Assembly of Ontario. The riding where my team and I had launched my leadership campaign.

Back then, in May 2017, pollsters gave us single-digit odds of winning. Analysts said I was too unknown, too inexperienced, too unrelatable. Columnists pointed to my turban and beard, and pondered whether a *very* visible minority could connect with all of Canada.

The past few months had been a blur of activity. In order to build the movement and create countrywide energy and excitement, we were holding events we playfully called "JagMeet and Greets" in communities as widespread as Duncan, BC, and Lunenburg, Nova Scotia. By that September day, my squad had signed up 47,000 new members—more than all the other NDP candidates combined. Our dream—to excite and invite a new generation of social democrats who believed in an inclusive Canada—was taking shape.

I felt my excitement building as I pulled into the park entrance and headed toward the recreation centre. We'd held events across the country, but this was the first official campaign stop in the city where it all started. Hosting an event in Brampton felt more like a homecoming party than another campaign stop. Behind the building's vine-covered glass walls, hundreds of our original supporters and volunteers, friends who'd been with me since the beginning, were ready to celebrate.

I glanced at my watch, a gift from my *bapu-ji*—my dad—on my sixteenth birthday, and saw that it was time to get inside. A volunteer in an orange T-shirt was waiting for me at the front. I turned the volume down on Post Malone's "Congratulations"— its contagious bravado and my non-stop playing of it made it our campaign's unofficial anthem—and rolled down the window. Before I could ask, he said, "Don't worry, I'll park it."

As he came around to the driver's side, I adjusted my bright yellow turban in the rear-view mirror. I hopped out of the car and hustled up the concrete stairs toward the rec centre doors. Before I reached them, though, a woman in a black T-shirt stopped me.

"Oh, hey," she said, casually puffing a cigarette. "Are you headed upstairs?"

"Yes, I am."

"Can we ask you questions?"

"Now?"

"No, during the event."

"Yes, you'll be able to ask questions."

"Okay," she said, and stepped aside.

As soon as I got inside, Hannah Iland, my campaign tour director, spotted me and escorted me to the ballroom. "Heads up," she said, "there's a local TV station that wants to broadcast the speech so we need you to carry two mics." She led me to the doorway. "We'll announce you in a few seconds," she said.

I peeked over her shoulder and scoped out a room filled with the bright faces of so many loved ones, and people who I had grown to know well over the past six years as a politician. I also caught a glance of the emcee, Gurkiran Kaur, the woman I was going to ask to marry me as soon as this crazy campaign was over. Hearing her introduce me to my supporters made the moment—and our future plans—all the more special.

When I walked onstage, the applause was overwhelming. Gurkiran handed me the two microphones with the signature affectionate look she gives me—a twinkle in her eye, a wink without winking. While trying to keep our relationship private so as not to cause any distractions from the campaign, we'd perfected our own sign language, a way of exchanging positive vibes without being overt about it.

I returned her glance and tested the mics on the crowd. "Wow, this is amazing," I said, taking a moment to try to pick out my parents in the crowd of a hundred. "First question, does my voice carry better this way, or—"

"It carries great," called a voice too clear to be from the crowd. I looked to my right and noticed the same woman who'd stopped me outside. She was striding over so quickly that her pace and proximity to me took me aback. As she spoke, her hands waved wildly and her head jerked from side to side. Her stream of words poured so fast I had a hard time grasping them.

"Hi, my name's Jennifer, I asked about a questions process, there isn't one, so I'm asking you now—"

"Hold on, one second, hold on," I said, squeezing out the words between hers. I turned to the audience and tested the microphones again so that I could figure out what Jennifer wanted.

She stepped closer, head tilted, angrily pointing up and down. "We know you're in bed with sharia," she said.

Of course, I thought. This wasn't the first time in my life I had been confronted with Islamophobia, or suggestions that there was something wrong with me because of the way I looked, or fears that I was a terrorist or terrorist-sympathizer.

"When is your sharia going to end?" she asked, wagging a finger in my face.

I'd encountered hecklers like Jennifer (many of whom were

worse) throughout my life. In fact, several months earlier, the media scrum for our campaign launch had been delayed by a similar incident.

In that moment, I purposely didn't explain to Jennifer that I'm Sikh, not Muslim. Though I'm proud of who I am, throughout my life, whenever I've been faced with Islamophobia, my answer has never been "I'm not a Muslim," because hate is wrong, no matter who it's aimed at. When it comes to stopping fear and division, all of us, no matter who we are, have to stand together. History has shown that if you allow any sort of hate to take hold, it spreads like fire, burning people for their race, gender, economic status, or sexuality.

Jennifer kept ranting. "We know you're in bed with the Muslim Brotherhood. We know by your votes," she yelled, still inches from my face. She disparaged Muslims and me, associated me with Islamic extremism, and said I didn't support women's rights, growing increasingly hostile with each new accusation.

I wasn't worried for my safety—much of my life has been spent disarming aggressive people, and I've gotten pretty good at it—but I was worried that she'd ruin our celebration. So many people on my team had worked countless hours behind the scenes, in offices, and on doorsteps, but hadn't had a chance to come to our gatherings before that day. They and the many other supporters in the room deserved better than having their optimism derailed and drowned out by bigotry. I feared they'd walk away with a bitter taste in their mouths.

I knew I had to cool Jennifer down and respond in a way that made the room feel positive again, but the chances of turning it around slimmed with every second she seethed. When two campaign volunteers approached Jennifer and tried to shepherd her away, one of them gently touched her back. Jennifer spun around and snapped at him. "Don't touch me!" she screamed. "Don't anybody touch me, or I will contact the police immediately."

There were rows of phone cameras pointed at us now. *Great*, I thought, *YouTube's about to blow up with an angry white woman shouting down a turbaned, bearded politician and threatening to call the police.* I could sense the audience's unrest, too, and I began to worry for Jennifer; I feared someone in the audience might direct their impatience or anger at her. I didn't want that negativity to dictate the day. I wanted us all to remember why we were there, why we were doing this.

The reason was spelled out in two languages on orange signs all around me, but it didn't sink in until I caught the eye of my *bebey-ji*—my mom—in the crowd. She looked at me with that calm wisdom that's always there. I could see just a hint of encouragement, too. Suddenly, I remembered the lesson she'd repeated so many times to me: "*Beta*"—dear—"we are all one. We are all connected."

Thanks to my mom, the right words finally came to me. "What do we believe in?" I asked the room. "We believe in *love and courage*, right? Love and courage!"

A dear friend of mine who runs a creative agency had helped develop "Love and Courage" for the campaign, but to me, it was more than just a slogan. When my friend presented the idea to me, I felt those two terms captured more than just my motivation, more than just my journey—they perfectly encapsulated the lessons life taught me, my values, who I am, and the way I try to live my life.

"Love and courage." I repeated it until the crowd echoed

the message louder than I could with the microphones. They chanted and clapped so powerfully that it seemed to surprise the heckler, who spun around with her arms up, cheering along. Did she not understand why the room was chanting?

"We believe in love and courage," I said to everyone. "We believe in an inclusive Canada where no one's left behind."

It was in that moment that I finally looked Jennifer in the eyes. She wasn't intimidating or scary at all. She was just a fellow human, one who maybe had been hurt or had faced hardships, or for whatever reason had grown resentful of people who looked different from her. When I saw that, I wanted her to know that I loved her. That *we* loved her. That we welcomed her and that she belonged in our version of Canada, too.

"As Canadians, do we believe in celebrating all diversity?" I asked the audience. "Give a round of applause for all diversity." As the crowd applauded, I felt truly blessed that our supporters were living our campaign message, rather than just putting it on signs and in hashtags.

I was proud that everyone in the room had met hate with love. It was the courageous thing to do.

While Jennifer went on about my fictional ties to extremism, I countered with, "We welcome you. We love you. We support you, and we love you. Everyone in this room loves you, we all support you, we believe in your rights."

In the days and weeks following the incident, many people asked how I remained calm in the face of so much aggression. My answer was always the same: Think about all the people who feel like they don't belong. In my case, I was set apart by my beard, brown skin, turban, and a different-sounding name, but it might be the clothes you wear or the accent you speak with or how much you or your parents earn. When you feel like you don't belong, you can become like Jennifer, or you can come up with positive ways to disarm prejudice.

After reflecting, I realized that people were really asking me where my love and courage in the face of hate came from. And that was a more complex question to answer.

Sometimes, loving someone, even yourself, takes a lot of courage. There isn't a single moment when I realized that. Rather, it was a lesson I learned and relearned my entire life, sometimes the hard way.

My story is a Canadian story, a journey in a country where people who are as different from each other as me and Jennifer can both find our place. It's a story of my family and the ups and downs we faced together. Some parts of it are hard to tell and could be hard for some to read. But most of all, this is a story filled with love and courage, and how I came to understand that these two forces are inextricably connected.

Part One

Chapter One

A NEW WORLD

M y parents had to make a lot of tough decisions to give my siblings and me the life they thought we deserved. One of the hardest was saying goodbye when I was just a year old.

In the late 1970s, my parents, Jagtaran, "One Who Uplifts the World," and Harmeet, "Friend to the Infinite Divine," were living in a one-bedroom apartment in Scarborough, at the east end of Toronto. While Toronto was on track to becoming one of the most multicultural cities in the world, it sure didn't seem like it at the time. Sometimes, in the elevator or on the bus, my parents would see another minority. But most of the time, my parents felt that they always stood out.

To help themselves feel at home, my parents sought comfort in the food of their childhood. The apartment was often filled with the fragrance of coriander, cumin, turmeric, and cloves from the dishes my mother made. That fragrance would follow us for the rest of my family's lives together, through half a dozen homes and five cities. But back then, while they marvelled at the cleanliness and amenities of their apartment, they couldn't imagine building a family in its cramped quarters, with only a single bedroom.

My parents, like many new Canadians, had found the transition to Canada from Panjab in 1976 difficult. It probably didn't help that Canada effectively recognized none of their education or international experience. They were getting by on my mom's meagre salary as my dad tried to pass the medical exam that would allow him to practise as a doctor in Canada. They each worked hours upon hours each day, trying to get ahead in their adopted country so that they could settle down and, hopefully, start a family.

Despite their precarious financial situation, my father was anxious to have children sooner rather than later.

"We've been married a year. What's the hurry?" my mom asked. But this, she knew, was my father's nature. He was always trying to dream bigger. He always wanted to provide more for his family; he was driven. He never wanted to settle. In a way this was the polar opposite to my mom, who was almost always content. She might be the only woman on earth to describe her labour and delivery as "not that bad."

I was born on January 2, 1979, a sizeable nine pounds and five ounces. (Seriously, Mom? "Not that bad"?) My mom named me by combining both my parents' names: the *jag*, pronounced "jug" (the world) from my dad's name, Jagtaran, and *meet* (friend) from my mom's name, Harmeet, meaning "friend to the world."

For the first months of my life, I slept on a stack of blankets by my parents' bed. Although we didn't have a lot of money, I never wanted for the important things—food, warmth, love.

Still, my parents wanted their children to more than survive—they wanted us to thrive.

So in the winter of 1980, as I was learning to take my first tentative steps, my parents took a leap of their own. My dad had applied to universities from one end of Canada to the other for his residency, flying between provinces for interviews. The travel was costly enough as it was, and my mom's maternity leave had long since expired. They couldn't afford a babysitter, so my grandfather came from Panjab to help look after me.

There was a lot of uncertainty about where my family would end up, so my dad suggested to my mom that my grandfather take me to live in Panjab for however long it took for my parents to get settled. It wasn't unusual in Panjabi culture for grandparents to raise a child while the parents got established, but there would be eleven thousand kilometres between my mom and me, her first baby. The thought of being away from her *beta* for a week, let alone indefinitely, made her heart heavy. But she also knew I would be better off living in one place with my grandparents until my parents were more settled.

So, in late 1980, my mom kissed me goodbye and sent me to the airport in a taxi with my grandfather. As the car drove farther away from their apartment, she could feel a hole open up in her heart and grow with every mile between us.

"I never knew it would be that hard," she said later. "I was broken."

I had barely had time to get to know my home in Canada. But as my name said, I was a friend to the world, and I was about to learn just how big that world was.

—⁂—

My first years in Panjab are impossible for me to remember. But I often wonder if they left some unconscious imprint on me, some deeper sense of what my parents' lives were like before they came to Canada.

My parents were born in Panjab, which literally translates to "five rivers": *panj*, meaning five, and *ab*, meaning river. The region stretches across the plains just south of the Himalayan mountain range and is surrounded by China and Afghanistan. It was the frontier land through which ancient travellers typically made their way into the South Asian subcontinent. It was home to the first Sikh kingdom, created in the early nineteenth century by Maharaja Ranjit Singh, a leader renowned for his belief in pluralism and diversity. Sikhs made up less than 10 per cent of the population of that first Sikh kingdom, but because the realm was based on Sikh principles of equality and pluralism, all spiritual traditions, faiths, and religions had equal rights and held positions of power in the royal court and army.

The Sikh kingdom was the last territory to succumb to the British colonialism that swept across the South Asian subcontinent. Eventually, though, Maharaja Ranjit Singh's kingdom did fall to the British in 1849 as a result of treachery and deceit, as opposed to military defeat. The ensuing century of British rule forced the hundreds of distinct and proud kingdoms across the subcontinent to amalgamate.

While the British were successfully pushed out of South Asia, they left collateral damage in their wake. The departing British, as they did nearly everywhere in the world, drew up on the backs of napkins arbitrary lines for countries, creating divisions and conflict. The same centralized power structures used by the British continued, so minority languages, tribes, ethnic communities, and spiritual traditions continued to be marginalized. Once again, the rights and dignity of the many diverse populations, languages, and spiritual traditions of the subcontinent were an afterthought.

Those one hundred years of British rule were culturally, socially, and politically devastating to all South Asians. The impact of that century is still carried, felt, and remembered to this day. It's a scar that has healed, to a degree, but the mark remains nonetheless.

My father, Jagtaran Singh Dhaliwal, was born in the city of Barnala, Panjab, in 1950. His father, Shamsher Singh, had served in the military as an engineer before settling into a quieter life as a farmer. Shamsher Singh enjoyed farming, but he wanted his children to get educations. They could help tend the cows and harvest rice, wheat, and cotton, but they were never obliged to do so, and only after doing their homework.

My grandparents encouraged my father to break from the family's military tradition. During my father's childhood, through a combination of poor management, bad business decisions, and a lack of government policies to support local farmers, my grandfather had lost a lot of his inherited land. The possibility of building a secure future as a farmer diminished with each passing year, so my grandparents encouraged my father to find another path. They felt that a career as a physician would provide a more stable and financially rewarding future than farming or the military ever could.

My grandmother Jaswinder Kaur never went to university, but she had a formal education in Panjabi literature. She'd stay up late to help my dad with his homework. Whenever his eyelids got heavy or he grew bored with the material, she'd bring

15

him back to the books. "Son," she'd say, "this is the only way to a better life."

My father took those words to heart. He attended medical school in the royal city of Patiala. He wasn't the first in the family to make their mark on the city. Walking through the streets of Patiala, my father often passed by a statue of his grand-uncle Sardar Sewa Singh Thikriwala. Sewa Singh was a renowned freedom fighter and activist who championed greater civil and legal rights for the under-represented in Panjab. He advocated for more democratic representation, and he insisted that the Sikh places of prayer—known as *Gurdwaras*—that were controlled by the British at the time should instead be run by the local community. Sewa Singh's actions eventually drew the ire of the local king and his British supporters. The king imprisoned him, but that didn't stop my great-grand-uncle's efforts. While in jail, he went on a hunger strike to protest the mistreatment of the less fortunate around him. The hunger strike cost him his life, but his efforts for democratic reform and social justice were memorialized in the statue that the city built.

Sewa Singh's advocacy against British rule, though, was unusual in his family. His brothers served in the British Indian Army. For many Sikhs—who at one point made up more than half of the British Indian Army—this was a pragmatic decision. Soldiers got up to fifty-five acres of land for their service after they retired. Favoured officers like my great-grandfather, who rose to lieutenant, earned even more.

My grandfather Shamsher Singh had followed my great-grandfather's footsteps into the military. Even after he settled in the outskirts of Barnala not far from his lands near his village of Thikriwala, he never shook the regimented military lifestyle.

16

Every day he woke, showered, polished his shoes, and went to work—either driving the tractor or supervising the workers. After lunch, he had to have his nap. And every evening, he drank from the same shiny teacup, feet up.

My father's family was better off than most, but my dad still struggled with contentedness. He felt ashamed about broken furniture at home that they were unable to repair or replace, and that he couldn't afford a bicycle to ride to school. He felt embarrassed by what he perceived as his father's failures, each of which resulted in less and less land for the family to farm, meaning the family had less and less income.

Sikhi—or Sikh teachings, practices, and the Sikh way of life—should have helped my dad avoid focusing too much on these worries. But at the time, my father didn't give spirituality a lot of attention, nor did his parents give it much emphasis. He hadn't walked very far down the path—not yet.

Some of you reading this may have a clear picture of what Sikhi is, but some of you may not. It's one of the world's youngest religions, started in the fifteenth century. The founding principle is a belief in oneness—or *Ik Oankar*. It's a belief that deep down we are all connected. In fact, it's a belief that everything is connected: each of us human beings alongside the life forms and forces we share this planet with.

A common analogy used to understand the principle of oneness is to see yourself as a drop of water in the ocean. Individually, you are unique and separate, but together with all the other drops, we become an ocean. The goal isn't simply to understand this connection but to live and experience it through love—love for the universe and all things in it, love for yourself, and love for others.

According to Sikhi, if others suffer, you suffer with them. When you help others, you're helping yourself as well—because we are all connected. A belief in the oneness of humanity means ensuring everyone has justice and fairness in their lives. If we are all connected, then injustice against one of us is injustice against all of us. This is why Sikhs categorically reject inequality. The belief in oneness in Sikhi also promotes pluralism and respect for different beliefs, spiritualities, and religions. Sikhi doesn't ever seek to convert. We can all be different, equal, and connected.

One particularly pernicious form of inequality that continues to persist in the South Asian subcontinent is the caste system, a system of inequality based on race and class. People of a higher caste, often people with lighter skin, have access to more resources, while those of a lower caste, typically those with darker skin, are denied those resources. At one time, this meant that only higher castes could learn to read and write. Today, some lower castes are still denied the right to access the local village well, and they experience significant barriers to attaining work, education, and other necessities of life. One of Sikhi's goals is to abolish the caste system.

The names Singh and Kaur replace family names that might otherwise divide society by class. Singh, a title of royalty, is given to men, while Kaur, another title of royalty, is given to women. While in some cultures, women's family names are omitted from history as they marry and take their husband's surnames, in the Sikh tradition, women keep the title Kaur throughout their lives. This practice represents the belief that women are sovereign and complete regardless of age or marital status.

All of these Sikh beliefs were familiar to my father when he was young, even though he and his family were preoccupied with their struggles rather than the teachings. They were losing more and more and more land. My grandmother was worried that their financial security was in jeopardy. She needed to make sure my father had a bright future. She believed that the only path to a secure future for her son was by him becoming a doctor. At first, my father accepted his mom's belief that becoming a doctor was the surest way to achieve financial success. It literally came with a title and access to a promising career. Later on, though, my father embraced medicine not only as a ticket out of insecurity but as a ticket out of India itself.

His determination to leave his homeland only deepened near the end of his medical degree. More and more, the ever-present corruption that penetrated almost every aspect of daily life in India was wearing on him. In the Indian bureaucratic system, you had two ways of getting ahead: paying someone off, or becoming a sycophant.

"If you wanted to get posted in a city, you had to bribe someone to do it. Sometimes a bribe wouldn't be enough and you were also expected to lick someone's feet," my dad said. "Why get stuck in this nonsense or waste energy on asking why things had to be this way?"

After he graduated in 1976 with his MD, my dad purchased an ad in the English-language newspaper *The Tribune* that combined his two priorities—leaving India and getting married—and kept his posting brief:

Young Panjabi physician looking for a woman living outside of India.

—m—

When my mom, Harmeet Kaur, first arrived in Canada in 1976, the thing that struck her the most was the freedom of women. She grew up in a place where women had to think twice about taking a bus. You literally had to weigh the risk of getting sexually harassed with the need to get to your destination. Walking down the street or being out after dark alone were calculated risks women had to make daily. Sikhi's feminist tenets had fought hard against this injustice, but misogyny was still alive and well in South Asia.

Given where she'd grown up, the first time my mom stood in a grocery aisle in southern Ontario, she was amazed to see women carrying sanitary pads in plain view of other customers. Coming to Canada gave my mom access to a freedom she had never experienced and probably never even imagined.

My mom had arrived in Canada on a family visa. She was sponsored by her brother, who was sponsored by his sister, who was sponsored by her husband. On it went and would continue to go, uniting relatives in their adopted home. In the decades to come, the number of Panjabi-speaking Canadians would grow to be one of the largest minority groups in Canada. While the majority of Panjabi-speaking people clustered around the greater Toronto and Vancouver areas, they had a presence in every province. My mom's family, like so many others, built their community one person at a time.

Unlike my dad, my mom had grown up on a multigenerational farm where the children *were* expected to contribute to the family business on top of their schooling. All of the work—picking cotton, husking corn, harvesting wheat—was done by hand. Luckily, there were four generations living in their two-storey farmhouse at the time.

My mom's parents, Sarup Singh and Gurbachen Kaur, loved farming, but they knew the future was bleak. They didn't have the means to buy any more land, and while the land they did have was incredibly fertile, twelve or so acres wasn't enough for the eight children to divide up and establish their own families on. My grandmother was ambitious and, like my paternal grandmother, she taught herself to read and write in Panjabi and Urdu, a rarity among women in their working-class farming community. My grandmother enrolled my mom and her siblings in the local village school and encouraged them to pursue education as a path to a brighter future.

My mom was probably the first woman in her family to get a university education. She graduated with not one but two degrees: a bachelor of arts and a bachelor of education. Despite my mom's credentials, though, it was tough for her to find work in India. There were limited opportunities. She found a part-time teaching gig, but it wasn't enough to earn a real living. Her siblings in Canada told her she would have a better shot there. They sold the land of opportunities and my mom bought in.

To her surprise and disappointment, though, when my mom got to Canada, she found that job opportunities weren't quite as plentiful as her relatives had advertised. Though she was educated in English, she, like so many other new Canadians, was told that her degrees weren't recognized. She looked into getting recertified, but when she found out how expensive it was, she knew there was no way she could afford it.

Hearing the stories of my mother from this time, I always thought of one word: *resilient*. My mom is pretty much always content. Whatever the weather, no matter if she's hungry or full, tired or rested, she is almost always happy. It's what has allowed her to overcome so much in life. My mom was a young woman in a new country who had just found out that her hard-earned education was effectively worthless. For many people, that would be cause to lose hope. But not my mom. In fact, my mom's story isn't unique. So many new Canadians arrive with so much hope, only to find that none of their education or international experience is recognized in Canada. I'm in complete awe of all the people who persevered and never lost hope despite the odds.

My mother found a job in a factory that made curling irons. After working there for a couple of months, she started taking an IT course on the side, hoping it would help her land a job at a bank. She finally got the job, an entry-level clerical position, and joined the throngs of commuters working downtown. Sometimes, when we drive through downtown Toronto, my mom turns to me and says, with a shy touch of pride, "See that tall building over there? That's where I used to work." And when she thinks my siblings and I can't hear, or that it won't get back to us, she'll say the same thing about us: "See those kids? I raised them."

Later that year, my mom's sister went back to India to visit family.

"I will find you a suitable boy," my aunt told my mom, almost in passing. *Oh no big deal I'm going to find you your life partner take care, talk soon.* Sometimes it's hard to imagine the different world our parents come from and the completely separate realities they experienced. There were no telecommunications between Toronto and the family farm, and my mom couldn't afford to fly back with her sister. All she could do was give some broad criteria for what my aunt should look for: well-educated, good-looking, a practising Sikh who, obviously, didn't drink or smoke, and was willing to live in Canada.

In Panjab, a couple of weeks later, my aunt opened up a newspaper to the classified section and found my dad's advertisement. She sent a letter to my dad, and a few days later, he arrived for a visit. As a physician, he was considered a good catch. He had received letters with marriage proposals from families in the UK and the US, but found that Canada's multiculturalism appealed to him most. And when he saw a photo of my mom, with her smiling eyes, he knew his decision was made.

When my aunt returned to Toronto two months later, she gave my mom a picture of her new husband. It could have been anyone. But my mom found the positive, just like she does in any circumstance. (I'm probably being a little generous when I say "any" circumstance. I mean, I would have loved for her to find the positive in me receiving an 80 per cent on my eighth-grade geometry exam instead of a 90 per cent, but I guess I wouldn't have had the pleasure of geometry tutoring after school.) She was content with what she saw: a serious face, strong nose, sharp turban, and classy suit. She took the picture to the immigration office and filled out a sponsorship application.

—⁊⁊⁊—

The guy who arrived on my mom's doorstep four months later, in April 1977, wasn't quite the man in the picture. Though my dad struck a strong figure in a turban, he had transitioned to wearing it only occasionally during his last couple of years at medical school, and he had cut his hair, which meant he wasn't a fully practising Sikh. Instead of a proud mane, his beard was also cut short.

My dad certainly didn't behave the way my mom imagined a doctor would act. Her first impression was that he seemed a little gruff and abrupt. *Maybe it takes a while to start liking him,* she thought.

My parents had a small wedding ceremony and moved into their apartment in Scarborough. My dad immediately got busy studying for the Medical Council of Canada exam and its US equivalent, which would allow him to recertify in Canada and practise there. Every day, he'd pack a bologna sandwich and board the bus to the University of Toronto library to study, while my mom went off to her new job at CIBC. It was supposed to be temporary. In a few months, my dad assured her, he'd pass the exam, find a residency, and they'd be living more comfortably.

But my dad failed his first attempt at the MCC exam. He was educated in English, but a second language is a second language. The rigidness of multiple-choice tests—something he wasn't accustomed to—stumped him.

They continued to scrape by on my mom's modest monthly salary. To help make ends meet, my dad worked as a security guard. He would study by day and then pull twelve-hour night shifts on weekends and evenings, trying to cram in study sessions during his breaks. It was a demanding schedule, and more than once, a supervisor fired him for sleeping on the job.

"I'm a doctor, but I can't use what I've learned to help people," he'd lament to my mom. More than just a blow to his self-esteem, it was a blow to his sense of self.

My dad thought he'd have better luck passing the American medical exams, so shortly after I was born, he went to New Jersey for a three-month course. When he returned, my dad was certified for a US residency. But both he and my mom were still determined to live in Canada, close to my mom's family.

To do that, though, meant saying goodbye to me for a time. That was when my parents made the decision to send me to Panjab to live with our family there.

"It will only be for a little while," my mom explained to me, my one-year-old mind unable to understand. "And when you come back, we'll have a beautiful new home."

Whenever my mom recalls our separation—even now, decades later—all her nervous tics come out. My mom, who fluctuates between being bold and opinionated or warm and fuzzy, instead goes quiet and softly taps her moccasins on the floor. She smiles awkwardly out of the side of her mouth, a thing she does to lighten the stress in her life. Over the decades, I've caught her making this expression a lot. Back then, when she'd first said goodbye to me, she thought it was the hardest thing we would have to do as a family. But she had no idea just how bad things would get.

Chapter Two

CHARDI KALA—RISING SPIRITS

The eight months without me were some of the longest in my parents' lives. My dad channelled his intense ability to focus and was single-minded about passing the exam to recognize his medical degree. He had a deep desire to succeed. In his mind, passing the exam would give us the financial security he had pursued for so long. But he also felt the pressure of proving himself, proving that he could make it. "It's okay if your medical degree doesn't work out," his in-laws would say. "You can always get a job in a factory."

I know comments like those hurt my dad. They flew in the face of all the long hours of study and sacrifice it had taken him to get this far. He badly wanted to work in the field he had dedicated the majority of his academic life to. Failure was not an option. What might have started off as his mother's worry over financial security had blossomed into a love for healing and curing. It was prophetic, given his name, Jagtaran—one who uplifts the world. His work as a physician would be his contribution to lifting people up.

He finally got his break when he got the results of his most recent exam. He opened the letter hopeful about the results but with guarded optimism, having failed to reach the passing percentage so many times before. This time, though, he felt he had poured that much more of himself into his studies, and he was confident he would pass. He unfolded the letter and read the results. He had passed, with a solid score. His heart beamed with the satisfaction and pride of achieving a hard-won victory. My dad was back on track, and he could finally earn his place in the Canadian medical practice.

My mom continued to work at the bank, but she had lots of time to herself. She wished she was spending it with her little baby, but instead, she was knitting clothes for me.

"How big do you think he is now?" she'd ask my dad at dinner, showing him the hat she had knitted that day. "Do you think this will still fit when he comes back?"

"Let's just focus on getting him back," my dad would say.

My dad thought the next step in his medical career would be easy, but it proved to be its own challenge. He had earned the degree, passed the equivalence exam, and gained local experience—he felt it should be easy to get accepted for a residency program. He applied to a number of schools in a variety of different specialities, completed his residency interviews, and awaited the results. The first responses that he received were all rejections. They were polite and nicely worded, but rejections all the same. As the rejections piled up, he started to feel a little panicked, but he reassured himself that he had applied to a lot of programs. Finally, in November 1980, my father received an acceptance letter from the medical school of Memorial University of Newfoundland, St. John's. It felt like he'd won the lottery. He quickly accepted the residency, specializing in psychiatry, and cancelled his remaining applications.

A few weeks later, my parents made the trek to St. John's. My mom and dad found a two-bedroom apartment and furnished it with a new mattress, a second-hand dining set, and a couch. Right after getting things settled in St. John's, my dad boarded another flight, this time to Panjab to pick me up from my grandparents, while my mom stayed behind to unpack the few boxes and suitcases in our new home. I can just imagine my dad's excitement and sense of accomplishment. He had made it, and now was going to pick up his son. He was well and truly on his path to a bright future in Canada.

—⁕—

We were all finally reunited in St. John's a couple of days before my second birthday. I was hobbling around in the snow and speaking full sentences in Panjabi.

"*Bhua*," I apparently said to my mom, using the word I would for my father's sister, "*aho soor morden chaliyeh.*" *Let's chase the pigs out of the field.* In Panjabi, there's a different word for almost every relationship. Aunts who are your mom's sisters are called *masi*, while aunts on your dad's side are called *bhua*, and grandparents are called something specific, depending on whether they're your mom's or dad's parents.

I'm sure it hurt a little when I called my mom "auntie" instead of "mom," but she let it go. My mom was just happy to have me back and loved that I was speaking Panjabi. My father, though, was a little more worried. He was adamant that we should speak only in English at home.

"How is he supposed to go to school?" he said to my mom. "The teachers don't speak Panjabi." My mom eventually conceded, and English became the first language in our house. Later on, though, my parents would regret their decision. Growing up surrounded by English, it was inevitable that I'd quickly adapt and learn the new language. But forgetting Panjabi meant I lost a little bit of myself and my ability to connect to my roots. It also meant I lost an important connection to my parents. My parents speak English fluently, but you can connect with someone on a completely different level when you speak in the language in which they feel most comfortable expressing themselves. There aren't any guidebooks on how to build a new life in a brand-new country in a language you've only ever studied in school. These were just the learning pains my family came to accept.

My first years in St. John's were blissful. As chance would have it, other South Asian doctors-in-training had found their way to Newfoundland. My dad was studying with a few doctors from different parts of South Asia, even a couple from Panjab. My parents had grown up in villages and cities where people from different faiths were neighbours and close family friends, and they were delighted to find out that St. John's was no different. My earliest memories were playing with the children of my father's colleagues, kids who were Hindu, Sikh, and Christian, and Hindi-, Panjabi-, and Telegu-speaking. All of our families regularly gathered for social evenings and delicious food. At least once a week, I'd stuff myself with chicken curry, aloo gobi (potato and cauliflower stew), saag (stewed spinach), and other delicacies.

I made my first friend in Canada in that St. John's apartment, too. Tim and I used to play with our toys in the stairwell until his parents or mine would call us home for dinner. While I was probably one of the only brown kids in the apartment, I remember playing with the other kids and never really noticing that I looked different. St. John's gets heavy snowfall, so we made use of the winter wonderland. We built snow forts and dug tunnels. I'd spend all day playing outside with the other kids in the building until my mom called out, "Jimmy!"

Yes, that really was my name growing up. My full name is Jagmeet Singh Jimmy Dhaliwal. When I was born, my parents were still struggling with their identity in their adopted land and were even more confused about the identity of their child. So, in order to keep my options open, my parents gave me a Western name in addition to my Sikh one. And when my siblings came along, my parents did the same thing. I was two years old when my sister, Manjot, was born, and they gave her the name Mona. Then, on Mother's Day in 1984, my brother, Gurratan— or Gary, as my parents called him—was born.

Each day, my world grew a little more. I started school not long after Gurratan was born, and I loved it. More important, though, I met my first crush. There was a girl named Sunali in my kindergarten class, and even though we were young, she carried herself with confidence. Of course, that meant that many of the other boys in the class bothered her non-stop—I think most of them had crushes on her and just didn't know how to show it. One day, a couple of boys were being more aggressive than usual toward her, pulling her hair and teasing her. I saw that they were upsetting her, so I walked up to them, pushed them away, and yelled, "Stop!" The boys looked stunned and shuffled away. Sunali looked over at me and thanked me, and I think my heart stopped for a moment.

My parents seemed similarly happy. The residency program at the university started my dad on a basic stipend, which grew a little every year. For the first time in his adult life, "Dr. Dhaliwal" felt good about his situation. We were financially comfortable, my dad had a car and a place for his family to live, and my mother was able to spend time with her children and especially care for Gurratan, who was still an infant just learning to crawl.

Though we were comfortable, our little family was growing fast and our apartment was getting a little cramped. So my father applied for a student residence on the hospital grounds and, not long after, we moved into a new home. The extra space was nice, but what I was most excited about was that our new house was literally across the street from Bowring Park.

When you're young, everything appears bigger than it actually is. But in the case of Bowring Park, my memory wasn't skewed by my youthful age—it really is massive, more like a conservation area than a park. For kids like me and my siblings, who'd only known cramped apartment buildings, this was like suddenly finding ourselves footsteps away from Neverland. Fitingly, there was a life-size statue of Peter Pan by the duck pond, an outdoor pool, as well as walking trails that wound through a forest of birch, maple, and spruce trees.

My dad loved having a family, and was always incredibly generous, but it was my mom who spent the most time raising us. She was basically a nutritionist, chef, driver, conflict resolution professional, and early childhood educator all in one. The last role, in particular, she embraced, as it allowed her to put her training as a teacher to work.

As soon as I could hold a pencil, my mom made me practise writing out the alphabet and the numbers one to one hundred. A common refrain from me and my siblings growing up was, "Why do I have to learn this? They're not even teaching us this in school!" But our complaints always fell on deaf ears. My mom had a passion for learning, and she was determined to pass it on to her children.

By the time I was in first grade, I was able to read Robert Munsch books on my own. When she saw that, my mom figured it was time to resurrect my Panjabi.

She started by incorporating Panjabi phrases back into our conversations. I don't remember the earliest phrases, but growing up there were a couple that stood out. One phrase in particular was one of her favourites, "*Do akhar pardia kar?*" (Why don't you study?) (Or, more literally, "Why don't you read two letters?") It was a phrase that came up often—my mom said it every time she thought we were wasting our time not learning something useful, but mostly it felt like she used it as a proxy for "study for your exams." It was her way to remind us to study so we would do well in school. I heard "*Do akhar pardia kar?*" throughout my educational life, from elementary school all the way to law school.

She even used it on me when I was a lawyer with my own practice. "*Do akhar pardia kar?*" my mom said one day while I was sitting on the couch watching a movie on TV.

I was caught off guard. I panicked for a second, thinking I had forgotten about an upcoming exam. I had been in school for so much of my life.

"*Bebey-ji*, I'm done with school, remember? No more exams, I don't need to study anymore," I replied with a smile and a light chuckle, relieved that there wasn't an exam I had overlooked.

My mom looked at me thoughtfully.

"So?" she said. "Just because you're done with school doesn't mean you stop learning. You should always be learning. Learning never stops."

She had me there. It's tough to argue with that. Here I thought she had momentarily forgotten I wasn't in school anymore. Instead she was still dropping wisdom on me.

Not long after reintroducing Panjabi into our day-to-day lives, my mom moved on to giving me actual Panjabi lessons. She started by introducing me to a little Gurmukhi, the alphabet and writing used in Panjabi but also in Sikh poetry. Beyond just language, she used Gurmukhi to help me better understand Sikhi. She began by introducing me to the Sri Guru Granth Sahib, the spiritual guide and teacher for Sikhs. Well, not the *whole* Guru Granth Sahib, which consists of 1,430 pages of love songs and poetry aimed at helping one walk down the path of love to experience oneness with the universal energy. She started me off with the basics. She taught me to read ੴ, *Ik Oankar*, the first word written in the Guru Granth Sahib. The symbol ੴ has two parts. The first is the number one, and the second is a character that means the infinite sound or energy of the universe. Read together, this has many meanings—"there is one infinite energy," or as my mom taught me, "we are all one." I didn't know it at the time, but I would spend the rest of my life hearing this phrase and reflecting on what it meant.

My mother also taught me a couple of other words, and we

would play a game. My mom would open up a page of a book containing excerpts from the Guru Granth Sahib and see if I could find the word, like literary hide-and-seek.

I loved the game, but improving my Panjabi was a slow process. My parents, who regretted not speaking Panjabi at home, had gradually transitioned back to speaking to us in a mix of Panjabi and English, but my siblings and I hadn't caught up. We were stuck in a communication stalemate—my parents talking in Panjabi, we kids in English. Even with my mom's patient teaching, I couldn't help but mix it with English. It wasn't a conscious decision. Hearing my parents speak it in public didn't embarrass me, as it sometimes can for the children of immigrants. The words just didn't feel natural anymore.

Still, I loved hearing the language around me, and the more my parents spoke it, the more it helped kindle a love for languages. Even knowing only rudimentary Panjabi, I had learned that certain phrases just couldn't be translated. One Panjabi saying in particular really made the point. If you want to really encourage someone, to give them that extra boost to take on a challenge or push themselves beyond their limits, you would say, "*Chakk de phatte.*" It was amazing how motivating the phrase was whenever I heard it in Panjabi. When I learned the English translation—"pick up the wooden boards"—I almost laughed. Needless to say, it doesn't quite have the same beauty or motivation in translation.

That love of language would follow me throughout my schooling. Years later, just before I entered high school, one of my teachers told me that I could move into an advanced French class the next year, but only if I took extra credits over the summer. She also recommended listening to French music and watching French television and films. I jumped at the chance. I had been captivated by Quebec history and saw a lot of similarities between the minority-language struggles of Québécois and what my parents experienced growing up as minority-language speakers in South Asia. I enjoyed speaking French and found it a beautiful language. I thought my parents might find it odd that I was so into learning French.

"You should absolutely do it," my dad said. "We'll even get you a tutor."

"Seriously?" I replied.

"It is a language you need in Canada," my mom said matter-of-factly, her eyes lighting up at the prospect of me doing something productive over the summer.

"The more languages you learn, the better," my dad added.

I guess their support wasn't really a surprise. My dad wanted us kids to have every opportunity and would sacrifice anything for his kids, and my mom was passionate about learning.

The next day, my dad gave me money so I could buy Patrick Bruel and Roch Voisine cassettes at the local mall, and over the coming months, my parents encouraged me whenever I turned the channel to Radio-Canada or rented a French movie from the library.

Later, my dad admitted he had an ulterior motive in supporting my French lessons. He thought that learning French might encourage me to learn Panjabi. I'm not sure how he drew that connection. There are some key similarities between the languages—they share the use of feminine and masculine prepositions and nouns. But it didn't work the way my dad intended. It wasn't until I was in university and became friends with more Panjabi people my age that I started speaking the language regularly, listening intently to my friends' words and trying to respond.

I wish I had learned Panjabi as a kid and that I had taken my mom's Panjabi lessons more seriously. I truly believe you can never fully connect with someone unless you speak the language they grew up speaking, the language they dream in. If you love someone's language, truly love it, then you'll find a door to their culture, identity, and what makes them who they are. Recently, in 2014, when I was hanging out with my parents and cracking jokes in Panjabi with them, what I'd been missing as a kid hit home. Not speaking my parents' language had left a gulf between them and me. When I finally spoke our mother tongue with my parents, I felt a new bond form between us.

I mentioned this regret in passing to someone. I can't even recall his name, but I wish I could because I want to credit him with what he taught me. He said that I shouldn't regret the fact that I didn't learn Panjabi growing up. I looked at him, confused, and asked, "Why not?"

"Your journey to learn Panjabi now has instilled a deep appreciation for the language. Now you see the benefit and beauty of the language in a way far more profound than you would have before," he said. "In a way, the lack of Panjabi in your childhood has helped create a love for the language in your adulthood."

—m—

There was another Panjabi expression I heard a lot growing up: *chardi kala*.

It was one of the phrases my mom taught me. At first, I thought it meant "happy" or "content."

I had just returned from a fun day hanging out with my friends when my mom asked me how I was doing.

"I'm in *chardi kala*," I said to my mom. I had been to the park.

"*Beta*, that's not *chardi kala*."

"What is it, then?" I asked.

She paused for a moment, searching for the words. "It's maintaining rising spirits when things aren't going well," she explained. "When the odds are against you, or you're feeling a bit defeated, but you still believe you can take that next step forward. That is *chardi kala*."

In 1984, when I was five years old, my parents tapped into the deeper meaning of this phrase.

It was that June that thousands upon thousands of Sikhs gathered to celebrate an annual commemoration at Sri Harmandir Sahib—the "Temple of the Infinite Divine," also commonly known as the Golden Temple, in Amritsar, Panjab. The complex includes the Sri Harmandir Sahib and Akal Takht Sahib. Together they represent the global Sikh centre of spiritual and political sovereignty. The Indian government claimed there was a group of political dissidents residing in the *Gurdwara*, and they launched a full-scale military assault on June 5, 1984. This was a day of historical significance for Sikhs, a day when thousands and thousands of attendees would be visiting the Harmandir Sahib. Harmandir Sahib is widely considered the most important *Gurdwara* to Sikhs.

The word *Gurdwara* literally translates to "gateway to enlightenment." But the thousands of people seeking enlightenment that day were trapped. Bullets and heavy artillery ripped through the crowds of innocent men, women, and children who were gathered there, while munitions devastated historic structures and tanks crushed the stone and marble floor. There was no reason for the full military assault. There was also no opportunity for attendees who were in no way the subject of India's concern to flee.

After the attack, the Indian government ordered a media blackout in Panjab. Human rights organizations and media were unable to provide any details on what had happened beyond the fact that the Golden Temple, along with approximately seventy other *Gurdwaras* in Panjab, were attacked. The exact loss of life was unknown and would long remain so. At the time, the Indian government claimed it was in the hundreds, but other independent estimates, given the number of people attending, placed the number in the thousands. To Sikhs, this was as heinous as if the Canadian government ordered the armed forces to attack a Roman Catholic cathedral during Easter Sunday mass.

Disturbed, terrified, and outraged at what had happened, Sikhs took to the streets of Los Angeles, Toronto, London— everywhere Sikhs had emigrated. Even St. John's. My parents and about twenty Sikhs gathered around the front steps of the Newfoundland and Labrador Confederation Building, picket signs in one hand, infants in the other. Those of us old enough to walk were sent to play in a nearby park while our parents chanted "Equal rights for Sikhs!"

It was a tiny but emotional protest that few would have noticed had a local news van not pulled up to cover it. The group asked my father to speak on behalf of them.

"How do you feel?" the reporter asked my dad.

"I feel terrible," he responded. "We're being killed, Sikhs are being killed. The Indian government ordered the military to attack a place of prayer. We still don't know how many people were killed. All I know is that it could have been me and my family if we were still living in Panjab."

My dad wasn't the only one who felt that way. Every Sikh, if they can, visits the Sri Harmandir Sahib, so the massacre cast a shadow over all of us. It would not be the last of the Indian state's brutality against Sikhs, either, though it was the last time my dad spoke openly about it for a long time.

My parents did their best to protect me and my siblings from their trauma, but even as a young boy, I could sense that, beneath their silence, they were deeply hurt and sad. There'd been genocidal campaigns of violence against the Sikhs in Delhi and throughout Panjab, including the Sri Harmandir Sahib and Alkal Takht Shahib complex. My parents would look at me and my siblings with profound relief and gratitude. We were safe. We were alive. In the years after the massacre at the Golden Temple, any time a news report about the incident resurfaced, they would hug us tight and say, "We're so happy that Canada is our home." Even as a young boy, I could sense that they didn't mean that lightly. They were thankful just to be alive and that we were all safe in a country that respected human rights and the dignity of life. Each day, my parents took another step forward, showing me that, in the face of trauma, there was only one response: *chardi kala*.

The Golden Temple Massacre was a front-page story, and led news segments. The footage flashed before my five-year-old eyes, although my comprehension was far from clear. While shots echoed non-stop like fireworks, soldiers stomped the ground with disturbing calmness. I saw flames spilling through the arched doorways and smoke billowing from every opening. Some walls were pocked with bullet holes. Others, completely toppled. Children not much older than me marched out with their arms over their heads, flinching from the sounds of explosions.

To say the massacre of the Sri Harmandir Sahib left an impression on me as a child is an understatement. It would be more accurate to describe it as a scar I carried with me, a reminder of the suffering and the horrible impact of hatred and violence.

Chapter Three

IMMIGRANT AMBITION

After my dad's residency in St. John's came to an end, we were on the move. With the help of our family friends, we packed a U-Haul trailer and drove four hours north along a scenic road to Grand Falls, a small mill town in Newfoundland. Grand Falls was the province's fifth-largest community and provided critical services for tens of thousands of people in central Newfoundland. My dad had been hired as head of the psychiatric ward. He felt immediately empowered by such an important job, which had him supervising social workers and psychologists. But it was also a temporary position, so we knew we wouldn't be there forever.

We didn't let that stop us from making new friends, though. The hospital put us up in a staff residence on a street with three or four other physicians and their families, all of whom were South Asian and who were also recent graduates from Memorial. Our families regularly gathered together, the parents bonding around dishes inspired by recipes from across the South Asian subcontinent while we kids watched Phil Collins and Madonna music videos in the basement. Other times, we'd venture out together to experience novel things like Bonfire Night. When we moved away from Newfoundland and Labrador a few years later, I was surprised and disappointed to learn that the province's tradition of massive bonfires, singing, and dancing in November hadn't made it to the rest of the country.

The kids on the block all played together in a ragtag group of mixed ages. They were happy to include Manjot and me. We rode our bikes, played tag, and got into all sorts of adventures. Gurratan was only about two years old at the time, so we played with him at home.

There were also two girls who I was always trying to hang out with. Fine, I had a crush on them, especially the taller one of the two. She would often ask me to run down to the nearby corner store to get some candy.

"Jimmy, can you buy us some candy with this?" she'd ask, handing me a $1 bill. (At 1 cent a piece, one dollar got you a lot of candy in 1985.)

I'd race down to the store and back. I'd return with a twisted-up sandwich bag bulging with candy, my heart pounding as I handed it over to my crush.

"Thanks, Jimmy," she said with a playful smile. "I guess I owe you a kiss. I'll give it to you sometime."

That was fine with me. And believe it or not, sometimes, when I least expected it, she would actually give me a little peck on the cheek when I got back from a candy run. And those moments were sweeter than all the candy in the world.

A few months later, toward the end of my dad's contract in Grand Falls, he sat us down at the kitchen table.

"I have a new job at a hospital in Windsor," my dad said, trying to put it in terms that my siblings and I would understand. "I'm going to be making more money."

"It will be good for all of us," my mom added. "It's a much bigger city."

"What about my friends?" I asked.

"You'll make lots of new friends," my mom said with a smile. "And we'll have what's most important—each other."

Groan.

I was a little sad when I heard that I'd be leaving my new friends so soon. But each night at dinner, we'd talk about what our new life would look like in Windsor, and I got more and more excited about what was in store.

Just before we left, my father's colleagues threw us a going-away party. My crush was there, and I knew it was probably the last time I would ever see her. I had a plan, but it took me all night to work up the courage to approach her. Finally, I found a moment when it was just the two of us alone in the kitchen. *Here goes nothing*, I thought.

"You know, you still owe me a lot of kisses," I said, trying to play it cool.

"You're right, Jimmy," she said, smiling. She looked around to make sure we were alone. "Come here."

My stomach was doing flips. "Okay—"

Before I could finish my sentence, she leaned in and gave me my first real kiss. It was still more like a peck, but it made my head spin nonetheless. My crush turned and walked back into the party, but I stood still for a moment. I didn't know what life would be like in Windsor, where we would live, or who my new friends would be. All I knew was that, thanks to the move, I'd got a kiss on the lips.

—⬩⬩⬩—

When we landed at the Windsor airport in 1986, the first thing that went through my mind was, *Wow, this is pretty fancy.* The cities I was used to seeing were much smaller by comparison, so the bustling terminal made me feel like we'd landed in an entirely different world.

Our home that first night was decidedly more modest: a motel close to the airport. Still, even that had an air of excitement to me and my siblings—in my seven-year-old mind, it wasn't every day you got to live in a motel. We stayed there for almost a month until my parents bought a modest bungalow, which meant I had to change schools again. I had been in second grade for only a month when I transferred to Sandwich West Public School to finish off the year.

My parents were actively on the lookout for another home, though, something that my dad really liked. And before long, they found it. As my dad tells the story, there was a newly developed suburb of South Windsor he particularly liked. He would drive through the neighbourhood regularly, and one day, he saw a FOR SALE sign in front of a two-storey home. He immediately called the real estate agent and put a down payment on the house. During summer break a few weeks later, we moved into our dream house.

I try to put myself in my dad's shoes in that moment. He had come to a brand-new country where none of his education and work experience had been recognized. He'd fought to secure a place for himself and his family. Finally, after all of his hard work, he had found a house for his family, one where we could now start to make a home.

Our dad took us to see the home for the first time just before he closed the deal, and I couldn't believe what I saw: a white brick house with red shingles on a huge corner lot. It was stately, with arched lintels and French panes on opposite wings. There were beautiful trees on the front lawn, which I immediately knew would be great for climbing. The inside was even more impressive in my eyes. A chandelier floated halfway to the floor from twenty-foot-high ceilings. Manjot, Gurratan, and I each had our own bedroom on the second level, which encircled a dark wood staircase draped in a royal blue carpet. There was a formal living room and a more casual family room on the first floor. The backyard was huge and wide—perfect for my dad's future plans, which included a swimming pool surrounded by a large wooden patio.

The end of second grade and the beginning of third grade meant some big changes for us as a family: a new house, a new school for Manjot and me. But it also meant a lot of changes for me personally. It was at the end of second grade that I made two big life decisions. I decided to change my name and stop cutting my hair.

Hair—or, more specifically, keeping it or not—was a special point of contention between my parents. My mom never cut my hair, but my dad didn't feel bound by that belief. When he brought me back from living with my grandparents in Panjab, my unshorn hair was tied up in a little bun on top of my head. Before we went to the airport, he took me to a barber to cut it off. Whenever my hair was cut, my mom would leave the room so we wouldn't see how upset she was. To her, hair was part of nature, and nature was a part of the universe, so our hair wasn't ours to alter.

But my dad was concerned with how I was perceived. He understood what it was like to feel like you didn't belong—because of your accent, the colour of your skin, or the country from which you obtained your degree. He didn't want to give people a reason to leave me out. He wanted me to know what it felt like to belong.

But I liked my hair. There wasn't anything particularly spiritual to my attitude—I just liked having my hair long. My mom subtly suggested that part of the Sikh tradition was not only keeping one's hair long but tying it up in a topknot.

"Do you want to start keeping your hair long and tying it up?" she asked me one day.

"Sure!" I said. Not long after, I started tying up my hair and wearing a *patka*, a smaller head covering worn by Sikh children. Though my mom encouraged me, it was a choice I was happy to make. Once it was clear it was what I wanted to do, true to form, my dad supported me without question.

There was something else on my mind, though. "I don't want to be Jimmy anymore," I told my parents. "I want to be called Jagmeet."

That surprised them. I had gone by Jimmy for my entire life until this point. I didn't mind the name—in fact, there was a WWF wrestler named Jimmy Superfly Snuka, and I thought it was cool that I had the same name as a wrestler. Still, I had always felt that Jimmy was more of a nickname than a proper name.

"Why do you want to change what you're called?" my mom asked.

"I just don't feel like a Jimmy anymore," I said. "I feel like Jagmeet."

Even at eight years old, I liked the idea of defying expectations, and I had always loved the fact that Jagmeet means "friend to the world."

When we arrived in Windsor, the automotive sector was still steady. The major employers in the city were the big three car companies: GM, Ford, and Chrysler. The working-class city had a strong union movement, and many people had access to good-paying jobs. Italian and Lebanese minorities had a major impact on the city—in our first year there, I was treated to the best pizza I'd ever tasted. The first time I ate pizza outside of Windsor, I remember being disappointed. *Maybe I'm just picky and used to the pizza at home*, I thought. But no: I learned Windsor pizzerias regularly won international competitions. It really was the best.

Our neighbourhood, Villa Borghese, would have been considered nice in any city. It was on the edge of town, a road intersecting with cul-de-sacs lined with custom-built homes. Most of the homes were a nod to the city's Italian heritage, but the people living there—teachers, doctors, successful business owners—had different backgrounds. I wouldn't call it diverse, necessarily, but there was some diversity. We got to know a South Asian family nearby who quickly became like family. The Alam family had two brothers and two sisters. One brother was about the same age as Gurratan; the older brother, Sohail, was a little older than me. One sister was a little older and the other a little younger than Manjot. Sohail introduced me to computers, adventure games like King's Quest, Space Quest, the Ultima series, and bulletin board systems—a fledgling version of the internet limited to message exchanges and file sharing.

Like most kids who have to move, I never thought I'd find friends like the ones I had. But it wasn't long before I was making new ones. There was Andrew, an Italian kid I played sports with, and Adam, who not only collected comics like me, but was a really talented artist who drew incredible comic book–inspired pictures. But there was one kid who stood out.

The first time I saw Walid Mansour was outside my family room window. I didn't know his name at the time—he was just the kid riding his bike up and down the street, busting jumps off the curb and popping wheelies. At the risk of now giving him a huge ego, I can say something about him just oozed casual confidence.

A little later, on my first day of school at Oakwood Elementary, my third-grade teacher introduced me to the class.

"Class, we have a new student," the teacher said. "His name is Jagmeet."

"Hi, Jagmeet," the class said as one.

I was about to quietly make my way to my seat, but the teacher hit me with a major curveball.

"Walid, can you show Jagmeet around and help him settle in?"

I looked around to see who the teacher was talking to, more than a little embarrassed that my teacher was essentially forcing someone to be my friend. Then I saw who it was: the kid I saw riding his bike in front of my house. What were the odds? Walid sat in the back row, a Lebanese kid with a strong jaw and a cool haircut.

"Sure, miss," he replied.

We ended up hanging out the whole day and at each recess. Walid was popular and seemed to be friends with everyone. Before I knew it, the last bell of the day rang and it was time to head home.

"Which way are you going?" he asked.

"Toward the church," I said as I pointed south across the schoolyard.

"Same here," he said. "Let's walk together."

When we got to the next intersection, I asked, "Which way are you turning?"

"This way," Walid said, pointing left.

"Me too."

We kept walking, talking about whatever seven-year-olds in the mideighties talked about (normally cartoons like Voltron or Thundercats, but with Walid it was probably something cooler like *Saved by the Bell*).

"I'm turning here," I said at the next street.

"No way—so am I!"

We turned onto Santo Drive and walked together to the cul-de-sac at the end of the road. "I live here," he said, standing at the edge of a long driveway to a red and white two-storey house.

I looked at him in amazement. "Are you serious?" I pointed to my house, right beside his. "That's me—we're neighbours."

Walid and I quickly became best friends, and from then on, we were a duo, hanging out pretty much every day. His younger sister became best friends with Manjot. Even his older sister would hang out with us sometimes to play basketball or foursquare. We often walked to and from school together. It was only a short couple of blocks to Oakwood Elementary. Our school backed onto a conservation area and a duck pond, so feeding the ducks and walking through the forest (or the bush, as we called it in Windsor) were part of our every day.

In our free time, we would spend hours just riding our bikes. We would cruise around town, exploring different neighbour-hoods or biking through the forest trails. That is, after I finished the readings or times tables or whatever my mom challenged me to study that day. My extra tutoring confused Walid.

"I'm going to stay back and do homework," I told him once after he asked me to ride bikes after school.

"Homework?" he asked. "We don't have any homework."

"Yeah, it's just some stuff my mom gives me."

What confused Walid even more was that I was happy to do it. Just as my mom had hoped, I'd come to genuinely enjoy learning. Take, for example, the yearly competition held in our school called Canada Quiz. It was an extracurricular competi-tion testing our knowledge of Canada. The prize? The winner had to walk up to the front of the entire school at the monthly assembly and take on the winners from the other grades. It sounded like a child's version of torture to Walid, but I thought it was awesome. I set a goal to be the winning competitor within the first year. When I found out I'd be quizzed at the assem-bly, I wasted no time going to the library to seek out books on prime ministers, provinces, and territories. I must have brought a dozen books home the first time.

I'll never forget the look on Walid's face when he saw the stacks and stacks of books on my bedside table.

"Let's go for a bike ride," he said.

"Actually," I said, "I'm going to stay back and study for this Canada Quiz."

"You're actually going to study for that? You know it's not marked?"

"I know, but I want to be good at it."

He looked at me as though I'd just told him I wanted to grow two heads.

Walid and I shared a love for riding bikes, playing sports, and spending time outside, but in a lot of ways, we were so opposite that it's a miracle we stayed lifelong friends. Walid might not have understood my love of reading all the time, but he never made me feel weird for it. When we were in grade school, there was a popular series about a young kid, nicknamed Encyclopedia Brown, who solved mysteries with his encyclopedic knowledge. The books had kitschy titles like *Encyclopedia Brown and the Case of the Soccer Scheme*. When he heard about the series, Walid started referring to me as Encyclopedia Jagmeet. He was the coolest kid in class, though, so if he thought it was cool that I liked learning, it meant everyone else thought so, too. I don't know if Walid even did it consciously, but come to think of it, he really did support me. I could imagine that in another circle of friends or without a best friend like Walid, my curiosity, passion to learn, and love of reading would have earned me the title of being a nerd. It was a big deal that Walid had my back. It's something I'm grateful for and will never forget.

The biggest difference between us, though, was in what we ate. Walid was a scarily picky eater—someone whose idea of adventurous food was dipping fries in BBQ sauce instead of ketchup—so he wouldn't come near my mom's chicken curries and *rajma chawal* (red kidney beans with rice). On the other hand, I ate everything and was always up for a food adventure. This pleased Walid's mom to no end because she truly loved to feed people. Grape-leaf rolls, *za'atar*, *fatayer*, and *labneh* were instrumental to our growth spurts. (When I say we grew up together, I really mean it.)

Walid was also always trying to live ahead of the curve. Once, I went over and said, "Let's go play."

"Hey, man," he said very seriously. "Let's not say that."

"Say what?"

" 'Let's play.' Kids say that. We gotta say, 'Let's do stuff' instead."

I thought about this for a moment. "Umm, okay. Walid, do you want to go . . . do stuff?"

Even in third grade, Walid wanted to sound older. Even though the stuff we were doing *was play*, he was always like, "Nah—what's the next move?"

Once, we were riding our bikes on a beautiful warm summer day, pavement speeding by and wind in our faces. I turned to Walid and said, "It doesn't get better than this, does it?"

"Imagine when we're driving cars, though," he said.

I humoured him with a smile, but in my head, I was thinking, *Cars? Who cares about cars? This is the life!*

Later, when we were old enough to drive, we would hit up all-ages parties in Windsor and Detroit. We were meeting new people, dancing, and discovering places for the first time. Despite how much fun we were having, every now and then Walid would still say, "Oh, man, I can't wait until we can go to real clubs."

"Sure," I said. "But let's just enjoy what we have right now."

Looking back, I guess I really focused on appreciating moments of joy because they took me away from the stress and worries of daily life.

Only once did we let our differences get between us. When

we were in fifth grade, for whatever reason, we got angry at each other and stopped talking, as kids sometimes do. Our spat went on for a few weeks, to the point that my dad took notice. He saw Walid outside one day and started up a chat.

"What's going on?" he asked Walid.

"Nothing," Walid mumbled.

My dad paused, then turned on his psychiatric interviewing skills.

"How do you get along with Tarek?" he asked, naming one of our mutual friends.

"Pretty good."

"And how do you get along with Aboudie?" he asked, mentioning another guy in our group.

"Good."

"And Jagmeet?"

Walid froze.

"Not so much, hey?" my dad said. He paused, gave Walid a few seconds to think, and continued. "You guys have a special thing. You're in the same school, the same age, same interests. And you're next-door neighbours. You're both very lucky to have a friend that you can talk to any time you want. Not all boys do."

That was it. My dad left Walid to reflect a bit. The next day, Walid came over to hang out, and we put the whole thing behind us.

When Walid told me this story many years later, it didn't surprise me. My dad loves helping people—that was what he did—and he loved his family dearly. He always wanted what was best for us. He was always incredibly generous with his time. He wanted us to experience everything the world had to offer. If it was in his power, he would make it happen. He always meant well—I knew that—even at times when it didn't seem like it.

—⁓—

It had been less than ten years since my father had immigrated with a medical degree he was told wasn't legitimate. In his residency, even though he was well regarded as a medical professional, he always felt like he had to prove himself knowledgeable because he was a foreigner. Money had been tight while we were in St. John's, but now that he was making a decent paycheque as the chief of psychiatry at Windsor Regional Hospital, no one could make him feel like he didn't belong.

Truth be told, nobody had to. No matter how hard my dad worked or studied, no matter what degree or designation he achieved, he couldn't shake the feeling of not fully belonging. I think part of the reason was his fear, drilled into him by my grandmother, of financial precariousness. My dad has always been driven. He learned to ski and swim in his forties. He came to a new country and didn't just get by but thrived. Maybe it was a by-product of his intense ambition, but as a result, my dad seemed like he was never satisfied. Whatever the case, his rebellious spirit meant that he was simply unwilling to accept things the way they were simply because people said so.

One way my dad pushed back against this feeling of not belonging was in the way he dressed. Many mornings, as I had breakfast before school, I'd often see him strut out the door donning an overcoat and English brogues that he had polished the night before. My dad couldn't control the colour of his skin or his country of birth, but he could control what his wardrobe said to the world, so he made sure his clothing never gave anyone a reason to think he didn't belong.

My dad signalled to me and my siblings that, as people of colour, we couldn't afford *not* to look good. He wanted to make sure we never felt the way he did: like we didn't belong. He thought one of the ways to achieve that was to expose us to as many different activities and hobbies as possible. At my dad's insistence, I learned how to mount a horse in equestrian lessons, carved the snow in ski classes, practised my golf backswing, and perfected my tennis volley. I even ended up taking some classes in squash and archery.

I found horseback riding to be sort of cool, and I transitioned from skiing to snowboarding, which I loved. But most of my dad's directed activities weren't my idea of sports. They were too technique-based for my liking. I preferred sports that let me release my energy, where I could out-hustle an opponent with speed and effort, like soccer or martial arts. To that end, golf absolutely infuriated me. It seemed the harder I swung, the more aggressive and less relaxed I was, and the worse my score.

My dad wanted us to be comfortable in any setting we could find ourselves in. So, partly as a treat and partly as continued preparation for life, each month, my dad would take us out to The Other Place, one of Windsor's finest dining establishments. Complete with valet parking, white tablecloths, and a touch of stuffiness, The Other Place delivered. It was an etiquette lesson and a family evening all in one.

The food at The Other Place was genuinely delicious, but my brother and sister and I preferred more casual dining. We all loved Swiss Chalet, Red Lobster, or pepperoni pizza from a local joint, eaten on the living room floor. Sikhi calls into question the taking of life strictly for pleasure, and it promotes a lifestyle of stewardship and a responsible use of resources. As a result many Sikhs are vegetarian. This would change later on, but growing up, we ate meat pretty regularly.

My parents invested a lot of time and energy in making sure we had every opportunity possible. At school, Gurratan, Manjot, and I became known as "Dr. Dhaliwal's kids," a title that brought a lot of high expectations from coaches and teachers. My mom made sure that summers included science camps, museum trips, swimming lessons, and sports. She continued to encourage our education and made sure we kept studying over the summer months. Manjot and Gurratan had also fallen in love with reading, a passion our mom encouraged with regular trips to the library. If I ever gave even the slightest hint of interest in a subject, she would start encouraging me, pointing out books about the topic, or bringing up bits of trivia to continue to spark my interest. And if ever I fell behind in a subject—translation, if I ever got less than a 90 per cent on a test—my mother would raise the issue with my dad, who would find me a tutor on the subject in no time.

My mom and dad had different approaches to supporting their kids. My dad would make sure we had access to any and every opportunity, and he was interested in how we carried ourselves. He wanted us to be confident. His philosophy could be summed up by his favourite phrase: "If my kids want blood, I'll give them the marrow." My mom tried to focus less on how the world saw us and more on how we saw ourselves. She would often say, "Happiness comes from the inside."

My mom often tried to pass along her wisdom through stories. One my favourites of hers was a story of Guru Nanak, the founder of Sikhi. In the story, Guru Nanak joined a group of people gathered in a river. They were busily cupping their hands with water and throwing it toward the sun. Guru Nanak did the same, only he threw the water in the opposite direction. The group laughed at Guru Nanak and said he was doing it wrong. Guru Nanak explained he was watering his fields.

"Your fields are hundreds of kilometres away," they said. "That's impossible."

"Where are you throwing the water?" he asked.

"We're sending water to our ancestors."

"How far away are the ancestors?" he asked them.

"Our ancestors are in the next world."

"If you can send water into the next world, then my fields aren't too far away," he said.

I enjoyed the spirit of rebelliousness and the willingness to challenge the status quo that these stories conveyed. Maybe in a small way, they inspired me to try to do the same. My mom also introduced me to something a lot of Sikh kids learn, *seva*. *Seva*, or "selfless service," is a fundamental part of Sikhi. A spiritual journey is incomplete if it doesn't also focus on what we give back to society and the world around us. At its core, *seva* is a lesson in love. The idea of serving others puts unconditional love into practice.

Mom started me young on *seva*. Every Sunday at Windsor's humble *Gurdwara*—a small, slipshod, cinder-block building on the outskirts of town—I'd work in the free community kitchen that all *Gurdwaras* must have, handing out napkins to the eighty or so attendees before food was served. *Gurdwaras* are supposed to be open 24/7, with four doors welcoming all people from the north, south, east, and west, without a specifically designated

59

spiritual day. But Windsor's Sikh population was too small to sustain an around-the-clock *Gurdwara*, so we got together mainly on Sundays.

"You are serving people you do not know with the same love you would serve your family," my mom explained to me as I handed out napkins and she filled people's plates with food. "As a Sikh, you have a personal spiritual journey. And that journey includes ensuring justice for all. It doesn't matter if that person is a Sikh, Christian, Muslim, Hindu, or atheist—the goal is to see everyone around us as one. To feel love for a stranger equal in strength to the love you have for your brother and sister."

My mom had a great fascination with other religions and languages, and would often remark on how beautiful the world was because we all looked different.

"Everyone has their own uniqueness," she said. "There is a place for everybody in the world."

Just as she did with our summer lessons in science and math, my mom left me room to explore Sikhi for myself. She encouraged me and my siblings to walk the path, but she allowed us space to discover a lot of it on our own.

Inspired by the stories my mom told, I began reading books on Sikh spirituality, and each discovery reinforced why I enjoyed it so much. I read about the Ninth Guru, who sacrificed his life for freedom of thought, defending a religion he didn't actually agree with. The story clearly showed the Sikh principle of pluralism, or respecting people no matter what they believed in. It made sense to me and was even a bit of a relief, as I thought about the fact that Walid and his family were Muslim, and how it had never seemed wrong that they believed something different from me.

Through my mom's teachings, the spiritual poetry I read, and *seva*, I gradually understood that the spiritual goal in Sikhi was to love unconditionally. But that's not something that happens overnight. It takes work to realize that we're all connected, to feel our connection to everything around us, to realize we are all one, and to love unconditionally. Just like working out in the gym builds the strength to eventually deadlift four hundred pounds, meditating, reading spiritual poetry, and *seva* all help to develop unconditional love.

"How can I be more connected to the world?" I asked my mom one night.

"You could try meditating," she suggested. "Meditation helps us connect with the infinite energy inside us."

She sat down on the floor beside my bed and patted a space on the rug beside her for me to sit.

"We're going to repeat the *gur mantr*," she said. *Gur* means "enlightened" and *mantr* is a word that one reflects on. In Sikhi, the *gur mantr* is *Waheguru*. It is contemplated and repeated out loud as a way to realize and experience the oneness of the universal energy.

I repeated the word *"Waheguru"* out loud. *"Wahe"* means "wonderful" and *"guru"* means "light in darkness" or "enlightener."

"Good, now say it with me," my mom said.

She began repeating the *gur mantr* rhythmically, in a sing-song manner. I copied her, trying my best to focus. I thought about the connection between this *gur mantr* and the one energy that I had learned connects, binds, surrounds, and constitutes everything—the energy that is everything and everywhere, the reason we are all one. Then, after a while, I stopped thinking and simply got lost in the repetition. I felt something new. It's hard to describe a sense of contentment and peace, but that's what it was. I felt grounded and motivated. I was hooked. I wanted to walk down the path of love and to connect with the world. I also wanted to live up to the meaning of my name.

But I would learn that being a "friend to the world" would be a lot harder than I expected.

Chapter Four

SAY IT TO MY FACE

Is he brown because he doesn't shower?" one boy said at recess.

"Dirty," whispered another.

At first, I wasn't sure if I was mishearing them, but then the taunts turned to my hair. I felt a shadow looming above me.

"I seriously can't tell if it's a boy or a girl."

"Should I?"

"Dare you to."

I kept my head focused straight ahead, trying to ignore the stares and the taunting, which I was now certain were directed at me. Suddenly I felt my topknot being pulled and then a hard shove knocking me to the ground almost simultaneously. I hit the grass hard and felt a sharp strain in my neck. I bit back the yelp, a mixture of pain and surprise, in the back of my throat. I snapped back to my feet and whipped around to confront my assailants. They were pointing and laughing at my *patka*, my small head wrap, half pulled off my head. My knees were covered in grass stains. I launched toward them with my hands up yelling, "Let's go!"

The bell rang to end recess and, with it, my hopes of settling the score, as teachers quickly began corralling students back to class.

When I had gone from Jimmy to Jagmeet, I had also gone from a regular bowl cut to wrapping my long hair in a *patka*. I thought I was making a personal decision about who I was, not inviting a new world of bullying. I was insulated from the bullying when I first started school at Oakwood. Recess was split up: kindergarten to third grade were on one side of the yard, and grades four through six on the other. As a third-grade student, I had been the biggest kid on our side of the playground, and I got along with pretty much everyone in my class. I also had Walid as my friend, so bullying wasn't an issue at school. Outside of school, I did notice that I was being stared at a lot, but things weren't that bad. However, as soon as I hit fourth grade, the bullying became relentless. It wasn't just at school but wherever I went. I was stared at, mocked, made fun of, and often assaulted just for the way I looked.

It started to feel like I didn't have many safe spaces. My own class was fine. Teachers were always kind and treated me well. I tried not to let things get to me. But to be honest, I was scared and hated the feeling of always being on edge. I started looking for escapes.

One of my favourite places was the library. Libraries weren't only my place of learning about the things that interested me, they were also an escape. I felt safe at the library, and I associated them with finding amazing stories that would take me to different places. I loved being transported to the worlds created by the words on the page.

The best library in town was Windsor Public Library's central branch. Going there was a treat. The library was huge—as a kid, I felt like it had every book I could ever imagine. That was where I headed when I was doing a research project or needed something hard to find. Whenever my friends and I had questions we couldn't solve, I'd say, "I'm going to get a book on that." That was the cue to ask my mom if we could take a drive there.

Most of the time, though, I would head to our local branch, Budimir Library. I regularly biked to it, a mid-century, concrete building next to a small plaza with a Mac's convenience store and a Little Caesars Pizza. I would lock up my bike outside, pull open the big wooden doors, and go burrow myself in the bookshelves inside, preferably the ones with the sci-fi and fantasy novels, my favourites. I was there so often that I was basically on a first-name basis with the librarians, all of whom were so friendly and helpful—in fact, one of them was also a fan of fantasy and science fiction and made amazing recommendations. I enjoyed Anne McCaffrey's Dragonriders of Pern series, which while probably technically science fiction blurred the lines a bit with its focus on dragons, as well as the Shannara series by Terry Brooks. I was also hooked on the Dragonlance series. I also enjoyed some classics like Gary Paulsen's *Dogsong* and *Hatchet*.

Each series opened up a new world, and I fell into each one, just like in *The NeverEnding Story*. As I turned the pages, the pink carpet and warm sunlight in the library slowly drifted into the background until I forgot they were there. The sometimes bizarre and unique nature of the fantastical worlds made them all the easier to get lost in. And I needed that safe place, away from the bullying.

Kids made fun of me for my name, calling me "Jughead" or saying I was a jug of rotten meat. Even the teachers who were well-intentioned would end up butchering the pronunciation.

"It's Jagmeet, like 'Jug-meet,'" I repeated, over and over, to little effect.

Every recess after that brought with it new insults.

"Hey, diaper head!"

"What's that stupid thing on your head?"

"Take that towel off."

The more I heard the taunts, the less I tolerated them. Though I felt afraid and wasn't completely sure of myself, I held my head tall, shoulders back, and was ready to fight back.

"What's up? You got something to say, say it to my face!" I said, shoving them and getting pushed back. Within seconds, we'd be swinging fists until a teacher broke up the fight and made us stand against the wall for the rest of recess.

I tried to keep my anger and frustration from showing. Whenever I got detention or was told to stand looking at "the wall" during class because I'd misbehaved, I'd stare at the wall, bored and a bit embarrassed. But I was never tempted to stop tying up my hair or go by Jimmy again. Changing my identity wasn't an option.

If anything, the teasing actually made me even more committed to standing out. To me, my *patka*, just like the turban I would eventually wear, represented that, as Sikhs, we stood for equality and social justice. In fact, the very act of wearing a turban in the Sikh tradition was an act of rebellion. Historically, turbans were worn by those of a noble class, and it was prohibited for lower classes to wear them. Sikhs defied that prohibition in an act of revolution, declaring all humans to be noble, no matter where they were born or what their gender was.

Besides, I knew that removing my *patka* wouldn't appease the bullies anyway. Kids didn't limit their bullying to my turban or name—they also attacked me for the colour of my skin. One of the most common slurs I heard—"Paki"—was a catch-all insult for brown people, whether they were from Pakistan, India, or Lebanon. Walid was exempt from it because of his fairer skin and hazel eyes, but his cousin Aboudie, who was a few shades darker, was called a Paki, just like me.

Until then, I was only vaguely aware that some of us were viewed differently. I had friends who were Italian, Lebanese, and Pakistani, as well as friends who didn't know the first thing about their ethnic origins.

My other friends didn't get bullied as much as me, but when it happened, they responded with wit. They disarmed bullies with insults. I wasn't funny and wasn't very good with words, so things escalated fast with me.

My mom knew about my fights (moms always seem to know what's going on, even when you don't want them to know). She wanted me to focus on my studies, use my energy more productively. But she never discouraged me from standing up to bullies. She was never willing to tolerate racism, and she didn't want her kids to have to put up with it either.

—⚓—

I don't remember which of the boys said it to me first. There were three or four of them. A couple of years older and a few inches taller than me. Sneering as they pushed me against the rusted chain-link fence that separated our school from the conservation area. They punched and kicked me. They held me back, got in my face, and mocked me in a cartoonish South Asian accent.

"Do you have curry for breakfast?"

"He sure smells like it."

"Get out of here," said one, before punching me in the chest.

"You don't belong here," said another.

"Terrorist!"

I had been called a lot of names. Though I was used to them, they still hurt. I had been physically attacked and had to defend myself. But there was something jarring about being called a terrorist. At age nine or ten I didn't fully understand the word. It was so serious compared to the usual insults flung my way, like "Paki" or "towel head." Obviously, I knew being a terrorist was a bad thing and had to do with violence, but I can't say for certain where kids in the eighties living in Windsor would have come up with that word. Maybe it had something to do with Canada's worst terrorist attack, the Air India bombing. Maybe that's why this unsettling term became the new insult to be hurled at me. I had no idea then that later, specifically after 9/11, this insult would be directed at me often. I didn't know that I would have to dig deep to craft my own response to the accusation, a response that would turn fear into courage and terror into love.

—⁓—

The Air India bombing killed hundreds of Canadians, which included Muslims, Hindus, and Sikhs. The horrific event occurred when I was six years old, but it continued to be in the news for the next couple of decades. The families of the hundreds of victims were reeling from the loss. And Canada itself was still reeling from this act of terrorism.

All of these details were lost on me as a child of nine or ten. But what was all too clear to me was that the media was painting Sikhs as terrorists and extremists. I knew people who believed in an independent land as an answer to systemic oppression and persecution in India. I also knew those who believed in working within the current framework for justice. But every Sikh I knew—universally and without exception—believed the Air India bombing was a horrible and cowardly attack on innocent lives. Everyone agreed: it was terrorism, plain and simple.

Despite Sikhs being thrust into the national spotlight, very few Canadians knew their story and why so many had fled India. There was some coverage of the June 1984 massacre at the Golden Temple; however, fewer people knew about what happened in November 1984.

Following the assassination of Indian prime minister Indira Gandhi, Indian elected government officials (including Member of Parliament Sajjan Kumar, who was recently convicted for his role in the genocide) used municipal public transit to convey busloads of goons to communities with high concentrations of Sikhs. These goons were armed with weapons and kerosene, and directed to attack and loot Sikh businesses, Sikh-owned homes, and *Gurdwaras*. Sikh men were dragged by their hair and arms into the streets, where they were burned alive. Children were bludgeoned with iron rods and women gang-raped.

From October 31 to November 4, 1984, the police and military stood by as the carnage continued. All told, the November 1984 Sikh genocide claimed the lives of thousands, while even more were displaced from their homes.

The situation for Sikhs in India continued to deteriorate after that. Back in Canada, my parents didn't know how to express the pain they were feeling. They closed up, perhaps wanting to shield us kids from the trauma they were experiencing. What made matters worse was the lack of information. Indian media censorship made knowing the truth difficult. Speaking to our relatives in Panjab felt unsafe, as my parents feared there could be reprisals.

Thankfully, there was still a safe place for us to express some of the difficult emotions: the *Gurdwara*. There, the pain was literally on display. One Sunday, I went to *Gurdwara* as usual. I noticed a new display case with pictures in it. Some of them depicted the ravaged structure of the Harmandir Sahib, the Golden Temple, in Panjab. None of the structures had survived unscathed—neither the *Gurdwara* itself with its beautiful gold-leaf dome surrounded by once-calm waters; nor the four towers at the corners of the complex; nor the Akal Takht Sahib, the "Seat of the Infinite" (one of the historic places of decision-making for Sikhs).

Seeing these beautiful buildings destroyed was a shock, but nothing compared to the shock I felt at seeing the other pictures that accompanied them. Most were photos of young men looking into the camera like you would for a school photo. One picture permanently embedded in my mind showed a man with a scar resembling an iron pressed into his stomach. I took it in, feeling horrified and concerned.

An uncle entered the *Gurdwara* and saw me.

"Are you okay?" he asked gently.

"I'm okay, but these photos. They're so painful," I said.

"These pictures have been smuggled out of India so that the

world can see what is happening," he said. "They're people who have been tortured or killed by the government."

I looked at the faces in the pictures again. Any one of those young men and boys could have been me.

The uncle waited patiently while I tried to process what I was seeing. Finally, he said, "These are cries for help. People in the West don't know what is going on. We have to find a way to make people care."

Thousands of young Sikh men were still missing. There were still active attempts to limit the flow of news coming out of Panjab, so taking photos of the violence, this uncle explained, was a risk, albeit one that was necessary if the truth was to be told.

I learned more about this hard historical truth thanks to the efforts of one of my role models growing up, Jaswant Singh Khalra, who was able to prove what people had widely known and communicated informally for years. His story was remarkable. He was a banker by profession who'd heard, as many others had, that Sikh men were being taken off the streets by government forces. It hadn't touched Jaswant Singh personally until the day one of his good friends was taken. Jaswant Singh then made it his mission to find his friend and uncover what was happening.

He eventually exposed that the police and paramilitary were conducting extrajudicial killings of the Sikh men in their custody and then cremating the bodies. For the first time, the Sikh community had proof of the injustices being carried out against them. For this, he received a threat to his life from the Indian police.

Many community members offered to help Jaswant Singh stay in Canada while he was in the country presenting his findings. But he declined, saying he had more work to do to expose the extrajudicial killing of Sikhs. He returned to Panjab. Soon after his arrival, he disappeared. Years later, a police whistle-blower revealed that he had been tortured and killed while in custody.

The horrible impact of that time had always been clear to me, but the exact details were not. Thanks to Jaswant Singh's sacrifice, we were one step closer to the truth being heard. But there was still a long journey ahead. I could see the frustration in the Sikh community—to have suffered so much, yet still the pain and trauma were not acknowledged.

Everyone who experiences pain and trauma wants healing and reconciliation. The first step to healing is receiving acknowledgement of the harm done. With no outlet for the pain and no acknowledgement of the trauma, those harmed often internalize the suffering and endure it in silence.

I was just a child, Jagmeet Singh, friend to the world. But I was learning that sometimes the world ignores people who need help, even when it's everyone's responsibility to stand up for those who aren't being heard.

Chapter Five

KICKS AND PUNCHES

It didn't take long to realize that I could embolden bullies or discourage them. It all depended on how I carried myself. If I walked across the schoolyard with my head down and hands in my pockets, a shy third grader trying to get home unscathed, it only made me a bigger target. That changed when I straightened my back, lifted my head, kept my fists in front of me. It didn't stop guys from picking on me, but I wouldn't take crap from anyone, even if I didn't stand a chance at winning the fight.

"Look, guys, it's Little Nipplehead," a kid once called me during recess.

Walid and I were playing one-on-one basketball. I swivelled around in the direction of the voice—a seventh grader on the other side of the court playing with his friends.

I threw my basketball to the side. It bounced in the grass as I marched his way. "What's up?" I yelled as I slapped the ball out of his hand and shoved him. "Let's go!"

I cocked back my fist. He flinched. I could tell that he and his friends weren't expecting me to fight back. They figured this nine-year-old would just walk away from harassment. They looked down at me: barely four and a half feet tall, skinny as a beanpole, mean mugging under my black head wrap.

"What the hell is with this kid?" the boy said to his friends. They shook their heads and picked up their ball from the grass.

I didn't hear another word from them. I was less and less afraid of physical confrontation, but my size got to me. I was average height and weight, and kids in my class, who knew me, didn't give me problems anymore. The people I was defending myself against were usually older than me—I was literally punching above my weight.

"When will I be bigger?" I'd often ask my mom.

"Don't worry, you will grow."

"When will I be stronger?"

"You'll be stronger."

There was more to it than that. More than I had the heart to say out loud, though I think my mom knew. Because deep down inside, it wasn't just bullies I wanted protection from anymore.

—⁂—

Manjot and I sat at the dining table doing homework and watching my dad through the kitchen doorway. He was aggravated, tugging a drawer out of the brown kitchen cabinets.

"Why is this so messy?" my dad barked. The drawer's contents jangled when he yanked it free, and he lost his balance. He caught himself on the oven, barely keeping the drawer from falling.

My mom entered the dining room, Gurratan following closely

behind, and he climbed onto the chair beside me. She stepped into the kitchen and calmly took the drawer from his hands.

"What are you looking for?" she asked my dad, as she riffled through it.

"I can't find anything in this filthy house," he shouted. He lurched toward the console, batting a pile of opened mail and flyers against the rose-patterned wallpaper. The papers cascaded onto the tiles. "What are we collecting all this for? And this—" He grabbed a stack of magazines with his two hands, lifted it above his head, and dropped it on the floor, where the magazines landed with a thud. My mom put the drawer on the counter and got on her knees to restack the paper. While my dad sifted through the drawer, my mom rose to her feet with the magazines and tiptoed toward the trash bin under the sink. He was in her way.

"Excuse me," she whispered, careful not to disturb him, but it was useless. There was no placating my dad when he was in one of his moods. He grabbed the drawer and dumped its contents on the tile. He kicked the scattered kitchen utensils around as he looked for something. My mom backed away to the corner, holding the magazines close to her chest.

All you could hear was the clinking and clanking of cooking utensils. I grabbed Gurratan's and Manjot's hands under the table. "Don't look," I said, turning my head to my notebooks on the table. In the corner of my eye, I saw my dad bend down and take what he was looking for.

"Clean it up," he said and stomped away.

Alcohol made my dad volatile and unpredictable. Some people get tipsy and become more agreeable when they drink. Others turn inward, quiet and reflective. But not my dad. He was a predictably belligerent drunk. My dad didn't have a mellow zone; even when he was sober, which was increasingly rare by 1988, he had gripes about whatever didn't meet his expectations at the moment. The living room wasn't tidy enough. His briefcase wasn't where he left it. The car was parked poorly. The fridge was empty.

But I still loved him—loved him with the most complex type of love that exists. The love you have for someone who has hurt you emotionally, who makes you feel afraid and angry, who fills you with spite and dark thoughts. But still, someone who you love regardless because you are a part of them and they a part of you.

There are no excuses for the anger my dad directed at us—my mom especially—but even as a child, I felt sorry for him. By the end of most nights, he'd be incoherent, slurring and staggering; obviously, this wasn't someone anybody would wish to become. It would take me many years to understand the root of his sickness, and even now, I'm not 100 per cent sure I understand it fully.

My dad grew up in an antisocial home with a small support network. My grandfather was a bit of a shell after his first wife died, so he kept to himself and interacted little with my dad. Meanwhile, his mom pushed away relatives out of paranoia that they'd try to exploit the family's modest wealth. As a result, I think, my dad's loneliness led to stress and depression. But, like his own father, he muted his sadness. He had never learned to talk through his problems or look for any other healthy coping mechanism. Some of us decompress by binge watching You-Tube. Others run or read or write rhymes. Personally, I cook—as late as three in the morning if I need to relax (the delicious meal a welcome bonus). But my dad's stress relief was the bottle, and he only tightened his clutch on it when the pressures got more intense.

He started drinking in Panjab during medical school, but only in social settings with professors and classmates. On those nights, he'd drink more than anyone at the table and need help getting home. But those nights were rare. His determination to become a doctor as fast as possible limited his youthful drinking. Similarly, when he first arrived in Canada and lived in Scarborough, he couldn't afford the time—or money—to get drunk regularly. Even in St. John's, when money wasn't as tight, he might unwind with a glass of cheap vodka but he didn't have the time to drink heavily what with his fifteen-day work streaks at the hospital and his assistant professorship.

After his residency, my dad's schedule allowed for more time to drink. The more structured days at the Grand Falls hospital gave him back his weekends for the first time in fifteen years. Still, he was self-conscious about consuming alcohol. My mom, especially, hated it—she, like most Sikhs, was against the use of intoxicants. My dad would never drink openly; he'd hide himself away. When he was done, he'd even hide his bottles in random places—in the washroom under the sink or behind the cleaning supplies in the laundry room cupboard.

My mom knew what was going on before she discovered the open bottles of Alberta Pure vodka tucked away with the Lysol and Vim. She smelled it on his breath. Saw it in his stumbles. Heard it in his mumbling.

She must have feared the worst when he got the job in Windsor. Barely making ends meet and a busy schedule had protected us against my dad's worst tendencies. Now, he'd have more time and money than ever, but there'd be more pressure on him than ever, too. To my mom, it seemed a dangerous combination.

The work would have been challenging for anyone. My dad felt the harshest judgment from patients who wondered aloud why a foreigner was looking after them. At the end of his days, all too eager to forget his frustrations, he drank heavily. Soon after we moved into the house in Villa Borghese, he built a bar for the basement. I don't remember what else he stocked it with, but I do remember his preferred bottle, Russian Prince vodka. There were always two or three bottles of that vodka in the cabinet. The label mascot—an unfriendly, bearded man in a tall bearskin hat—looked extra menacing to my childhood eyes.

As a kid, it seemed to me that my dad drank Russian Prince like water. So, I wondered, what if we could fool him into actually drinking water, not vodka? I hatched a plan with my siblings one day while we were messing around in the basement.

I positioned my brother at the foot of the stairs. "Watch the door, Gurratan," I said. "Manjot, come here—hurry." She followed me to the bar, where I took bottle after bottle of clear liquor from the cabinet and handed them to her to pour down the drain.

"Do you think it will work?" she asked, as she refilled each empty bottle right to the lip.

"Maybe he'll think, *Oh, it's just not working*, and give up," I explained.

What did I know about the taste of vodka? It smelled like hairspray, that much I could tell, but I couldn't imagine my dad would drink something that tasted as putrid as it smelled. All I knew was he'd drink the stuff and that made him act crazy. So

I figured we were getting rid of the problem, making the home safer, and probably helping him, too.

It didn't take long to realize how wrong we were. We were in the living room when he arrived from work. I heard him hang his coat in the closet and drop his keys in a bowl on the console. The basement door creaked open and his footsteps softly echoed downstairs. Seconds later, I heard his footsteps thumping upstairs again.

My dad entered the living room wearing his blue suit with an unbuttoned shirt collar and loosened tie. He held two bottles by his side. His lips were wet. Water overflowed down the Russian Prince's menacing face. I slowly gazed upward, expecting an angry outburst. My dad's look, however, was one of embarrassment. As a father, he should be entitled to parental authority *and* moral authority—the wisdom and power to tell kids what's right and wrong. But he knew he couldn't reprimand us for what we had done.

"Dad, you're mean when you drink it," said Manjot.

"We want you to get better," I said. "What you're doing is wrong."

"I know," he said.

"You're scary," Gurratan said.

"I'm know, I'm sorry," my dad said with a big exhale. Despite the apology, he grabbed his overcoat and walked out the door. The Mercedes backed out of the driveway and returned twenty minutes later. Through the windows, I watched my dad walk over to the passenger side and lift two plastic bags off the seat. He came inside, and I heard the glass bottles clang together as he kicked off his shoes. The basement door creaked. His footsteps faded as he walked farther down the stairs.

"I wanted my mind to slow down," he'd later tell me. "I'd come home, take my medicine, and have a good night's sleep. Then, the next day, wake up and prove I'm better than the others. But why did I have to prove I'm better than others?"

My dad's balanced perspective was years away, though, and after our failed attempts to replace his vodka (we tried several times), things remained the same. Nobody was immune to his drunken outbursts. No one was safe from the airborne objects he'd throw, the insults he'd hurl. The man had everything: good house, good car, good pay, smart and obedient kids. A country that gave him a chance to thrive. Yet he was impossible to satisfy. A clean-freak who was himself a mess. A perfectionist who was profoundly imperfect.

He took it out on my mom the most, constantly nitpicking about her cleaning abilities and appearances.

"You don't dress properly," I overheard him yell at her in their bedroom one Saturday afternoon. "Put on something nice for once," he shouted.

"Let's go somewhere else," I told Manjot and Gurratan. I gathered my siblings and took them to our favourite spot, a little ledge at the top of the basement stairs that we would often sit on and dangle our legs off of.

I closed the door to the basement, dimming our parents' voices to a muffle. I tried to act like nothing was happening.

"Let's go downstairs," I said. I helped Gurratan off the ledge and led him and Manjot into our basement, where we sat cross-legged on the vinyl flooring. We arranged ourselves in a triangle facing each other. We started meditating together, repeating *Waheguru.* After a while, I pulled out a book of Sikh poetry, unwrapped the cloth binding, and read it out loud. We were far from enlightenment, but in that moment, the three of us were connected, which was good, because it felt like we were all each other had.

—∿—

Looking back, I recognize that this time was tough for my mom. Things were scary and we were all trying to figure it out.

As a kid, escape was the only protection I could see. But I vowed to myself that one day I'd be tough enough to protect my family from my dad.

"When will I be stronger?" I asked my mom for the umpteenth time.

"Do you want to learn how to be stronger?" she asked.

"Yes!" I exclaimed.

"Maybe we can sign you up for tae kwon do."

The next week, my mom drove me to a plaza in a commercial part of town. The gym was sandwiched between a nail parlour and a tailor, with a plastic sign over the door that read TAE KWON DO. The dojo in a plaza reminded me of the Cobra Kai Dojo in *The Karate Kid*.

My mom dropped me off in front of the glass door and told me she'd be back in about an hour. I opened the door to a wide-open room decorated with Bruce Lee posters and framed photos of fighters kicking and punching through bricks and wood. There were different-size punching bags dangling from the ceiling by chains, and stacks of wood boards, which immediately excited me—I thought I'd be smashing them with my fists in no time.

A man in a white uniform—the baggy pants and shirt of Korean martial arts—greeted me with a handshake.

"You must be Jagmeet," he said.

"*Jug-meet*," I replied. "Hi."

"Jug-meet, you're early. I like that," he said. "I'm your instructor, Mr. Reginald Neilson."

Mr. Neilson wasn't the tae kwon do master I expected. To me, he looked like a bald old man with barely noticeable grey hair behind his ears. When he showed me to the change room, I noticed he had a limp. But he did wear a black belt, so that was something, and there were pictures of him smashing bricks on the wall outside the washrooms.

He opened a locker. "What size are you?" he asked.

"Medium."

He pulled a folded uniform halfway out the locker, sized me up, then returned it and searched for another. "You look like a small," he said, handing me a uniform and rolled-up white belt. "This is how it starts," he said, tightening his black belt.

He left me to change. It felt powerful as I pulled on each piece of the uniform, like I was piecing together armour. I returned to the main room and sat on the hardwood floor as other students trickled in. They all noticed me sitting cross-legged on the mat, waiting for class to begin. I remember a muscular guy with big glasses and an Afro, a chubby teenager with long hair, and James.

James was the last to arrive, wearing a Lycra shirt and shorts. He carried an angular bike helmet under his armpit as he pulled the Velcro straps on his cycling shoes and placed them against the wall. The rest of us were suited up and standing shoulder to shoulder by rank, a dozen young men, a few young women, a couple of high school–age guys, and me at the very end—the lowest in rank and size.

"Sorry," James said, panting. "Police pulled me over. They said I was riding too fast. They almost gave me a speeding ticket!"

He quickly changed into his uniform and returned, taking his position at the very end of the line. His red belt had a stripe, meaning he was one level away from his black belt.

We stretched and mimicked Mr. Neilson's movements together—front stance, back stance, leg swings—poised with our fists in front of our chests, ready for combat. I kept glancing over at the highest-ranking students, trying to imitate them and change positions with the same slow-motion gracefulness they used. Mr. Neilson started calling out movements and strikes to practise with more force and guttural releases.

"Front kick."

"Side kick."

"Vertical punch."

We practised the different forms—series of strikes and blocks that simulate a fight—that would carry me through the ranks. The most basic white-belt forms were simple turns, steps, and strikes that I mastered quickly. It only took a couple of months for me to get a yellow stripe on my belt, and then I earned the yellow belt itself. With each upgrade or each new piece of armour I strapped on—like boxing gloves and shin guards—I felt a sense of accomplishment. Most of all, I felt more powerful.

I trained more intensely than the other students because I could release all my might without hurting the other, bigger club members. My sparring partners saw me as the kid brother of the tae kwon do club, so they treated me kindly, letting me punch and kick as hard as I wanted. It was great practice, but what I really wanted was to break boards like James did. During his black-belt test, I sat cross-legged on the sidelines, rapt with attention. I admired how fluidly he pounced through the air before doing a jump kick and chopping the wood with his fist, and how straight the broken edges of the boards looked by his feet. He had to spar with all of us at once to earn the highest ranking. He moved with speed and grace.

That's the kind of skill I need, I thought to myself as I watched him.

James was a superstar who crushed opponents at tournaments. I didn't have to compete to earn my coloured belts, just learn the forms and self-defence techniques, and pass the exams. While belt examinations were formal, Mr. Neilson was relaxed about levelling up. What mattered more to him was our dedication to the martial art. I spent a lot of time at home practising my forms, which got more complicated with each new colour and stripe.

Forms force you to visualize mock fights, like playing out a match in your mind. I remember once practising in my bedroom as my mom leaned against the doorway watching. I didn't mind the audience, and she appreciated me doing anything physical or academic with my time. My arms glided from reverse punch to outer forearm block, reverse punch and knife-hand strike, moving in slow motion but delivering strikes with enough force to give my uniform sleeves a satisfying snap. I blew exhales with each strike, trying to stay focused, but her smile distracted me. My stone face broke, and I started fighting my mock opponent with a huge grin.

Over the next couple of years, I graduated from yellow belt

to orange to blue. I was eleven years old and four levels from black belt. Finally, I was ready to start breaking stuff.

"I'll grab a board," I exclaimed the first time Mr. Neilson mentioned it.

"Hold on," he said. "I don't want you punching through wood just yet. It's too hard on your knuckles, and your bones are still developing."

I liked the way Mr. Neilson appealed to science and biology with his lessons, but I was disappointed—I kept thinking about James's black-belt test and how mesmerized I'd been. Mr. Neilson must have sensed my impatience, because he eventually relented and laid a thin board down across cinder blocks, like a bridge. He walked me through the method, showing me how to hammer through the board with the blunt side of my fist. It cracked under my force like an eggshell.

I couldn't wait to show off to my friends. That weekend, we scavenged the neighbourhood for construction materials and collected sturdy branches around the ravine. My friends held them out for me to break with my feet, elbows, and hands.

"Let me try," said Walid. I held up a branch, and he hit it with all his might. The wood barely cracked. Walid yelped and fanned his hand in pain.

We all laughed, and as we left the ravine, I snapped the branch over my knee. I really was getting stronger.

—⁓—

My training in the dojo carried over into the streets, and the more I trained in tae kwon do, the more my fighting style changed. Before, if kids tried to shove me or pull my hair, it devolved into an unsophisticated scrap—headlocks, kneeing, rolling on the grass, and pulling at each other's jackets. Now I had technique.

One recess, toward the end of fifth grade, a kid started ridiculing my *patka* again. "What's that bandage on your head?" he taunted. "You get hit in the head? Are you covering a lump? I'll rip that thing off your dumb head."

I marched right up and challenged him. "If you're going to do it, do it, then." As soon as the boy grabbed me by the bun, I channelled my inner Jean-Claude Van Damme. Normally my instinct would be to get his hands off my head, but I let him have my bun. It meant I had two free hands and he only had one. While he tried to tear my *patka* off, I threw a reverse punch to his solar plexus, then a straight punch to the same spot. I landed a couple of side kicks, and the boy crashed to the floor.

My fifth-grade teacher, Mr. V, barrelled toward us to break up the fight. But there was nothing to break up. I stood still as the other kid lay on the floor, holding his stomach and gasping for air.

Mr. V helped the boy to his feet, then grabbed hold of me by my arm. He took me to "the wall" and ordered me to stand against it until the bell rang. I stared at the wall, unblinking. I looked around to make sure no one was looking. I then turned back toward the wall as a couple of tears slid down my face. I wasn't hurt and the other guy had started it. But picturing the older kid on the ground gasping for breath, I felt bad about what I had done. I didn't want to hurt him. I quickly rubbed my eyes with both hands and slipped my tough-guy mask back on. The recess bell rang. I was free to go. As I walked back to class, kids who'd seen the fight looked at me with more respect. I gave them the barest hint of a nod and continued on my way to class.

After recess, Mr. V marched me to the office, where he called my parents and asked them to meet with him after school.

I thought I was going to be suspended. But when my parents and I walked into Mr. V's classroom that evening, he acted very warmly. Mr. V lived in our neighbourhood and was friendly with my parents. Whenever my dad saw him washing his red Mazda Miata in his driveway, he'd walk over for a quick chat.

Mr. V offered my parents coffee from the staff room. They declined and squeezed themselves in two little kid desks on either side of mine.

"Jagmeet is an exceptional student," Mr. V said. "He always has the right answer. Always. He throws his hand up so often I worry he's going to hurt it. Maybe we should get you a little buzzer, like *Jeopardy!*, hey buddy?"

I blushed.

"So what is the problem, then?" asked my dad.

"The problem, Dr. Dhaliwal, is that I'm worried about Jagmeet wasting his potential. He has a great appetite for learning, but he's distracted by all these fights."

My mom and dad spoke a few words to each other in Panjabi.

"Perhaps things might be better if Jagmeet was at a different school?" my dad said. "We've heard of a good school in Detroit. A few of my colleagues send their kids there."

"A change of scenery might not hurt," Mr. V said.

"What do you think, Jagmeet?" my mom asked.

"Let's see what it looks like," I said.

The next day, my mom picked me up from school early so that we could tour Detroit Country Day School together. The name was a bit of a misnomer; the hundred-year-old preparatory school was actually in an affluent suburb of Detroit called

Beverly Hills. It took my mom forty minutes to drive there, across the Ambassador Bridge, north on the I-75 and continuing north on the M-10.

The first thing I noticed was how big the complex was. There was an elementary school and a high school all on the same grounds. There were several soccer fields and a big outdoor field with lots of seating.

We walked into the building just before the final bell. The students broke free into the halls. They were all wearing uniforms. The boys wore khaki pants, the girls grey or plaid skirts, and everyone wore a white shirt and a striped tie. Some of the high-schoolers wore varsity jackets with gold letters. I was always the type of kid who found shopping for new school clothes annoying, so it appealed to me that here I wouldn't have to think about what I wore each day.

I also noted the ethnic makeup in the student body. At Oakwood, a number of my friends were Lebanese, and I knew an Asian girl and a Tamil girl. But that was it for diversity. Here, there were crowds of Arab, Asian, black, and brown kids. It looked like a TV school cast by a director with minorities in mind.

The tour rubbed off on my mom. My dad had already made up his mind—he always wanted his kids to have the best, and he was already planning to start Manjot and Gurratan at the school once they reached sixth grade. My mom was less impressed by the perceived status that came with the school. What appealed to her was how eager to learn these students appeared. Many were loudly discussing class lessons as they moved textbooks and binders from their lockers to their bags.

As we drove home, one thing lingered in my mind. The entire time we'd been there, no one had said anything about my *patka* or stared at me for more than a moment. And when they did look at me, it was more, I think, to note that I wasn't wearing a uniform than because I was wearing something different on my head. Until then, the feeling of being an outsider had weighed heavily on me, occupying a huge part of my mind. With that weight lifted, I hoped I would now be free to excel at academics and sports. Maybe, just maybe, I could make my dad proud enough that he'd finally feel satisfied.

Part Two

Chapter Six

POINT SYSTEM

M r. Neilson gathered us together at the end of a practice to tell us the news. I had sensed something was up before he sat us down to make the announcement. The Bruce Lee posters were rolled up and set against the wall, and throughout training, he hadn't called out strikes with his usual vigour. We sat cross-legged on the hardwood before him while he fidgeted with the ends of his belt.

"This is a little bit awkward for me," he said. "But due to some financial difficulties, I'm not able to hold on to this place anymore."

"You're closing the gym?" I asked in alarm.

"No. No way. Not closing anything. Just moving it." He paused. "To my house. For a while—just until I figure out the next move."

I sat back in relief—we would still have a place to train. But I noticed other, older students looking at each other through the corners of their eyes. The idea of training out of a basement was a little disappointing. A lot of tae kwon do purists, valuing the prestige of a dojo and its instructors, would have stopped attending after hearing an announcement like that. Lucky for Mr. Neilson, his style of training was less traditional and more focused on street fighting, so most of us were looking for practical training more than prestige.

"We'll continue with classes at the same times on the same days," said Mr. Neilson. "I'm moving all the bags and equipment there. Your rankings, wherever you are, none of that changes. It'll be just as good as this." He laughed. "You know what? It'll be better. Who needs a fancy place? The martial arts are supposed to be humble."

We bowed to our instructor, and he bowed back. I could tell that he had lost a few students with the news. Not me, though.

When my mom picked me up, I told her Mr. Neilson's dojo was moving to his house.

"What does his wife think of him bringing the class to their house?" my mom asked.

I shrugged. "I dunno."

"Does he have any kids?" she asked.

"I don't know."

"How many people are in the club? Do you have any friends there?"

"They're all my friends," I said. She shot me a dubious expression as she turned the Volvo onto Santo Drive. "*Bebey-ji*," I groaned. In two short years I'd watched my strength and speed improve manifold, and I was eager to see what more years of practice would earn me.

She grew even more suspicious the next week when she

dropped me off at the new dojo. Mr. Neilson lived in a run-down, two-storey house off Tecumseh Road, around the corner from an auto shop and bottle depot. Mr. Neilson had asked us to enter through the alleyway and backyard, but my mom wasn't having it. She parked on the street, walked me to the front door, and rang the doorbell.

A very old lady in a floral dress answered the door. "Hello?" she asked, her voice as thin as a ghost's.

"Is this Mr. Neilson's dojo?" my mom asked.

"My son's downstairs, but you're welcome to come through the front."

"Mr. Neilson's your son," my mom noted. "This is *your* house?"

"Lived here for almost fifty years."

"You and . . . your son."

I pulled at my mom's jacket to stop her pestering. Just then, Mr. Neilson popped his head around the corner of the back-door entrance. The baggy sleeves of his uniform swished in the air as he waved. "Hi, Mrs. Dhaliwal. We're down here." He disappeared around the corner. I gave my mom a look: *Relax.*

As I shuffled to the back of the house, I overheard the old lady offer my mom some tea.

"If it's no trouble, thank you very much," my mom said as she removed her shoes.

The dojo was an open basement with concrete floors and exposed steel support beams. Punching bags hung from the un-finished ceiling. Mr. Neilson had tried to make the place feel the same as it had in the strip mall, with martial arts posters on the walls and a big, rubber, blue mat covering the floor to protect our feet. But there was no way to disguise it: we were training in his elderly mom's basement.

Mr. Neilson continued to try to make the place seem cooler than it was. Before our stretches, he showed us his pet piranhas in a big neon aquarium. "I think it's just about suppertime," he said, scooping a goldfish from a separate tank with a net and plopping it into the piranhas'. They attacked the goldfish, chased it, tired it out, and nipped at its fins until it flopped into a corner, and the piranhas set upon it.

We put on our uniforms and stretched together. Mr. Neilson held himself up on the ceiling beams to stretch his body, trying to make the exposed construction seem like an advantage. As we practised axe kicks, his foot flew over his head and hit the ceiling. He chuckled and said, "Must be a good day for me."

By the end of the hour, the piranhas had chomped their prey to a skeleton, I'd forgotten about the weird scenario, and my mom was satisfied enough with Mr. Neilson's operation that I was allowed to return the next week. I was relieved to know that I'd still have my chance to earn a black belt and to break more than a single board—maybe even with my knuckles, like my older classmates.

But with each practice, the class got smaller and smaller. None of the women had followed over to the basement, so we started changing out of our streetwear and into our uniforms in the open. Unfortunately for me, one of the students who remained was a boy who'd been picking on me and trying to ruin what was otherwise a great training experience: Eric.

Eric was a heavy-set teenager with long hair, and he had been mean to me since I had earned my first colour. I was incredibly committed to tae kwon do—I still practised every day at home. Sometimes, I'd get a slap on the back or a quiet nod of approval from one of the older students.

One day, Mr. Neilson overheard Eric calling me a loser as he held his sparring gloves high above his head where I couldn't reach them. "Is that guy bothering you?" Mr. Neilson asked me as I took a break, my frustrations showing. Normally, I liked to handle those sorts of problems myself, but Eric had been bullying me more than usual all practice. I nodded yes.

"Thought so."

Mr. Neilson told the class that we'd be working on some new self-defence techniques for the rest of practice. We gathered around to watch him demonstrate.

Mr. Neilson picked Eric as a volunteer. "I want you to bear-hug me from behind," he said, turning his back to Eric. "Tighter," he said. "Tighter—don't be afraid. I can . . ." Mr. Neilson gulped for air. "Uh-oh. How do I get out of this?" he asked.

Mr. Neilson threw his head back, surprising Eric with a whop to the nose. "First, head-butt—sorry, buddy. I should have called that out."

Eric rubbed his nose on his shoulder to soothe the pain.

"After you've hit them in the nose, you want to get into a horse stance," continued Mr. Neilson as he crouched forward, pulling Eric nearer to the floor. "You can grab his hair and yank it to help pull him down, but be careful not to lean too far, because if he's a bigger guy, like Eric, then he's going to put all his weight on you. If he takes you right down—you're finished. Instead, make sure you got a good stance like this and—see, what's right here?" Mr. Neilson nodded at the open space between his legs.

I stared in disbelief. *No way*, I thought. *There's no way he's going to . . .*

I watched as Mr. Neilson struck a quick blow between Eric's legs and dropped him flat on his back, striking Eric once more in the stomach as he hit the floor.

Mr. Neilson released Eric and slapped his hands together. "Let's try that—everyone grab your sparring partner. And be careful not to actually hit each other."

When practice was over and we'd changed into our plain clothes, Mr. Neilson asked me to stay behind. "If Eric gives you a hard time again, let me know," he said.

"Okay, thank you."

"You know, Jagmeet, you're getting really good at this. Have you thought about trying out for tournaments?"

I shrugged. "Maybe." I was trying to play it cool, but inside, I could feel myself getting fired up—the idea of competing was really exciting.

"Think about it. You'll need more training, but I can give you more training on the weekend, free of charge. One-on-one lessons so you'll get better."

"Really?" I asked, not believing what I was hearing. The idea of more training to get even better quicker was exactly what I wanted. "Yes, I think I would really like that. I mean, I want to be best. I want to earn my black belt," I said.

At the time, a black belt summed up everything I wanted. It was the pinnacle that would mean I was the best, the toughest. What I wanted was to be so tough that bullies would think twice about teasing me or laying a hand on me. And, truth be told, I wanted to make my dad think twice about laying a hand on any of his family.

"Good—let your mom know and think about what I said."

"Sure thing, Mr. Neilson."

It didn't take much convincing for my parents to agree to extra training. Since I'd started tae kwon do, my parents had noticed a change in my confidence, something my dad had tried cultivating for so long with activities I hadn't cared for. Now that they'd finally found something that stuck, they were thrilled to hear I wanted to do more of it.

The first time I arrived for a weekend lesson, my mom dropped me off in the alley behind Mr. Neilson's house. This was the usual way we entered the house to get to the basement— we'd walk from the alley through the backyard to the back porch, and then down the stairs to the gym in the basement. When I walked up the backyard gate, though, I noticed Mr. Neilson was already in the backyard. He was sunbathing on a reclined patio chair.

"You're early," he said, sitting up in his chair. I looked at my watch—*not really*, I thought, *I'm just on time*. I was more surprised to see that the only garment Mr. Neilson was wearing was a leopard-print Speedo. He looked down, registering my surprise, and laughed. "If I wore these in the winter, my neighbours would think I'm crazy."

He stretched a little before opening the back door and gesturing me to head inside. Before I could take my first step downstairs, though, he stopped me with a hand on my back. "Nope, this way," he said, pointing upstairs. "You'll see—this is a very different program."

As we headed upstairs, Mr. Neilson started chatting more.

"It's interesting the way people's perspective changes how they see something," he said.

"What do you mean?" I asked.

"Take my swim shorts, for example. In the summer, if I was sunbathing or at a beach, people wouldn't think much of me wearing these swim shorts."

I nodded as though I understood, even though I had no idea where he was going.

"But imagine if I was walking around in my underwear. All of a sudden, people would think it was a little weird."

"Okay," I said, still confused.

"But if you think about it, what's really so different about wearing swim shorts or underwear? Why should one be considered strange and the other accepted as normal?" he concluded.

In the back of my head, I knew that there was something off about this conversation, but he left it at that.

When we made it to the top of the stairs, I had the distinct feeling that his mother wasn't home. It was the first time I'd been in any part of the house other than the basement, and the house was quiet as a vault. He walked into his bedroom and asked me to sit on the rug at the foot of his bed. As he rifled through some books and magazines at the bottom of his closet, I looked around his room. It was very tidy and filled with tae kwon do pictures, weapons, and memorabilia. There was another fish tank on the dresser alongside photos of his younger, more muscular self posing with his friends. A long *bō* staff hung above the headboard, and *nunchuks* were displayed on the wall beside other traditional tae kwon do weapons. On the bedside table, I spotted a black club about the size of his forearm.

"How much do you know about the body?" he said, sitting across from me on the floor, still wearing nothing but his Speedo. On his lap was a stack of books. He turned them 180 degrees so I could read the titles. They were about human biology and health.

"A lot, I think," I said. "I want to be a doctor."

"So you know about muscles?"

I nodded.

"Oh, yeah?" he asked, opening the top book to a spread of a front-facing and back-facing skinless man, nothing but muscle and tendon. "What do you know about them?"

I started naming out the ones I could point to—hamstrings, Achilles tendons, triceps—but he cut me off.

"No, no," he said. "Not do you know the muscles—what do you know *about* them? About what they do?"

"They do everything," I said. "They let me move, jump, pick things up. Whatever I need."

"Nice. And minute things too, like blinking and chewing. You know that if you work them out they grow, right?"

I nodded.

"But muscle tissue gets help from a hormone called . . . do you know it?"

I shook my head.

"Testosterone. Now there are natural ways and unnatural ways to build testosterone. Unnatural ways are things like steroids. Guys will inject it right into themselves, but it's terrible for you. It'll kill you. Never do that. Natural testosterone, though, is great. Natural testosterone is something we can build every day, and it's actually not that hard."

"Okay."

"You can take these home," he said, setting aside the books atop the stack of his literature. Underneath the books, he was holding a magazine. I'd now recognize it as a *Penthouse* or a *Play-*

boy, but as a kid, it looked to me as though it might be a lingerie catalogue. He licked his finger and pinched the top corner. "Do you know the differences between male and female anatomy?"

"Kind of," I said.

"Let me explain it to you anyway." He showed me some pictures of naked women and then naked men and women together, named the private areas, and then returned to the male parts with more detail. "Any muscle can get stronger and healthier with more testosterone. When you get aroused, you get more blood flow, which is also great for muscle development." He looked at me with a smile. "It's probably working already."

I looked away and adjusted the way I was sitting, embarrassed.

"Relax," he said. "You're about to go through puberty, which is when your body starts producing lots of testosterone naturally. Actually, you're probably already there. Do you ever touch yourself? Does stuff come out?" I looked at him blankly. "Well, I can help you get through puberty faster, and puberty will make you taller, stronger, and faster."

He waited for me to show some interest as I mentally assessed him. Mr. Neilson had a stern, unfriendly face with bushy eyebrows and coarse skin, so he didn't naturally stir up feelings of trust and safety. But he'd protected me in class and taught me skills to fight bullies. I thought of him both as mentor and protector. After a long pause I said, "Okay."

"Okay. I have a program that focuses just on enhancing testosterone and blood flow," Mr. Neilson continued, making it sound like some "special ops." "It's kind of like a new medicine, so you won't find it anywhere else. And, to be honest, it's not something I offer to everyone. Just the star athletes. James—you remember James, right?" I nodded. "He was a part of this program."

"He was?"

"Yeah, but don't tell anyone. If everyone knows, then I have to offer it to all the members. I don't have time for that."

"Okay."

"Okay, I'll show you how it works."

Mr. Neilson asked me to rub on top of his Speedo. I didn't do it very long before he said it was now my turn. "It's better if you take everything off," he explained.

While Mr. Neilson rubbed me, he explained to me in medical terms what he was doing. He spoke as though I was doing it to myself: "You're stimulating your blood flow," "You'll notice a difference in yourself almost immediately," "Sometimes you might ejaculate—that's normal."

It was difficult to hear a word of it over my own thoughts. Some of what he said made sense because it appealed to my love of science. But why were we up in his room? Where was the old lady? Why did I have to take my underwear off? If this was normal, why were we alone? Then again, he had made it pretty clear to me that this was a "special program" that only the very best were allowed to participate in.

He took his hands away after a few minutes. "It's always better to do it with your trainer, but you can practise this at home, too," he said. "It all helps with passing the program. Here's what you do: any time you come over for practice on the weekends, you get points. Any time you get an erection, you tell me and you get points. Any time you rub yourself, you get points. If stuff comes out, you get points. Any time you get a wet dream, you get points. Most of all, any time you come for special training, you get points. We count all of your points each week and add it toward getting your black belt. Make sense?"

"I guess," I said.

"I know you want to get stronger and fight better," he said. "I know you want your black belt, so you really need to be in this program, Jagmeet."

I nodded. He told me to get dressed. As I reached into my bag on the floor to put my uniform on, he stopped me. "No, no. Get your pants on," he said. "We're done; I'll see you next week."

"I don't need my uniform?" I asked.

"No, not for this program. But you know what? Always bring your uniform, just in case."

And that was it. The hour was up.

—⚊—

It's obvious to me now how much strategy Mr. Neilson used to manipulate me—not just to groom me, but also to make my parents comfortable with me going to his house alone. He made sure they always saw me with my uniform in my bag—the uniform I never actually put on during weekends. I think he may have also exploited a blind spot: while my mom was a little suspicious about the club being in the basement, she probably didn't even imagine that a boy could be sexually abused, and I avoided giving any clues or hints about what was going on.

Mr. Neilson knew my own insecurities and aspirations, maybe better than anyone else. He studied me as closely as I studied tae kwon do. He knew I was in a hurry to get my black belt, but he also knew I knew that the level progressions would slow down once I achieved a blue belt, and that the skills I would have to master to level up would get more complicated. His "points," he promised, would help fast-track me.

But most of all, he knew I wanted results. I wanted to be bigger. I needed to be stronger. Mr. Neilson tied his perversion to my performance, my primary motivation. And as the weekend sessions continued on top of my weekly training, I convinced myself that I was improving.

It didn't take long for the abuse to seem normal. I went over for an hour every Saturday afternoon, always while Mr. Neilson's mother was out. He'd start each session by asking, "What's your update for the week?" I'd report what "points" I'd earned, and he would tick lines on his clipboard chart and take a few notes. Sometimes, I'd lie to him, telling him I'd masturbated when I hadn't or that I had a wet dream when I still didn't know what that was. Finally, he'd ask me to "help" with his testosterone, then he'd help me with mine. He never removed his underwear; I always removed mine. He never went further than that.

There was only one time when the program overlapped with the weekday club. We were stretching together, lined up by ranking, myself in the middle, facing forward as we tried to get into a low stretch. Normally, I could get down into a near split, but that day, for some reason, I couldn't.

"It's not working," I said as he came around to inspect our stretches.

"Come upstairs, I'll give you a hand," he said.

I went to his room, where we went through his program and he helped me stretch. When it was over, I got back in my uniform and returned downstairs with him.

Eric was watching as I tried again to get into a lower stretch, this time dropping closer to the floor than before.

"Hey," said Eric. "How'd you do that?"

I didn't say anything. Neither did Mr. Neilson. This was "special ops."

—⁓—

Between Mr. Neilson's abuse and my dad's worsening alcoholism, I had a lot on my mind when I began sixth grade at Detroit Country Day School in September 1991. Very quickly, however, the demands of going to the new school busied me to the point that I could hardly think about anything but my academics.

My school day started at 6 a.m., when I caught the early carpool with a handful of other Canadian kids who also went to the prep school. All of us were doctors' kids, and we crammed into a minivan for a thirty- to forty-minute commute. After-school activities and sports meant I often wasn't home until 4:30 p.m.

The school made extracurriculars mandatory. In order to graduate from one grade to the next, I had to earn one "white point" for doing a certain amount of community service, a "gold point" for joining a club like chess or the school newspaper, and two "blue points" for sports (it could be an individual sport, like weight training, but at least one had to be a team sport). I now spent some evenings volunteering with elderly people at my dad's hospital to get my volunteer hours, and I stayed after school for sports. All of that was on top of my assigned homework, routine reading of fantasy novels and Sikh spiritual poetry, and Sunday services at *Gurdwara*. I enjoyed the unique challenge each activity brought, and I appreciated the distractions they offered from my home life. Most of all, though, I liked that I didn't have to fight anymore.

For the first time in years, my identity and appearance didn't feel like a major barrier. Detroit was a diverse city to begin with, but Country Day was exactly the kind of school that upwardly mobile immigrants desired for their kids. I was no longer the only one in class with a head covering—along with my *patka*, there were also *kippahs* and *hijabs*. Practising different traditions and observing different holidays was normal in class. The notion of mocking kids because of their identity was ridiculous. There was still ample bullying and snobbery to go around, all of it centred around your "coolness" factors—having the right or wrong brand-name shoes, or being helplessly dorky—but I was never bullied for the way I looked at school again.

The one time I did get in a scrap, the experience was night and day compared to my days at school in Windsor. I can't remember the exact reason this boy was picking on me, but he was pushing me and acting aggressively. I tried to get him to stop but he wasn't interested in talking. He was a lot bigger than me, too, so physically, I couldn't avoid him. He kept on getting in my face, blocking my way and trying to intimidate me. Finally, I'd had enough. When he pushed me again, I threw a burst of rapid punches to his abdomen. Instantly winded, all of his aggression deflated.

I scanned the faces of students that had gathered around us. Had we been at Oakwood, had any of them been Walid or even a random bystander, I would have earned their respect and maybe a couple of pats on the back or a high-five for standing up for myself. But the response I received was the furthest thing from praise. People looked at me like there was something wrong with me.

"That's kind of violent," a girl said, totally appalled.

"But *he* was picking on *me*," I tried to argue back, to no avail. The kids watching all dispersed as if they had just watched a horrible car crash.

Country Day was like a separate society that I was driven in and out of each day. While I had a lot of acquaintances there and the kids were generally friendly, I couldn't break through the already established cliques, so I didn't make any close friendships for a while. But I didn't mind—I already had a lot of friends in my completely separate world in Windsor, as well as a best friend, Walid.

As close as I was to Walid, I never opened up about what was going on with me during that time. I never complained about stuff at home. I remember one summer day when we were about eight or nine years old. We were hanging out in the backyard by the pool. My dad came outside. He was clearly really drunk. Walid said hi politely. And before my dad could engage with him, I went toward my dad and said, "Get back inside."

Dad didn't listen, so I started pushing him toward the garage and then up the stairs that led into the house, yelling at him the whole time. At some point, my dad yelled, "Up yours!" back at me.

When I came back outside, Walid looked shocked.

"Why were you so rude to your dad?" he asked. He liked my dad and my dad liked him.

I explained to Walid, for the first and only time as a child, that sometimes my dad drank and was difficult to deal with. We never spoke about my dad's problem again until we were thirty-nine years old.

Maybe it never came up again because I was worried that to Walid, my dad seemed perfect. To Walid—to most of my friends—Dr. Dhaliwal was like a sitcom version of a dad. When in public view, he was sober, charming, charismatic, well-dressed, and eager to share many wisdoms. It would have been nearly impossible for Walid to match up the dad I knew behind closed doors with the one who bought us the best video camera on the market and let me and Manjot film mock television shows and news reports that we would star in together.

And I definitely didn't want to tell Walid about Mr. Neilson. That's the thing about abuse—it can make the victim feel an overwhelming sense of shame, a shame so disabling that one suffers in silence. I somehow blamed myself for what had happened, and while I knew what had happened was real—I didn't imagine it—part of me didn't actually believe it. And if *I* didn't believe it, how was anyone else going to? So I carried the shame and stigma; I buried it deep. I told no one, and I told myself not to think about what had happened. In a way, I prevented myself from actually accepting the truth. But here, now, is the truth of the experience: abuse doesn't just go away, even after it ends. The consequences linger. They take a toll, even if it's invisible for a while. By not speaking up, by convincing myself that nothing had happened, I got through—in the short term. But in the long term, I would have to face the truth. I would have to unearth it, bring it to the surface, and examine it. I would have to face the fact that I was the victim, not the perpetrator. I was not to blame. I would have to accept that the abuse really did happen and that it had taken a devastating toll on me.

—⋙—

When I started sixth grade, I was too tired on weekends to go to my special training anymore. With school starting up, tae kwon do was going to be hard to squeeze in with my new academic demands. And, honestly, I'd been losing interest in it ever since I started Mr. Neilson's "special program." I was a few levels from earning a black belt, but my passion for martial arts had been stamped out by conflicting feelings about my training. The other sports I was playing and my new school were better ways of building my confidence, and the feeling of specialness that Mr. Neilson initially groomed had slowly faded. Without it, his testosterone training didn't feel like "special ops" anymore. It felt like a chore that I dreaded having to do and that made me feel uncomfortable with myself afterward. It also didn't seem to get me any closer to a black belt, as he'd promised.

I don't know if I was consciously avoiding training, but one day my mom asked if I wanted to go and I said, "I don't think I have time anymore."

That was the end of it. She never asked me again. I never saw Mr. Neilson again. And I never heard from him, either. But I did hear *about* him.

About a year later, I was hanging out in our backyard when my mom called me in for dinner. When I went inside, the table hadn't been set yet. My mom sat alone at the table and seemed a little on edge. My mom was a lot of things, but she had never come across as uncomfortable toward me. Whatever was up, it was serious.

"Jagmeet," she said.

"Yes, *bebey-ji*," I said, standing at the doorway.

"Sit with me," she said. I did. "This probably didn't happen, but did Mr. Neilson ever show you any pictures?"

I shifted in my seat a little, immediately flushed with shame about myself and worry for my mom. I believed I'd done something wrong, something about to make her already stressful life worse. I knew where her question was leading, but I felt she had enough on her mind with my dad's addiction, so I played dumb. "What do you mean?"

"Any pictures of men and women together in magazines?"

"No."

"They're saying that . . ." She trailed off. She was so uncomfortable it was hard for her to say the words. "The police called your father. Apparently there have been complaints of Mr. Neilson behaving inappropriately with children, so they're checking in with anyone who took classes with him."

As my mom spoke, I immediately understood what Mr. Neilson had been doing to me. I just hadn't had the words for it until that moment. Still, I wasn't quite ready to use them.

"Mom, nothing like that happened to me. Don't worry," I said, trying my best to calm her worries.

"Okay," she said, reaching the limits of her comfort. "It's just about suppertime."

And that was that. She'd tried. She'd asked, and I'd said nothing. Why? I was worried about how she'd take it, worried that she would feel like she'd let me down. I was worried that maybe she would think I was tainted or dirty because of what had happened. And, of course, part of me wondered if it had all been my fault. Maybe I'd let this happen. Maybe I should have prevented Mr. Neilson from doing what he did. The swirl of guilt, shame, and blame took hold, and it made me turn to stone.

The next day, Walid was waiting on his front porch when the carpool driver dropped me off at home. He'd started taking classes with Mr. Neilson a few months before, and now that I could see clearly what Mr. Neilson was doing, I knew I had to warn Walid.

"You have to stop going to Mr. Neilson's classes," I blurted out as I ran across his front lawn.

"What do you mean? Why?" Walid asked.

"He got in trouble for doing something with students," I said, purposefully trying to be vague.

"Did something happen to you?" Walid asked.

"No," I said without a millisecond to spare. I couldn't admit to it. The way I saw it back then, I had done it to myself. *I didn't stop Mr. Neilson*, I thought. *I let him do this*. I didn't want Walid to think I'd let that happen—I just wanted to make sure the same thing didn't happen to him.

"Did he do anything to you?" I asked.

"No," said Walid. "He offered me private lessons, but I didn't want them. I guess I'll have to find a new club now."

"Good idea," I said.

We hung out a little longer and talked about other things until my heart rate returned to normal. I was relieved that nothing had happened to Walid. If anything had, Walid would have told his parents and he would have told me. I felt a little reassured, and the feeling of guilt and shame momentarily subsided.

I never heard anything more about Mr. Neilson or a police investigation. It would be another fifteen years before I talked to my family about what happened. That's how long it would take me to understand it wasn't my fault and to come to some self-knowledge. It took me even longer to work through the trauma he caused. Mr. Neilson's abuse would affect my self-esteem, my self-love, and my ability to be intimate. That night, all I could think about was how ashamed I was for continuing to go back to his club. I'd always thought of myself as a mature kid, a bit of an old soul who had a lot of control. I had agency over my academics and the bullies I successfully defended myself against—so how could I have let this happen if it wasn't my choice?

I wish I could go back and tell my younger self, "It's not your fault." But at the time, I never heard those words. So my coping mechanism was simple: don't think about it. Whenever I felt the shame or the guilt creep up, I would have a conversation with myself.

All right, Jagmeet, something happened and it was messed up. I'm not sure how to fix it or make it go away. We made it through, that's all that matters. Now don't think about it.

I carried out the same conversation with myself that night in bed, trying to push the sound of Mr. Neilson's voice and the feel of his touch into a black hole of amnesia. The shame was too much. One thing was certain to me: I couldn't ever let anyone know about it.

Chapter Seven

THE LAND OF FIVE RIVERS

Weekends were the worst. My dad would either be stumbling around the house drunk and out of his mind, or passed out on the couch. He was very particular to hide his bottles and his actual drinking, but whenever he drank too much, he ordered pizza. If we came home to a scene of empty pizza boxes strewn about, we knew that things were going to be bad. Empty pizza boxes and bottles are the image permanently etched into my mind of things being bad.

My dad's behaviour, as unfair as it sounds, also appeared to have an impact on how people perceived us. As in any close-knit community, the rumour mills were in full effect. Word got around that my dad had a drinking problem. Even though I was considered a good kid, we were tainted by my dad's alcoholism. We started to get the feeling that people wanted to avoid us.

After my dad had gotten his residency in St. John's, my mom stopped working. She volunteered for community activities every now and then, and became a full-time mom. Once my siblings and I were more self-sufficient, she started helping out as my dad's office manager, but that job obviously depended on him having a practice. She got so wrapped up in trying to take care of him that she didn't think she could do anything else.

Each time my dad finally sobered up, I would sit down with him and deliver a long lecture.

"Dad, we have to talk," I'd start.

"Sure, *beta*, what is it?" he replied.

"Dad, when you drink, it's scary for everyone. You're not yourself. You get angry and you break things. I know you don't want to do that."

"*Beta*, I'm so sorry. I never want to hurt you or our family; that's the last thing I want to do," he said each time.

"I know, Dad, but when you drink, that's what happens. You scare us. You scare me."

His eyes would fill with remorse, and I'd feel as though I was getting through to him.

"Then I won't drink anymore," he'd promise. "I hate drinking, if that's what it does to you and our family."

"Do you promise? Do you promise, Dad, that you won't drink?"

"Yes, I promise. I promise that I'm never going to drink again," he'd declare with an intense solemnity.

Each time he said it, I would believe him with the same hope as if I was hearing the promise for the first time. And each time he made that vow, he broke it, sometimes the very next day. But no matter how many times he said the words, I always believed that this would be the time he kept his promise.

Sometimes he was still a little drunk when we had those chats. Overcome with guilt, he would try to make it up to us by being suddenly and unbearably kind—hugging us, slurring that he had the best children and the greatest family he could ask for.

I'm ashamed to admit that I became meaner to my dad the older and bigger I got. I rarely yelled at him unless he actually became physical—gesturing aggressively, yelling, or throwing things. "Go away—you're drunk!" I yelled one evening, pushing him and his horrible breath away. A pathetic frown washed over his ruddy face. His eyes welled up as he pouted helplessly. I immediately felt awful.

My siblings and I relied on each other to get through. I saw myself as their protector. Many times, things became scary as my dad was yelling or moaning, or we heard our parents arguing and screaming and things being slammed, dropped, or broken. In those moments, I brought my brother and sister together and we weathered the storm by reading spiritual poetry or meditating together. We were afraid and traumatized, but we found fleeting glimpses of peace in those moments together, and it helped us understand the idea that we are all connected, that we are all one.

While the turmoil brought my siblings and me closer, it severed us from our peers. Windsor's Panjabi community was small to begin with. Our extended family was smaller still. Our community seemed to be shrinking around us.

We had some family in the Toronto area who we visited now and then. Over the years, my mom's eldest brother or brother-in-law stepped in a few times to try to get my dad to stop drinking. I don't know how much my mom shared with them, but they knew how bad it was from what she described to them.

When I was younger, we would visit family in the Greater Toronto Area at least twice a year, and one of my cousins would
visit us regularly in Windsor. But as we got older, his parents
didn't let him visit anymore.

"Why don't you ever send him here?" I remember my mom
asking my aunt on the phone. "He wants to see Jagmeet." My
mom went quiet as my aunt tried to make an excuse, and from
then on, I rode the Greyhound to Newmarket any time we
wanted to visit. I understood my aunt's concerns. I wouldn't
have wanted my kids exposed to my dad's crippling alcoholism
either. It was scary.

Our dad's reputation followed us to *Gurdwara*, too. On the
one hand, they respected my dad—the only Sikh doctor in
Windsor, a mover and shaker, a benefactor to the *Gurdwara*. On
the other hand, he was an embarrassment to them—a caution-
ary tale about the perils of alcohol.

People outside the Sikh community noted the contrast
between my father and me. One day, I was having dinner at
Walid's house, when one of his uncles asked about my Sikhi.

"Why don't you cut your hair?" he asked.

"Because it's part of my belief," I said.

"Why doesn't your dad follow the same teachings?"

"Maybe he doesn't have the same strength of belief. But
that's okay, that's his decision."

Walid's uncle froze, then broke out into a good-natured
laugh. My precocious answer surprised and delighted him.

Later that summer, I called Walid to see if he had plans.
"Want to hang out?" I asked.

"Sure," Walid said.

"I have some homework to do, but come over after lunch."

There was a pause on the other end of the line. Finally, Walid said, "Yo, why don't you come over to my place instead?"

It dawned on me—Walid's parents didn't want him coming over either. Even though Walid and I had never talked about my dad's behaviour, there were just a few metres between our houses, so it seemed Walid's parents knew that our idyllic house on an idyllic street was anything but that. Walid's parents could be strict at the best of times—he always had a curfew and boundaries for how far he could ride his bike. Once, Walid and I spent an entire day building a raft to cross a creek near our neighbourhood. We didn't get home until dark. It wasn't unusual for me to leave the house during the day and come back at night. I don't remember ever having a curfew or any restrictions on where I could ride my bike or how far I could go. When I got home that night, though, my mom was frantic.

"Where's Walid?" she asked the moment I walked through the door.

"He's heading home. Why?"

"His mother called the police. She was worried because he was gone all day."

I wanted to laugh—we had spent the whole day no more than a five-minute walk from our house, and my mom wasn't worried. But Walid's had been so concerned that she'd called the police.

I didn't take Walid's reluctance to come over anymore personally. In some ways, I was relieved—I didn't want friends coming to our house because I was worried about what state my dad would be in, and what he would say or do.

Manjot seemed to think the same way as me, as she'd often escape to her friends' houses. I started bringing Gurratan along

119

to Walid's house more often, just to get him out of the negative environment. Gurratan was thrilled—he usually wanted to tag along with me wherever I went. He was content just hanging out with Walid and me, watching us play video games, and listening while we big kids talked about whatever thirteen-year-old boys talked about in 1991 (Paula Abdul, probably).

I never minded having Gurratan around—he was pretty low maintenance—and I never saw him as an annoying little brother. Quite the opposite. I liked having him around. If I said, "Would you go get that for me?" he went to get it, not out of fear, but out of brotherly love. Back home, Gurratan often wanted me to play toys with him. Gurratan had taken over my action figure collection and had added to it. We didn't keep each toy carefully wrapped up and packaged, or on display never to be used. Instead, we acted out action scenes. Even though I was past the age of buying action figures myself, I actually enjoyed listening and adding to his elaborate stories and quests. Together, we created whole mythologies, an entire world built exclusively from our own imaginations.

While we enjoyed the stories we created, there was always a minor point of contention. "I want to be this guy," he said once, clutching one of his favourite figures: a two-headed ogre with bulging muscles. Each of the ogre's two faces had menacing eyes and an angry scowl.

"Sure," I said, taking a muscular warrior from the pile. "I'll be the white ninja."

"My guy's the good guy."

"He's clearly not," I said. "He's scary looking. He's supposed to be the bad guy."

"No, he's the good guy."

"Look at his fangs, Gurratan. Good guys don't have fangs."

"Good guy," he insisted.

Gurratan was a cute kid, chatty and confident, but sometimes, I worried about him. If Walid and I tried to hand him a
Nintendo controller to have a turn, he would be too afraid to
play.

"No," he protested. "I don't want to die."

"It's okay," I said. "We have a bunch of lives saved up."

"It's too scary."

"We'll just start over if you die," Walid assured him. It was
futile. Maybe my dad's erratic behaviour and frequent outbursts
were having an impact on Gurratan. Truth be told, it was probably affecting all of us. The only difference was that Manjot and
I were old enough to have some memories of times before my
dad's sickness. But for my brother, this was all he knew.

I'd become good at compartmentalizing my troubles and
suppressing negative thoughts. Too good. While I couldn't control my mind from sometimes bringing up what Mr. Neilson
had done to me, I was able to successfully prevent myself from
spiralling down a hole of guilt and shame by constantly repeating "Don't think about it, just don't think about it" like a mantra
whenever bad memories flashed back. My dad's alcoholism and
abuse, though, were far too present and fluid to simply think
away, so I relied on my safe spaces.

Walid's house was one such place. My go-to escape, though,
was still my fantasy books. Libraries continued to hold a special
place in my heart. They were safe spaces filled with stories that
could transport me far away, and the librarians acted as gate-
keepers to those portals.

On weekends, I'd wake up and start reading. Sometimes I

would skip breakfast and then bike to the library, skip lunch, and only come back home in time for dinner, dizzy from living in an imagined place for ten straight hours. One series that consumed me was Robert Jordan's Wheel of Time, a masterpiece with its sprawling worlds and detailed magic system. I latched on to its vision of the universe as a tapestry into which everyone is woven, from the past to the future and back again. It was an infinite cycle, like the universe, and also like the circle of the *kara*, the steel/iron bracelet I wore on my wrist.

As much as I enjoyed escaping to other worlds, though, I still wanted to explore the one around me. One of my favourite things about my new school was the number of field trips and outings to cultural institutions it offered. Museums, galleries, historical sites—our class regularly piled into the school bus and headed to one or another. I even had the opportunity of travelling to Paris, Normandy, and a few small towns for a week with my French class.

That trip was special to me. It was my first time travelling without my family. Before I left, my dad gave me a present: a journal in which I could keep a record of everything I saw and did. My dad was very thoughtful that way. Any time he thought there was something that would help us kids out, whether it was a tutor or an experience like skiing or a tool like a journal, he tried his best to make sure he provided us with it. I made sure to jot down every sight, smell, and sound I came across, many of them entirely new. I rode an underground subway for the first time. I ate my first crepe ever, and when I tasted the Nutella inside it, I was immediately hooked. I wrote down how cool I thought the French kids' style was.

Monsieur Tremblay taught at our school in Detroit, but he

was originally from Quebec. He was a bald, burly, rough, and rugged-looking man, but his appearance contrasted completely with his kindness and gentle warmth. Monsieur Tremblay took us to markets and stores, and let us roam around to practise our language skills. His chats about Quebec culture and history got me reading more about what the French in Canada had faced throughout history. The more I read, the more parallels I saw with what my parents had faced growing up speaking Panjabi, which was seen as a language inferior to the official languages of Hindi and English. My decision to learn French was an act of solidarity with the people of Quebec as much as it was me falling in love with the language. I credit Monsieur Tremblay with planting the seed for my love of the French language and understanding of Quebec culture.

That trip was the first time I had been away from my family for so long on my own. I had visited relatives in Toronto, but that wasn't the same thing. Here I was away from everyone I knew in a country thousands of kilometres away. Coming back home was a special experience. It was really only when I saw my family again after so long that I realized how much I had missed them.

After a while, though, the bad days started to take their toll again. The mall was a shelter from the turmoil at home. Walid and I spent many weekends there, just a couple of mall rats walking around, hanging out, looking for friends, and, if we were so lucky, spotting a crush from school. Still, though, it was far from a safe space. Often, some jerk would call me "Paki" or make fun of my *patka*. "Do you have a brain injury?" they might yell. "What's that weird thing on that kid's head?" others would say in obnoxiously loud voices.

What hurt the most, though, was the pointing and laughing. It was such a common response, and every time it happened, I felt the same flush of shame. Laughter isn't innocuous. Every time I heard it in a public place, I would start to doubt. *Maybe I do look funny*, I'd think. *Maybe I deserve to be laughed at.* I had a tough shell. I could steel myself against insults, but laughter slipped through the cracks in my armour and soaked me in shame.

I'll never forget this one time when Walid and I were walking through the mall. Out of the corner of my eye, I saw a little kid laughing at me. It was just him laughing—it hurt more when it was a big crowd—and he was close to our age, so I didn't give him much thought. But then I noticed he was with his parents. The boy gleefully pulled on their coat sleeves to bring their attention to me. You'd think they'd have stopped his teasing. You'd think they'd say something like, "Honey, that's not nice—don't make fun of how he looks." Instead, they looked in my direction, pointed, and laughed even harder.

A hot flush of shame mixed with a cold, sinking feeling that I didn't belong there. The fact that the parents were laughing along with their child was chilling. I always figured parents would correct their kids when they misbehaved, or at least provide some protection. But I now saw that I wasn't always going to be safe just because parents were present. If even the parents, who were supposed to set the right example, thought it was okay to laugh at me, then maybe, I thought, there was no safe place.

Their laughter rattled me. But, like other things that had shaken me before, I pushed the feeling down and tried to ignore it.

"Want to check out if there are any new arcade games?" I asked Walid.

"Sure," he said. We turned down the hallway leading to the less travelled part of the mall, away from the laughter and shame.

Experiences like that were still better than being at home. At home, I had to steel myself from the pain and humiliation caused by my dad. At home, I felt like I had to take care of my mom, brother, and sister. At home, I needed to show my mom and siblings that I had the strength to carry them, that they could rely on me.

When I reached the limits of my strength, though, I'd sneak off to a quiet corner where no one could see or hear me—my bedroom, the washroom, the basement storage closet, wherever I was least likely to be found. When I was sure I was alone, I'd cry. In those moments, it seemed like there was no end in sight to the difficulty. I felt alone because there was no one I could turn to. I was too embarrassed and ashamed to tell Walid or any other friends. I couldn't speak to any relatives about it. My family was living it too, and I needed to be strong for them. So I bore it in silence, my crying muffled in dark rooms, hiding my sadness and fear as much as my shame.

—⁂—

One summer day in 1993, I came home and immediately noticed something strange was going on. My dad was unusually sober. Instead of being grumpy, angry, or belligerent, he seemed different. Calm? No, he was sad. My dad had always been emotional. He was the first to get teary-eyed during the sad scene of a movie. But this was something more than that.

125

"Jagmeet," he said quietly. "Come sit down."

"Are Gurratan and Manjot okay?" I asked.

"Your brother and sister are fine. It's your *dada-ji*," he said, referring to my paternal granddad. "He died of a heart attack yesterday."

I sat there quietly, unsure what to say or feel. Though my grandfather had been an integral part of the first years of my life, I'd hardly seen him since. He'd visited once or twice in New-foundland and even after that, but we hadn't bonded in any lasting way. I was conflicted, thinking that I should have been sadder than I felt. But the only emotion coursing through me was guilt. Guilt for not feeling any sadness at all, and, I think, for not building a connection with my grandfather when he was alive.

After a few quiet moments, I asked, "Are you okay?"

"We have to get to Panjab," he said. "Your *poa-ji*"—my pater-nal aunt—"is already on her way and they will start the funeral rites soon. I have to be there for my duties."

In Sikh tradition, the body is just a shell housing the one energy, that energy that connects all humans and everything around us. When a Sikh person dies, the body is burned. As the eldest son, albeit from my grandfather's second marriage, my father felt it was his responsibility to see to the final rites and take care of his mother and sister.

"Our flight is in two days, but we could only get three seats, so your mother and Gurratan will meet us there next week."

The immediate excitement I felt about going to Panjab—reconnecting with my history and identity—was sapped dry by the realization that my sister and I would be alone with my dad. *Was he even capable of looking after us?* I wondered. After seven years of watching his heavy drinking, I'd almost forgotten there was a public version of him that *wasn't* under the influence. A couple of times in early high school, while volunteering at the hospital, I'd witnessed him running the psychiatric unit with total control, knowledge, and proficiency. It was cool to see him like that, making confident decisions for a massive operation, but more than anything, it was simply surreal. I couldn't reconcile the man I saw in those brief moments with the one I knew at home.

I couldn't remember the last time I'd felt secure around my dad. Now we'd be alone with him in a foreign country? A place where visitors could be easily taken advantage of? Where police might harass us identifiable Sikhs? I was worried, but I didn't know what to do.

I approached my mom later that night, when I was packing. "*Bebey-ji*, when are you going to get there?"

"Like your father said, *beta*, I'll arrive a week after you."

"I know, but when exactly? Do you know what day?"

Sometimes, even when you think moms don't know, they know.

My mom drew closer, gave me a hug, and said, "Don't worry, Jagmeet. Everything is going to be okay. Just make sure you look after your sister."

I hugged her back. "Don't worry, *bebey-ji*," I said. "I will."

As our departure inched nearer, I slowly started to think I could trust my dad. He was grief-stricken, yes, but he had the presence of mind not to get hammered. He took the responsibility of caretaking for me and Manjot seriously. It fascinated us to see him take charge of each situation the way he did—driving us to Pearson Airport in Toronto, guiding us from Pearson to

Heathrow, then Heathrow to Indira Gandhi International Airport, all with ease. This wasn't my dad; this was Dr. Dhaliwal.

We'd travelled a lot before as a family, but always to safe, familiar places—to California once, and to Florida semi-annually. Even from the air, I knew this trip would be profoundly different. The flight across Asia seemed to go on forever, and since there was just one Disney movie playing on the bulky TV aisle screens, I spent most of the trip watching the land transform beneath my window. In my head, I thought about our destination. Would I recognize anything from my childhood? Would anything feel familiar?

"What do you think India is going to be like?" Manjot asked.

"I don't know," I replied. "I don't remember anything about it."

"Of course you don't, you were just a baby. But do you think there will be camels?"

"Maybe," I said, shrugging my shoulders.

"I'm looking forward to making new friends," Manjot said.

As soon as we stepped off the plane and saw crowds swarming at the end of the jet bridge, my dad put a firm hand on our shoulders. "Be careful," he said.

My dad hadn't been to India in twelve years and for a moment, his face betrayed the sense of calm he was trying to create. Taxi drivers and baggage handlers pushed toward us, vying for his business, talking and stepping over themselves for his attention. My dad tried to negotiate a fair price for the three-hundred-kilometre trek to our family's village, but the drivers' aggressive bartering frustrated and flustered him. "Let's look at the buses," he finally said, holding Manjot's hand while I pushed our luggage on a dolly.

I'd imagined something like a Greyhound charter, but when

we went to the station, what we found was closer to a rusting school bus you might see for sale on the side of a highway. Inside, every bench seat but one was filled by travellers, almost all of whom were men. My dad was worried about Manjot, so he sat immediately next to her so he could make sure there wasn't anyone else touching her. The only space left for me had me leaning precariously close to the gearshift, halfway between the driver and the door. That part of the bus must have been in contact with the engine because it got hotter and hotter as the trip continued.

It was nighttime when we left, but the combined summer weather and body heat radiating off the sixty densely packed passengers made it oppressively hot. Sweat poured off my face as I switched between sitting against and standing on the burning steel.

Looking outside as we drove north across New Delhi, I felt like we were going back in time. People and vehicles shared the roads with animals—bull carts with straw carriages, camels pulling two-wheeled wagons, old men walking alongside their donkeys, chickens roaming between their feet and tires. Bells and horns drowned out the crowd with their hierarchy of noises—bikes ringing, scooters squawking, and our bus belching the mightiest trumpet (instead of, you know, using a turn signal) each time it changed lanes.

The drive was eight hours long, with about six stops. It was daytime when we finally arrived. I blinked groggily and saw we were in the middle of what looked like a bustling town. There were people everywhere, walking in front of stores with peeling paint and battered-looking signs. The honking of cars and smell of animals filled the air—it was overwhelming.

I carried our bags to the shade, noticing my dad's furrowed brow as he looked in each direction, stroking the stubble on his face. "Are we okay?" I asked.

"This is new," he said. "There used to be a different bus station here." He paused. "I don't know my way home."

"Didn't you grow up here, Dad?" Manjot asked.

"Everything is so different," he said, half to himself.

My dad asked around the bus depot for directions to his family's farm, in between nervously checking the time on his watch. We were afraid we might miss the ceremonial washing and dressing of his dad's body because we hadn't gotten an early enough flight. He worried that the cremation would begin without him, and hoped that they'd hold off for him. Precious time passed as he tried to orient himself and piece together the directions offered to him based on his description of the farm. If only it were as simple as giving an address and taking directions like "Go left on Ouellette Avenue, right on Wyandotte Street." But the instructions people gave were more like "Go down that road, there'll be a baker, then take a left and go past so-and-so's house."

It turned out that the bus station wasn't far from our family's house. The outskirts of Barnala, where my dad grew up, had been developed into housing and businesses since his last visit. He'd been looking for a farmhouse on the outskirts of the city, as he remembered it, but the city had long since enveloped the farmhouse.

We carried our suitcases through the surrounding area, a subdivision of concrete shanties inhabited by families struggling to survive on the margins. Kids younger than Gurratan waved gum packets and corn at us for sale. When we said no, they stretched out a palm for money.

I'd never been hit by so many scents at once. Our North American environment seemed positively sterile by comparison. The air carried the familiar scent of Panjabi cooking and spices, but it mingled with burning wood stoves and manure patties, open sewage dumpsters, and live animals. It was sensory overload.

There wasn't a spot of grass or plants on the ground, just garbage and bones and crushed plastic bottles. Dust rose behind us as we dragged our bags through the dirt road. When we finally arrived and stepped through the gates, the place had a vague familiarity, not from any personal memories, but from pictures I'd seen in photo albums. There was a large courtyard with one structure on either side: one was a newer building where my grandparents had been living, and the other—the one where my dad grew up—was rented out to some people who worked for my grandparents. A vegetable garden filled the courtyard between the houses, along with flowers and the first trees I'd seen up close since arriving in India.

As we approached my grandparents' cute little house, my dad recited memories as they activated before his eyes, pointing out the places he'd played and studied, husked corn, and learned to ride a bike. There were a couple of parked cars belonging to relatives and loved ones who had arrived to give their condolences. We removed our shoes outside the house and stepped barefoot onto the concrete floor inside.

We looked around, but there was no one to be seen. Suddenly, my dad realized—the cremation had already happened.

"They didn't wait for me," he said sadly.

My dad felt as though he hadn't fulfilled his responsibilities as the eldest child, but to me, he'd finally risen up and met his responsibilities as a father. I couldn't remember the last time I'd felt so proud of him. He'd been sober for five straight days and was extremely "with it." He'd brought Manjot and me here on his own, negotiated our travel to his village, and kept us safe throughout the adventure. I'd thought we were travelling with Dr. Dhaliwal, but the love and care he showed made me realize it was my dad all along.

Chapter Eight

THE RUSSIAN PRINCE

The loss of his father somehow had a life-changing impact on my dad, and it didn't stop after our trip. He returned to Windsor motivated to get clean, reconnect with his Sikhi, and be a role model to his kids. Sometime during the trip my dad had let his beard grow out and started tying a turban.

It had been years since I'd been in the presence of my dad's true personality. He was charming, smooth, and a little goofy. It was during this time that I really got to understand him. He talked about growing up in Panjab, the fears of growing financial uncertainty as his dad kept losing land, and the pressure he felt to achieve more security. It relieved me to have the 2.0 version of my dad, but it filled me with insecurity, too. I feared he could relapse at any moment.

Our home felt more secure as his sobriety continued into 1994. The length of my dad's hair was like a litmus test for his health and well-being: the longer and more luscious it was, the safer I felt. Having never seen my dad with long hair, it was a little confusing to catch sight of him one day at the kitchen table with a *patka* tied on his head because he was going to play tennis. I hadn't really ever seen a grown man wearing a *patka*. I thought that it was only something little kids wore. I think he was a little uncertain about the *patka* as well, but he didn't have a sports-style turban. He was still figuring it all out, but I guess that's just it: he was a grown man awkwardly growing into his faith in middle age.

My dad had started going to work in a turban, too. I had started tying my own turbans in ninth grade, two years before our trip to Panjab for my grandfather's funeral. Usually, as Sikh kids get older, they start wearing one, and I felt beginning my first year in high school it was definitely time. Funnily enough, even though my dad hadn't worn a turban when I was growing up, he was still the one who taught me how to tie one. He showed me how to fold the turban cloth in pleats called a *pooni*. It takes two people holding the cloth stretched out to its full length. Then he taught me a little turban-tying hack. Usually after doing a *pooni* or pleating the cloth, you sit or stand in front of a mirror and tie the turban one wrap or *lard* at a time. My dad taught me a technique where he stood still, holding one end of the fabric, while I slowly spun, winding the turban around my head until we got closer and closer. It took some coordination, but it usually turned out surprisingly all right.

The first time I tied it was the summer before ninth grade, and I immediately went to show it to Walid. He was always honest with me, so I knew that when I showed him my turban for the first time, he would tell me straight up what he thought.

I knocked on Walid's door, and when he opened it, I spread out my arms. "What do you think?" I asked.

He looked at me very seriously and solemnly. Finally, he said, "I like it. It suits you."

I sighed with relief. "Really?"

"Actually, can I be honest with you?"

"Of course."

"I think it looks a lot better than the other thing you used to wear."

I laughed. "You mean my *patka*?"

"Yeah. This one you're wearing looks better."

That was it. I switched to a turban and never looked back.

My dad reconnected with his roots in more ways than faith and culture. For Manjot's tenth birthday, he surprised us with a puppy—a tiny German shepherd curled up in a kennel, his golden paws folded over his little black snout. My sister shrieked with joy, startling the pup. His floppy ears flipped up and his eyes shot open. When we looked into his big brown eyes, Gurratan immediately ceased being the baby of the family.

"What's his name?" Manjot asked.

"Jugnu," said my dad, pronouncing it *Joog-new*.

"Why Jugnu?" she asked.

"That was my dog's name when I was a boy."

"What's it mean?"

"Firefly."

"That's cool!"

My dad created a schedule for us kids, making sure we each did our part in taking care of Jugnu. Manjot and I didn't mind taking Jugnu for walks, but Gurratan could be a bit lazier about it. Jugnu didn't care who took him, just so long as he got out. There could be a blizzard outside, and Jugnu would be going stir crazy in the house, begging to be let out.

"Who is taking Jugnu for his walk?" my dad would ask, staring out at the falling snow as Gurratan did his best to fade into the background and avoid eye contact.

"Jagmeet, it's your turn," my dad said. As the oldest sibling, the buck often stopped with me. I loved being outside, so although I sometimes grumbled, I didn't mind. I enjoyed the walk and the retreat into the trees around our neighbourhood. Walks with Jugnu gave me some time to myself. Even when the sun was setting and the long shadows gave the forest a more ominous look from the outside, I still felt like I had a safe refuge within it.

My dad was definitely the alpha to Jugnu, who was most obedient to him, but I was a close second. Jugnu was a peculiar dog, one who liked being around people but still liked his space. Manjot always wanted to cuddle, but Jugnu wasn't the most snuggly. Whenever she tried to get close to him on the couch, he'd pick himself up, hop to the floor, and sashay away.

On walks, neighbours tried to coo and baby-talk to him. "Is your dog friendly?" they'd ask.

"No," I'd say.

"Can I pet him?"

"Definitely not."

Jugnu would lose his mind at strangers through the living room window, let alone ones passing him on a sidewalk. Inside the house, we could get him to bark like crazy and run up to the nearest window simply by saying, "Look, look."

That training came in handy once when I took Jugnu for our regular walk around the block. We passed by a teenage guy who was walking on the street and singing along to "Losing My Religion" on his portable stereo. He stopped singing when he saw us and called out to me, his voice dripping with sarcasm, "Hey, man, are you losing your religion?"

I turned to him with a raised brow, said nothing, and continued walking my dog. Out of the corner of my eye, I noticed him walking toward me.

"What do you got on your head?" he asked with a sneer.

I clenched my jaw.

"Is that a towel?"

I turned around to face him. I knew he was making fun of me and that it was likely only going to get worse. He walked toward me with a smirk on his face, about to spew his next line of insults.

Jugnu was quivering beside me—like many dogs can do, he could sense my tension. He had a strong, sturdy build thanks to all of the walks we took him on. So when I said, "Look, look," under my breath, he was ready to act. Jugnu lunged toward the man, jerking me forward by the leash. He growled and barked like a canine bodyguard. The guy—stiff as a fence—turned 180 degrees on his heels and walked back the other way. I crouched down and soothed Jugnu. I scratched him behind the ear the way he loved. "Good boy," I said. Jugnu was a little unpredictable and probably not the best-trained dog for living in a neighbourhood, but he took care of me in a lot of situations that would have been much worse without him. Having him around expanded my safe spaces to include any I was in while walking with him.

137

Between the sudden stability at home and unexpected fun of Jugnu joining our family, 1994 shaped up to be a welcome respite from the chaos of the past few years. Going into tenth grade, I decided I would finally try out for the soccer team. Despite some stiff competition, I was excited to find out I'd made the cut. I'd played hockey for a year when I was younger and tried my hand at seemingly every sport short of lawn bowling, thanks to my dad's encouragement. I liked some sports more than others, but I absolutely loved soccer. I yearned for that feeling of pushing my body to its limits, and I loved those plays when I could turn a tackle into an attack—chasing down the ball alongside an opponent, legs pumping like pistons, searching for that perfect opening to a teammate across the field.

"Keep that up and you'll be playing varsity in high school," my coach told me after I pulled off a particularly nice play.

The year kept getting better. Late in the school year, our parents delivered some welcome news to me and my siblings: we were heading back to Panjab. The previous summer trip had been bittersweet because of the funeral, and it had been a whirlwind given the number of familial duties we'd packed into a single month. This time would be different. It would be a guilt-free family vacation.

Instead of going straight to Panjab and concentrating our trip there, we flew to Delhi and stayed there for a few days to enjoy some sightseeing, shopping, and family activities.

I don't think the beautiful colonial streets of Connaught Place in New Delhi will ever leave my memory, nor the majesty of the Lal Kila, the Red Fort. We also visited Bangla Sahib, one of the oldest and most impressive *Gurdwaras*, as well as the other Sikh places of meditation and learning in the capital. I marvelled at the *Gurdwaras'* geometric designs, ornate domes and arches, and cool textures and materials. I didn't expect ordinary *Gurdwaras* to be so impressive. In comparison to Delhi's *Gurdwaras*, the cinder-block temple I was accustomed to in Windsor looked like a big, grey milk crate.

Afterward, we made our way to Panjab in time to celebrate the one-year anniversary of my grandfather's death. In true Sikh tradition, there was little crying or grieving; instead, a couple hundred people gathered under a big outdoor tent to sing positive songs and do group meditations with traditional instruments.

"Why is everyone suddenly so happy?" I asked my mom as I watched our family celebrate.

"Because," she said, "life continues. Energy isn't created or destroyed, it just continues in a different form. Your grandfather may have passed away, but his energy continues, and he remains in our memories."

—⁂—

Joyful as that day was, though, there was still unspoken tension on my dad's side of the family. Consequently, we didn't spend as much time with my paternal relatives this time as we did with my mother's side of the family. My *nana-ji* and *nani-ji*—my maternal grandfather and grandmother—had visited Canada a lot for months-long stays, rotating between our house, my uncle's in Newmarket, and my auntie's in Scarborough. We'd naturally become more comfortable around them, but now I was on their turf and was able to bond with my *nana-ji* Sarup Singh in new ways.

My *nana-ji* was remarkably fit for a man in his eighties. Each day, he'd take me on a long, scenic walk around Ghudani, his rural, calming village surrounded by high rivers and tributaries. Unlike his wife, my *nani-ji* Gurbachen—a serious woman with little time for folk music, cultural superstitions, and other "frivolous" things—*nana-ji* Sarup was a lighthearted man who delighted in sweets and adventures. Though I didn't understand every word of the stories he told, I loved hearing about all the places he'd travelled by bike. In his prime, he'd biked from Ghudani to Lahore, a distance of two hundred kilometres on rough and muddy roads, for no other reason than to visit old friends.

One morning, while we played *seep*, a card game similar to casino, I asked him about his *amrit*—the ceremony when a Sikh is initiated and becomes a *Khalsa*. A *Khalsa* is one who is sovereign, or free. A *Khalsa* should be free from any ideas that oppress or discriminate. *Khalsas* reject superstition, dogma, and any forms of oppression, and they celebrate the equality of all. The initiation ceremony is available to anyone, regardless of gender or age, provided a person is old enough to make the conscious decision to participate. My *nana-ji*, however, had only recently got around to it.

"What's *amrit* like?" I asked.

"It's very important in the life of a Sikh," he said. "It's an emotional experience. It shows you're committed to a path of justice and fairness for all. You commit to training to understand that we are all connected, that we are all one." He smiled playfully.

"I'm thinking about taking *amrit*," I said.

He was obviously happy that I wanted to make the decision.

"Why do you want to do it now?" he asked.

I reflected on the question. I had already begun wearing four of the five articles of faith, known as the five Ks, and I was practising Sikhi regularly. I had *kesh* (my uncut hair), an acceptance of my natural form and reminder of my connection to nature. I wore a *kanga* (comb)—on a practical level, it helped me to keep my *kesh* neat, but it was also a reminder that cleanliness wasn't about just appearance and health, but about remaining internally committed to principles of justice and fairness. My *kara* (steel/iron bracelet) reminded me of the infinite nature of life and energy—no beginning, no end. And my *kachera* underwear was a reminder of modesty. Taking *amrit* would mean adding a *kirpan*, a traditional sword. The word *kirpan* comes from *kirpa* (grace) and *an* (honour). The *kirpan* represents the oath of *Khalsa* to defend the rights of all people.

I thought about the idea of the *Khalsa*. The *Khalsa* was the culmination of Sikhi. It was a commitment to continue to walk down the path of love and to work for the betterment of all. The word "*Khalsa*," besides meaning one is sovereign, means being free from ideas or beliefs that enslave, but more than that, it means being committed to working for freedom and justice for all. Becoming *Khalsa* meant making a lifelong commitment to doing what I could to defend the rights of all and work for fairness and justice. Seeing that my *nana-ji* had just done it reminded me that it was never too late or too early to act.

I finally answered my grandfather. "I truly believe that we are all connected and that we are all one. That we have to take care of each other. I want to make a commitment to doing my part to make the world a little better."

"We can make it happen," he said. "Where would you like to do it?"

Any *Gurdwara* in Panjab was a possibility. I could have done the ceremony back in Windsor. But I had my heart set on Anandpur—the city where the *Khalsa* was inaugurated. Anandpur was where Guru Gobind Singh—the tenth and final Guru of the faith—initiated the first group of Sikhs.

A couple of days later, my grandfather took me there on a bus. We arrived after a few hours of travel, but as soon as I stepped off the bus, I realized that while I had four of my five Ks with me, I hadn't picked up a *kirpan*.

"*Nana-ji*, I didn't bring it with me!" I said.

"No problem, we'll find one here." He took me to a bustling market teeming with colourful trinkets, textiles, and burlap sacks overflowing with bright red peppers. Several stalls sold exclusively traditional weapons—polished swords, pole arms, and *katars* (armour-piercing daggers). *Nana-ji* helped me pick a simple *kirpan*, with a wood and steel sheath and unadorned steel blade. I solemnly strapped the fabric holster diagonally across my *kurta* pajama, a plain white cotton fabric that's the daily wear for a lot of people in Panjab.

We arrived at the bleach-white *Gurdwara* and registered my name for the initiation. We sat cross-legged in an open area under domed ceilings until I was finally invited into an exclusive area reserved for existing and soon-to-be *Khalsa* members. Guards holding spears stood outside a tall, ornate wooden door, which they pushed open with their free hands to allow me to enter.

"I'll wait for you here," said my *nana-ji*.

Inside, a range of men and women, teenagers, and elderly folks waited for *amrit*. The ceremony is carried out by five *Khalsa*, who are referred to collectively as the *panj pyare*, or the five lovers. They can be from any gender or age, but they are usually people who are well respected and can act as mentors or guides.

Together, we read aloud the five *banis*, the spiritual poems I recited every morning, while one of the *panj pyare* stirred a bowl of sugar water with a double-edged sword. The blade scraped the bowl rhythmically while we finished our last words.

Another *panj pyare* explained the *Khalsa* code of conduct in Panjabi. I understood only half of it, but I grasped the essence: the path of Sikh spirituality is connected to love. To realize we are all connected takes love. To fight against injustice requires a deep act of love. Everything in Sikh spirituality is based on this idea of love combined with the belief in the oneness of all things.

Finally, we took turns drinking from the water and eating handfuls of *karah prashad*, pudding.

I left feeling entirely different. I didn't necessarily feel reborn, but I felt grounded and committed to a path. I rejoined my *nana-ji*, my body tingling with a sense of excitement and achievement, but also a sense of responsibility.

—⁓—

When we returned to Canada, I tried to bring that same positive energy with me. But after we got back, I went through a downturn. There were things weighing on me that, had I had the vocabulary for it at the time, I would have called the early signs of a depression.

Several weeks went by, and I didn't reach out to Walid once. I didn't call, walk over, or even say hi. Manjot tried to gently nudge me.

"I was hanging out next door with Walid's sister," she said to me one evening. "Walid says hi."

"Tell him I say hi, too," I mumbled.

A few more days went by, and Manjot came up to me again.

"You're not hanging out with Walid—is everything all right?" she asked.

I didn't have a reason, or at least, not one I could put into words. Everything I was feeling was only made worse by the embarrassment I felt at not being able to reach out to my best friend. When Manjot confronted me about it a third time, I finally broke down and admitted that I felt weird because we hadn't spoken in so long.

"Just reach out to him," she said. "He's your best friend, he's not going to mind."

I knew she was right, but I couldn't muster the courage. But the next day, I was sitting on the porch when Walid walked up to me.

"Hey," he said quietly.

"Hi," I replied.

We started chatting, and the next thing I knew, we picked up right where we'd left off. Manjot never said anything, but I'm sure she had something to do with our reunion, and I said a quiet thank you for her help.

My dad had also been reconnecting since our return. Whether it was because of regrowing his hair, returning to Panjab, or having Jugnu in his life, my dad continued to try to embrace his roots when we got back to Canada. He also seemed to want to set some new roots of his own. One evening during dinner, he made a surprising announcement.

"We're moving to a farm," my dad said.

I dropped my fork. Manjot looked at me nervously. "Like, with cows and stuff?" she asked.

"No," he said. "Just forty acres or so and some crops."

"Crops?" I asked. "That kind of sounds cool."

"But . . . my friends," Manjot said.

"We won't move far," he said. "Just outside the city. A ten-minute drive, at most. Just wait until you see the spot—it's beautiful."

We looked at my mom for a reaction. Was Dad serious?

"It will be a nice farm," she said, the flatness of her voice at odds with her words. "Why don't we go see it tomorrow?"

I tried to imagine what had given my dad this idea of moving to a farm. My dad and I had watched the movie *Far and Away* together. In the movie, the main character hears repeatedly from his father that "A man is nothing without land." My dad didn't watch many movies, and that line stuck with him, I think. He'd also learned that we had been effectively cut out of his father's will, and so he wouldn't inherit any of his ancestral lands.

Whatever the reason, the next day we went as a family to *Gurdwara* and, after the program, drove to the southern tip of Windsor along a gravel road called Disputed Road. The street earned its name because it was the subject of a long-standing dispute over property boundaries between Windsor and the town of LaSalle. It was in limbo, and for us teenagers, it felt like that was exactly where we'd landed. We tried to keep an open mind about it, but there wasn't much to get excited about: a long, flat plot of land blanketed in snow, with nothing more than a rustic red barn. There was, maybe, one house in sight, a few hundred metres down the road.

"Are you sure about this, Dad?" I asked, standing at the side of the road and stamping my feet to keep warm.

145

"We are going to build the biggest house you've ever seen," he said. He pointed straight ahead. "You know what's back there?"

"Nothing?" Manjot said.

"Bean fields," he said. "And farther back, there's a creek you can play in." Manjot and I traded skeptical glances. I was almost sixteen now, and she was thirteen, so this wasn't exactly a sell to us. Gurratan, however, perked up at the idea of having his own little ravine to explore with Jugnu.

"Great," Manjot said. "What about our pool?"

"We'll build another one."

I had to admit, the more my dad described our future home, the more romantic it seemed. I could imagine planting some saplings so that I could take long walks through the country-side the same way I had with my *nana-ji* on his farm in Panjab. I mentioned as much to my dad and, in his typical fashion, he went overboard with the idea, this time for the better. He said he'd contact the ministry to get us connected with a reforesta-tion project so that we could plant an entire forest.

"This might actually be kind of cool," I said.

"No fair," Manjot cried, glaring at me. "Jagmeet's getting his driver's licence next year, but I'll be stuck here in the middle of nowhere."

"Jagmeet will drive you wherever you need," said my mom, without so much as looking at me for approval.

"How big of a house are we talking?" I asked my parents.

"Big as you want," my dad said. "I want you and your sister to help design it."

"Awesome," I said, finally sold on the idea.

My dad stayed true to his word and let us kids have a say in the planning. Manjot and I each got to design a bathroom and our rooms. Inspired by my love of the woods, my room had forest-green marble counters, stained wood cabinets, and beige tiles. Manjot's was a funky black-and-white room—right down to the toilet seat in her ensuite bathroom—with black-and-white-checked tiles. I wasn't sure if her monochrome modern design was really her preference or passive rebellion for having to leave behind her friends and our walk-friendly neighbourhood.

My dad worked with a custom builder on the floor plan. The front door would open to an airy vestibule and handcrafted, curving wood staircase. The living room, dining room, and kitchen were in one open wing of the house, under a high, sloping ceiling, with a sliding door to a spacious back porch. My dad spared no costs, building a dream home on flexible steel-joist floors so it would never shift or sink with time. My mom, as always, was unnerved by these luxuries, but she made sure to plan a meditation room upstairs, looking out toward the street.

The further along the project got, the more I was convinced it was a good idea. But nobody was more excited about it than Jugnu. My dad had bought me a car when I got my licence, so I often took Jugnu to the construction site so that he could run free—he was clearly enjoying all of the extra space.

It had become a habit of mine to take Jugnu on long walks like that, late at night or through the forest by our home. As we walked, I'd scratch behind his ears and quietly tell him what I was going through and how it was making me feel. He'd sit or jog beside me, cocking his head occasionally. He was the perfect listener. No matter how anxious or sad I was feeling, I knew that I could count on Jugnu simply to listen and be there for me. When I looked into his intelligent brown eyes, there wouldn't be any judgment or fear—only love. He was my lifeline in some of my darkest moments.

One day, late in the construction process, I brought Jugnu to the site for one of our usual walks. As he sniffed around the front lawn, I headed up the freshly dried concrete stairs under the front archway and opened the towering wooden door. A worker standing atop a tall stepladder was installing the base of a chandelier. I gave a wave and carefully walked around him over the blue Italian tile mosaic. My hand traced the fine details of the solid oak door frames as I moved from room to room, opening and closing the doors, impressed by their weight. Even the bathroom cabinets were solid oak.

I went up to the washroom on the second floor that I'd designed. I pulled the knobs of the drawers, satisfied with the smoothness of the ball bearings. I opened the cabinet beneath the sink—and immediately slammed it shut. I stepped back, then opened the cabinet again slowly. My old nemesis—the Russian Prince—scowled back at me from an empty bottle tucked behind the plumbing.

Chapter Nine

DISPUTED ROAD

When my dad relapsed, the first thing I noticed was his beard. He started by trimming it shorter and shorter until he finally just shaved it off. When he shaved his beard, he stopped tying a turban as well.

But I didn't need the beard or turban to tell he had relapsed. Since I had to continually assess my dad's sobriety, I developed an incredible sensitivity to the slightest signs of him drinking. I could tell he was drinking by minor changes in the way he stood, whether his eyes were glassy or alert, whether he avoided everyone and went straight to his bedroom or spent time hanging out on the main floor.

He started drinking heavily again. First, it was just the weekends. Then it became some evenings.

He stopped going to *Gurdwara*, too. "Dad, did you drink?" I asked once after we got back from services.

"No, no, I didn't," he said. "I'm fine."

I stared at him suspiciously, noting his flushed cheeks and heavy eyelids.

"Smell my breath," he said. I leaned toward him, inhaling the abundance of cologne on his neck. He opened his lips, but barely, as though he was about to whistle, and blew out what he thought was a scentless whiff. I could smell the alcohol immediately.

"Dad, you promised never to drink again!" I said solemnly. I looked my dad in the eye. He looked away. Our interactions were often the same at this time. I would point out how his drinking was something that was hurtful to me and to our entire family. He would be ashamed and promise not to drink again. Though I was heartbroken, I would confront him and try to get him to promise again. I never gave up, and I never stopped believing that he would honour his promise to me despite all the evidence to the contrary.

My dad was a fairly high-functioning alcoholic. Even though he was getting drunk regularly on weekends and some evenings, he was still always able to make it to his office Monday to Friday and work unaffected.

Despite how much my father earned, even when he was healthy and working regularly, my mom was always worried about money. Maybe "worried" isn't the right word; she was very cautious. She was careful not to spend too much because she was always afraid we would not have enough money. Maybe it was her farmer upbringing. Times were often tough for her growing up, so the idea of not wasting money and being careful about expenditures became a part of who she was. My dad tried to reassure her that things were okay and that we were doing fine. No matter how convincing my father's arguments were, my mom couldn't shake the fear of financial insecurity. Looking back, maybe it was her intuition foreshadowing what was to come.

She became increasingly worried about my dad's decision to buy the farm and build the farmhouse.

"We don't need to move into that house, we're fine where we are," she said. "Why don't we just sell the new house we built?"

She tried, but she couldn't change his mind. In April 1996, renters took possession of our house on Santo Drive and we moved into the farmhouse on Disputed Road. Things immediately went from bad to worse.

My dad's drinking ramped up after the move. Soon, he was getting so intoxicated that he'd moan all night, an ominous and creepy noise that coursed through the halls and under our doors, no matter how hard we all pretended not to hear it.

Living on a farm can cut two ways: it can be beautiful and relaxing, or it can be terrifying. For twelve-year-old Gurratan, especially, it felt like we'd moved into the haunted hotel from *The Shining*. Where I looked out my bedroom window and saw a tranquil environment and an escape from what was happening under our roof, Gurratan looked out and saw a sea of unknowns. From the perspective of my anxious little brother, we'd moved to the middle of nowhere, with no one for miles that he could run to, should he ever need it.

My sister hated it, too. As predicted, our new home messed with Manjot's social life. She used to walk everywhere in Windsor to meet with friends. But from Disputed Road, if she couldn't get a ride from me or my mom, it would take her thirty minutes just to reach town on foot, and that included walking along a gravel road covered in snow and ice for almost half the year.

After just four months in the new place, my parents tried to sell the house. Times were tough in Windsor, so it wasn't a seller's market. The few buyers who did come by all had the same question: "You just built this house, Dr. Dhaliwal. Why are you so quick to sell your home?"

My dad's answer never changed. "We're running out of room—we need a bigger house."

—⁓—

Back in school, I was in eleventh grade and really wanted to earn my first varsity letter. Soccer remained my favourite sport, but I was starting to fall behind my friends' ability level. I relied on hustle and grit, but I was getting out-skilled. I didn't make the varsity team and instead made the cut for junior varsity. It wasn't a varsity letter, but I still enjoyed it, so I played out the season. Not making the varsity team turned out to be a blessing, though. I wanted to earn my letter and doubted I could do so in soccer. This forced me to try out for another sport—I still had to earn my mandatory blue point—which is how I discovered wrestling.

It had been five years since I'd quit martial arts, and I had been missing a more productive way of releasing my energy. By eleventh grade, I'd been in my fair share of street fights, but I'd never fought a formal match with rules and a referee, not even in tae kwon do. I was inspired to join the team after watching some of my favourite martial artists compete in the Ultimate Fighting Championship. Inspired by fighters like Royce Gracie and Dan Severn, I tried out for the wrestling team on a whim.

I loved the physical grit and utility of grappling. I loved the technique, strategy, and skill behind the takedowns. I enjoyed the intensity of going for the pin. I also liked how practical it was to learn how to wrestle. Grappling was an incredibly important skill for a well-rounded martial artist. I knew its importance to be true from first-hand experience: a lot of street fights ended up in grappling on the ground, so there was a functional benefit to learning techniques that I could use to disrupt my opponent's balance and take him down. In that sense, wrestling was another way to develop the skills I needed to stand up for myself. And never far from that thought was my ever-present worry that I should be able to protect not only myself, but my family.

On the advice of my coach, I took up weightlifting, strength, and fitness as my secondary-school sports. My body seemed to change overnight. Gone was the gangly boy. Suddenly I was a seventeen-year-old with a strong core and powerful legs, back, and chest.

"You clearly enjoy wrestling," my coach told me after a mid-season practice leading up to our first tournament. I was sitting cross-legged on the mat, and I grinned at the thought of my first fight ahead.

"There is one problem, though," my coach said.

"What's wrong?" I asked.

"The refs won't let you fight like that," he said, pointing at my head. My hair was wrapped up in a cloth and covered by my wrestling helmet, and I had a modest goatee with a moustache and light beard just covering my chin. "It's against the rules to have any facial hair in high school tournaments."

The news worried me. I wasn't going to cut or shave my hair, but I wanted to compete. Neither my coach nor I knew what to do.

"I might have an idea," he said. "Put this on."

My coach handed me a round, rubbery mask with a hole for my mouth and giant circles for my eyes. I held the mask in my hands, confused as to how it even went on and even more curious about how it would look when it did.

One of my teammates walked by and saw the mask in my hand.

"That's scary as hell. You're going to have all of your opponents psyched out," he said, slapping me on the back in encouragement.

Maybe he has a point, I thought. I could turn the mask into an advantage. I figured out how to thread my wrestling headgear straps through the mask and put it on. It was a bit claustrophobic, but when I checked myself out in the bathroom mirror, I had to laugh.

"It's actually kind of intimidating," I said, before lunging at my teammates with a growl.

I would need all the help I could get. For my first match, I was scheduled to face one of the highest-ranked high school wrestlers in Michigan. Like most of the top wrestlers in my division, he'd probably been training since elementary school, so he had years of experience on me. He was a great finisher—a master at turning his opponent's mistakes against them for a quick pin.

I stepped into the blue circle as the favourite to lose. He must've known it, too, because I got a quick takedown in before he knew what happened. We got up and I hit him again. And again. He kept hitting the floor, over and over again, until he was so worn down that I could go for the pin.

It was a bit of beginner's luck, so the rest of my first wrestling season was up and down. Each loss was a learning opportunity, a

chance to literally and figuratively pick myself off the mat. Looking up at an opponent from your back, knowing you've lost, is
an awful feeling. But it just made me want to work harder, and
every victory inspired me and buoyed my confidence. So much
was changing for me. Just a couple of years before this, I was so
shy I couldn't even pick up the phone to order a pizza for dinner. I dreaded the idea of talking to a stranger at the other end
of the line. I'd have Gurratan make the call, and then, because
he was only a little kid with a squeaky little voice, the vendor
would think the call was a prank and no pizza would arrive. My
mom would ask what happened and I'd have to confess that I'd
made Gurratan make the call.

Now, though, because of wrestling, I felt a stronger sense of
self. I wasn't as afraid to speak up or to be seen. I'll never forget how overjoyed and humbled I was when, at the end of the
season, my coach asked me to be the team captain the next year
and awarded me my first letter. Earning my varsity letter and
becoming captain of the team, no less, was an awesome feeling.

"I want the team practising during the off season and it's
going to be your job as captain to help me keep them motivated."

I was all for that. That summer, my coach arranged for me to
go to Ann Arbor, Michigan, to attend a wrestling camp. I went
all on my own, and I loved it. I trained hard and earned the
respect of high school students like me who loved the sport and
who had come from all across the state. I also earned the respect
of college wrestlers and coaches. Away from the pressures of
home, I felt grounded and strong. But, naturally, the experience didn't last forever.

Once I returned home, it was back to reality. My dad's drinking was worsening. Home was full of mess and uncertainty and a series of battles big and small. When I stepped onto the wrestling mat, though, all of that dropped away. It was just me and my opponent, the rules defined, the boundaries clear. For the first time in years, I had a place again where I could be confident, where I could feel in control of my mind, my body, and my future.

It seems wrestling made a real difference at the right time, and people around me noticed the change in me. My brother and I hung out a lot during this time. One night, we went to watch a movie, *Liar Liar*, starring Jim Carrey. For some reason, my newfound lightheartedness came pouring out of me. In the past, I had been pensive and serious, but not anymore. I was laughing so hard at Jim Carrey's antics that Gurratan was actually worried I was choking. I assured him I was feeling fine, better, in fact, than I'd felt in a long while.

—m—

When it came time to consider universities, my school counsellor helped me put together a thorough application for a bachelor of sciences, majoring in biology. My goal was still to get a medical degree. The counsellor suggested I apply to the University of Michigan, the default school for Detroit Country Day students. It was renowned for its science research excellence and sports programs, including a wrestling team with seventeen national championships.

I thought about it. I had come to realize that, wherever I went for university, I wanted to live away from home. At the same time, I didn't want to abandon my brother and sister. I also knew that I wanted to go to school in Canada. Going to school in the US was my parents' decision, and I understood why they had made that decision, but for me, I wanted to be back in my own country. Eventually, I applied to the University of Toronto, the University of Waterloo, and Western University in London, Ontario, all just a few hours away. As I waited for responses, I grew increasingly conflicted between the desire to get away and the need to be able to come home quickly if my family needed me. And the closer I got to graduation, the more I sensed they'd need me a lot. Especially my mom.

Gone was the woman who'd raised me to be studious and resilient, to be disciplined and tough, to steel myself from pain, and to keep my head held high. Now she was fragile and defeated, completely worn down. Her deep, husky voice was higher-pitched and strained, and it often cracked as she pleaded with my dad through tears.

"You're so mean to me," I overheard her say to him one morning after a particularly bad night of his drunken behaviour.

"I'm so sorry," he repeated over and over, their voices muffled.

"You hurt me so much."

Though he kept saying sorry, he truly didn't know what he was apologizing for. He had no recollection of their screaming match the night before, the crashing and banging, her begging him to stop drinking and him yelling, "Get off my case!" His kids remembered it, though. I heard every word of their arguments through the pillows I pressed against my ears.

My mom started to have regular meltdowns. It wasn't just heartbreaking to witness, but surreal. My dad had always been the emotional one. I'd always thought of my mom as gruff and stoic, a bit of a Superwoman. Now, when something set her off, she'd dissolve into tears. It wouldn't even have to be about my

157

dad's alcoholism or our finances; it could be a totally innocent argument about Jugnu.

"We can't keep opening and closing the door to let him in and out of the house all winter," she complained to me. "The house is freezing."

"What should we do?" I asked. "He's high energy—he needs to blow off some steam."

"Jagmeet . . ." Her voice cracked on my name. Her eyes turned red and watery.

"What's wrong?" I asked, hurrying toward her. She melted in my arms, shaking and sobbing. I held her tightly as she cried.

"It's so tough, Jagmeet, it's so hard," she said. "He's so bad to me."

"We'll get him to stop drinking," I said.

"He won't."

"He will. He still loves his family, I know he does."

"I've tried."

"I'll talk to him," I said.

"It won't work. I don't know what to do."

I felt awful thinking of being away from her. "I won't go away for school. I'll say no to London and Toronto," I said.

"You have to get your education."

"I'll go to university here, so I can help us get through this."

"*Beta*, no. You have to live your life."

And then, just when it seemed like the burdens on my mom couldn't possibly get heavier, they did.

—⁂—

A few days later, a man in a suit visited my dad's office unannounced. He introduced himself as an inspector from the College of Physicians and Surgeons of Ontario in Toronto and shook my dad's hand.

"What is this about?" my dad asked, closing the door behind them and gesturing for him to take a seat opposite him.

"Dr. Dhaliwal," he said, "we have a report that you have a problem with alcohol that may affect your ability to practise medicine."

"A report from whom?"

"I can't say, but we take these claims very seriously."

"Has there been any complaint about my patient care from a patient or their family?"

"No, there hasn't, but we have to follow up on the claim."

"They're making it up," my dad responded. "Anyone can make a report and I can just lose my licence?"

The inspector held up his hands to calm my dad down. "Nobody's suspending your licence. That's not why I'm here. But I have credible claims that your drinking might affect your ability to deliver care and I need to ask you a few questions."

He opened his notebook and asked my dad about the frequency of his drinking, where he drank, and how he'd been affected by drinking. My dad answered honestly.

"From what I'm hearing it sounds like you need help," said the inspector.

"No, no," my dad protested.

"You need to see an addictions specialist and—"

"I don't have that kind of a problem," interrupted my dad.

"Dr. Dhaliwal, if you don't cooperate, this becomes an investigation," he responded. "Do you understand me? We'll go back as far as we have to in order to get to the bottom of these claims. And we'll suspend your licence if we need to. There haven't been any patient complaints at all, so you still have options." He let my father think about it for a moment before continuing. "For your own sake, take the easy route."

The inspector explained that on top of getting treatment at an addictions centre, my dad would have to enter a physician monitoring program. My dad would be assigned a colour, and each weekday morning he'd have to call an automated line that announced one of five colours. If the voice message said "blue," "green," "yellow," or "white," he'd continue with his day. If the voice said "red," he'd have to go straight to a medical lab and leave a urine sample. The system was random. He could go ten business days without hearing "red," or he could hear it two days in a row. If he wanted to drink excessively, even in the privacy of his home the night before work, he'd have to play the odds.

He told my mom what had happened as they drove home together after work. "How long will they monitor you?" she asked.

"Five years," he said. "How do they expect anyone to last that long without making one mistake?"

"You have to get clean, Jagtaran," she said. "You have to manage it."

He squinted at my mom, assessing her silently. My dad found her calmness and lack of shock suspicious, but he didn't say anything until they got home.

They removed their shoes and hung up their jackets. Manjot and I were out, probably tied up with after-school programs at school, but Gurratan was home from school.

"Take Jugnu outside," my dad told him before following my mom into the kitchen, where the ingredients for dinner were chopped and prepared to cook.

"Look me in the eyes," he told her.

My mother froze and slowly turned to him, unable to meet his gaze. He slammed his fist on the counter. "You betrayed me," he said. "Do you realize what you've done? We could lose everything—this house, the car, the children's education, all our savings."

"I didn't know what else to do," she said, sobbing.

As Manjot and I pulled into the driveway and parked, we saw Gurratan on the front steps with Jugnu huddled against his legs. "What's going on?" I asked.

"I don't know," he said. "Mom and Dad were fighting."

When I entered, my mom immediately hurried upstairs. "What did you do?" I asked my dad.

"Ask your mother," he said angrily.

I found my mom hyperventilating in the meditation room. She explained what she'd done.

"I'm sorry, Jagmeet," she said through her tears.

"Never apologize," I said gently. "You did the right thing."

I put a comforting hand on her back and held her tightly. "We'll get through this together," I said. "We are all connected." I repeated the words and teaching my mom had taught me my whole life, passing them over to her with all the love I could muster.

Chapter Ten

ROLE REVERSAL

I threw a duffle bag of clothes over my shoulder, lifted a box from the trunk of my vehicle, and shut the trunk with my free hand. My eyes met those of another student in the parking lot whose parents were struggling to pull some large boxes out of their minivan, and I nodded to say hi. I turned to my new home: Saugeen-Maitland Hall, two L-shaped towers housing 1,200 young adults on their own for the first time in their lives. As the biggest coed residence in North America at the time—nicknamed "The Zoo"—Saugeen single-handedly put Western University on a variety of "best party school" lists.

Music, whistling, and orientation cheers from the front parking lot reverberated off the residence's concrete, beige walls. On my way in, I dodged students in neon T-shirts chasing each other across the lawn with Silly String. "This is awesome," I said to myself.

The main floor carried the aromas of the cafeteria (which

turned out to offer pretty good food). I lined up with the other students and received my student residence orientation package, including the keys to my room. As I headed up the stairs to the first floor, I felt the excitement mounting. I couldn't wait to figure out what my room would be like and who my roommate would be. I had reviewed the room layout so I knew that rooms in Saugeen would be two to a room, with a common bathroom and cafeteria. Saugeen had actually been my last choice; I had chosen two other residences, both of which had four private bedrooms with a common living room and kitchen. When I opened the teal door of my suite, I saw two single beds. One bed was empty. The other already had sheets on it, and the wall above was plastered with Marilyn Manson posters. The "Antichrist Superstar" sneered at me behind white contact lenses, his emaciated, nearly translucent body smeared with black paint. "That's going to give me nightmares," I said to myself and chuckled.

I unpacked some of my clothes, freshened up in the communal bathroom down the hall, and returned to find my roommate sitting on his bed under his goth art. To my relief, my roommate looked nothing like the guy in the poster. Mike was a friendly, jolly dude who loved philosophical conversations. He had a kind face and a strong, stocky build.

Mike and I quickly became close friends. You wouldn't think that would happen since on the surface it seemed like we had nothing in common. We liked different music—I was into hip hop, R & B, and reggae, which he thought was the most painfully boring kind of music, with unoriginal repetitive beats. Meanwhile, Marilyn Manson, Megadeth, and other forms of rock sounded like loud screaming noise to me. He liked bars while I liked dance clubs. And we didn't like any of the same sports or activities. Despite all that, we regularly stayed up until the early morning hours engaged in debate about the origins of the universe and faith itself. A staunch atheist and rationalist, Mike saw spirituality as mythical mumbo-jumbo, and he wasn't afraid to press me on my beliefs.

"How do you know there's an energy, Jagmeet?" he asked me one evening as we lounged on our beds. "How do you prove it?"

"I believe there's a connection between us all," I said.

"What's your proof?"

"I don't know if there's a concrete thing I can point to," I admitted. "I just think there's something uniting us all. Even if you think about it scientifically, we're all made up of matter, and all matter breaks down to neutrons, electrons, and protons."

"You totally just made that up on the spot," Mike said with a kind laugh. "But fair enough, when it comes down to it, we're all made of the same thing."

My science might not have persuaded Mike, but what I liked about our discussions was that, although we had very different opinions, he always took the time to genuinely listen to and consider my perspective.

"I haven't even been here for a full month, and already you've got me rethinking my whole world view," I joked to him after I came back from class.

I was helping Mike think in new ways, too. I was listening to a lot of Bob Marley at the time, which meant Mike was hearing it, too. He'd sometimes break out his guitar, singing and playing in our dorm room. He had a nice voice and could play guitar well. Mike surprised me during the Saugeen residence talent show by singing "Redemption Song."

Basically, being at university was like I'd flipped a switch.

While I had overcome difficulties, I still had a lot of insecurities. Wrestling had really helped me find myself again, find that inner confidence. But there was something about coming to a new city, a new school, that allowed me to shed whatever was left of my insecurities and immediately adopt a truer version of myself. I had the chance to be myself without the baggage of previous expectations and insecurities.

I quickly made friends and had different circles, many of which overlapped. My friends and I would get into all sorts of adventures together—partying at the campus club during "Soca x Bhangra" nights, joining intramural basketball, going on road trips to other universities, or checking out the local restaurant scene. My parents supported me with my tuition and living expenses, plus a monthly spending allowance that made my student life very comfortable.

I quickly got caught up in Saugeen's prankster culture. It wasn't long before I was embroiled in an all-out prank war with my residence friends. It started when one of them left a box of chicken wings and pizza crusts beside my head while I slept (I dreamt about food all night). I woke up surprised to see the boxes around me and laughed to myself. Eventually, some of my friends let slip who did the prank. The next day, another friend and I snuck into the culprit's room and silently arranged ourselves around his bed.

"Ready?" I mouthed. "One, two, three."

In one fell swoop, we flipped the culprit's mattress over—with him sleeping on it—sandwiching him between his bed and the box spring. We raced out of the room, laughing our heads off, while our friend yelled at us from his tangle of sheets.

And so it went, tit-for-tat, each of our friends one-upping

each other with increasingly complicated schemes, like rigging water buckets on top of rez doors to collapse on the person living there when they left for first class.

To me, university wasn't just about having fun. And it wasn't just a place where I was going to take courses and study to become a doctor, either. It was a place where I could shed whatever residual shyness, awkwardness, and insecurities I still carried with me.

One evening, I was sitting with a friend in our common room, talking about everything and nothing in particular. He and I were sharing stories of our childhood, when my friend turned serious.

He ended up sharing an account of sexual assault. I listened quietly while my friend spoke about his struggles.

"I understand," I said when he was done.

"I don't think you can," he replied.

"Actually, I can," I said. "Something similar happened to me."

This was the first time I ever admitted to another human being that something had happened to me. It was seven years since I had been assaulted, and I could only talk about it in general terms. But even this minor step of admitting out loud that something had happened felt like a little weight lifted off my spirit. I still had a lot of healing to do. But this moment was another step down the path.

Years later I spoke about what happened to me in more detail to someone very special to me. This person told me that it wasn't my fault. I had told myself that a couple of times when the thought of what happened resurfaced and I couldn't push the memories down, but there's something very different about saying that to yourself when you're alone versus hearing someone else say it. Hearing those words unlocked a flood of emotions I had buried for over a decade. I had tried to convince myself the abuse wasn't my fault, but I don't think I fully believed it. When someone said it to me, I think I began to believe. I don't have the words to express the gratitude I feel to this day for this kindness. People may have caused me pain, but people have healed me as well.

Over the course of my first year, I continued to build my confidence and form new relationships with the people around me. Growing up, I didn't really have a lot of friends from the same spiritual background, nor did I have many Panjabi-speaking friends. At Western there were many Sikhs and Panjabi-speaking students. When I was a kid, my parents would listen to Panjabi music at the odd party, but at Western, I was surrounded by people who loved it. I even joined a bhangra dance team.

The first time I showed up to our dance group's practice, one of the upper-year students walked up to me the moment I came through the doors.

"Hey, you're new. I'm the best dancer on the team. Stick with me and I'll teach you everything I know," he said.

I wanted to laugh, but I kept it in. It turns out, he could walk the walk, and he took the time to teach me what he knew.

When I started going to clubs off campus it didn't take long to notice that bouncers regularly patted down my brown-skinned friends and me. They hovered by our tables, while my other friends who weren't visible minorities walked around unchallenged.

Sadly, I'd already become accustomed to that sort of heavy scrutiny by authority. A couple of years earlier, just after getting my driver's licence, the police in Windsor pulled me over. I was driving my dad's Mercedes with the windows rolled down on a summer day. When I saw the flashing lights in my rear-view mirror, I felt myself break out in a cold sweat. I immediately pulled over and turned down Nas's "If I Ruled the World," then stared straight ahead with my hands on the wheel. As the officer walked toward the driver's side, my mind raced with possible infractions. *Did I forget to signal? Was one of my rear lights out?*

"Hello, sir," I said, trying to keep my voice even.

"Can I see some ID?" he asked.

I reached into my back pocket and fumbled for my driver's licence. As the cop took it from me, I asked, "Did I do anything wrong?"

He walked to his car without a word and returned a few minutes later. He handed my ID back through the window. "This is a routine stop," he said. "You're free to go."

Afterward, I tried to put the incident out of my mind. I figured the officer suspected me of being a car thief. *It probably wasn't every day he saw a seventeen-year-old driving a luxury vehicle*, I thought. But then the same thing happened a few months later while I was in my Explorer. And then it happened again. And again.

The supposedly random and so-called routine stops continued when I got to London. Each time, the cop would take my ID, run my licence number through their system, and send me off as though nothing had happened. They weren't always polite, either; more than once, they told me to keep my mouth shut. "We'll ask the questions, sir."

I was driving a vehicle, so police officers could legally stop me under the Highway Traffic Act. That wasn't exactly the same thing as "carding." However, since I hadn't committed any offence, in effect, I was being "carded"—though the term was years away from entering my lexicon—being arbitrarily stopped because of the way I looked. My information could potentially be recorded in a database, even though I'd done nothing wrong.

One day, after another stop on my way back from class, I vented about it to my friends Steve and John.

"Isn't it so annoying when you get pulled over for no reason?" I asked them as I flopped down beside them on a couch in the student centre.

They looked at each other with raised brows. "To be honest, that's never happened to me," said Steve.

"Yeah, me neither," added John.

"You've never had cops check your ID in the street?" I asked.

"Like, without speeding or whatever?" Steve asked.

"It's happened to me at those police checkpoints where they watch for people drinking," John said. "But never just out of the blue."

"Huh," I said, leaving it at that.

Steve and John were both white. They hadn't experienced what I had. Later that day, though, I told the same story to a couple of our racialized friends. They knew exactly what I was talking about—they'd been pulled over routinely, too.

"Bro, you're being profiled," they explained. "It happens to brown guys all the time."

In those early years, I didn't think much about my rights or the responsibility of the police to treat everyone with fairness. Instead, I internalized the experiences and considered how I could counter the negative stereotypes that were being held against me and my friends.

"We should start a club," I said to some friends one evening as we sat around in our common room.

My friends nodded and murmured their agreement, but nobody seemed as enthusiastic about the idea. Then one of them, Gurpreet Kaur, jumped in.

"Let's do it," Gurpreet said. Together, we spent the next few months laying the groundwork for Western's first Sikh Student Association.

I had an idea of events we could hold and how we could recruit members, but I needed help with the execution. Gurpreet brought the get-it-done mentality, so together we mobilized a couple dozen of us to volunteer at soup kitchens or to get together for meditation sessions. We staged a pop-up *langar*, a community kitchen like what you'd find in a *Gurdwara*, in the student centre. We even brought in guest speakers and held community events that introduced the broader community to Sikhi. We discussed the teachings, beliefs, and practices, breaking down myths and misconceptions, replacing them with knowledge and understanding.

Working for the association energized me in a new way that my classes or sports team hadn't before. For so long, my identity had been the target of so much negativity. Suddenly, I had the opportunity to change the way people saw Sikhs. In addition to working to change the perspectives of people looking at Sikhs, it was an opportunity for rewarding internal debate, too. It was a chance to work through different perspectives and opinions held by our own community's members as well.

During one exhaustive planning meeting, our members couldn't agree on where we should hold an upcoming function.

The group was split between a local bar and a room in the student centre. Some members thought the bar was a good attraction for hesitant attendees, but I and others thought it could just as well discourage them.

"Sikh teachings criticize the use of intoxicants, not on moral grounds as much as on the grounds that they act as an obstacle to the pursuit of truth," I said. "As Sikhs we're 'students,' we're seekers of the truth, and I don't think a bar promotes that mission statement. Besides, *Gurdwaras* were designed to be safe and inclusive spaces. Bars aren't very inclusive for people who don't drink, but a room on campus can be safe for everyone."

"So what?" asked one of the guys on the other side. "Lots of Sikh events have bars, even weddings."

"It's just not in sync with our goals," I said.

"But you eat meat. You're judging alcohol because you don't drink, but you're just doing what's convenient for you."

"Eating meat is debatable," I said. "It comes down to understanding the value of life and not needlessly taking it."

"According to some, but not everyone. You just don't think it's critical because it doesn't work for you."

"That's not true," I said.

"I bet you couldn't even be vegetarian."

"Sure I could."

He grinned smugly. I already knew what he'd say. "Okay, well," he started, "I dare you to be vegetari—"

"I'm vegetarian—done," I said.

He laughed. "Are you serious?"

I was. From that moment on, I never ate another bird or mammal, and later on, I cut fish and eggs out of my diet, too.

I would love to say I acted on principle. Truth be told, though, I became a vegetarian because I wanted to win that argument.

After a couple of weeks, though, I quickly found being vegetarian very rewarding. I felt good, like I was lighter and had this really positive energy. Later on, the ethical treatment of animals, reducing my carbon footprint, and protecting the environment became my motivations for continuing this as a life choice.

—ɯ—

Most of the fun I had at school happened on weekdays, because on Fridays, I jumped in the car and headed west on the 401 highway. I'd follow the signs for Windsor, and the first glimpse of the "Welcome to Windsor, the Rose City and the Automotive Capital of Canada" sign would fill me with warm (positive) nostalgia. But the feeling quickly morphed to concern when I turned onto Disputed Road and our farmhouse came into sight.

Things weren't good. My dad was usually too drunk to leave his bedroom on the weekends, and would only see me when he came down to forage food from the kitchen. Sometimes he tried to engage with whoever was there, despite no one wanting to talk with him. He would dredge up issues that were well past discussion, or revert to his obsession with tidiness. "The house is a mess," he grumbled.

"Go back to your room, Dad," I told him.

"No, the house is a mess," he would shout, and then swipe his arm across the living room coffee table, slamming books to the ground with a crash and sending papers flying everywhere. His sudden motion and anger would leave him unbalanced, and he would stagger as he tried to keep himself upright.

"Go to your room," I said more firmly.

His Sunday hangovers were brutal. He had the presence of mind not to drink on those days, lest his random monitoring colour come up Monday morning. But the fight against his impulses turned him prickly and belligerent. We had the same conversation again and again—me lecturing him to get help to stop drinking; him downplaying his disease—until I got back on the highway. Every Sunday evening, I'd drive back to school wracked with a mix of relief and guilt. Relief because I'd have five days of peace. Guilt because I didn't think I deserved to have any peace while the rest of my family suffered.

Still, my siblings and I looked forward to each weekend visit. Since our time together was so limited and precious, I regularly turned down offers to hang out with Walid and the guys in favour of going out to the movies to catch rom coms with Manjot (her choice, not mine—though I secretly enjoyed them) or just to stay home, chat, and catch up with Gurratan.

I also made sure to spend time with my mom each weekend. I was worried about her. Her sense of purpose had diminished over the years. All of us kids had outgrown her tutoring, although it was largely thanks to her efforts that we were all doing well in school. Still, we didn't depend on her to get around anymore, now that Manjot could drive herself and Gurratan wherever he needed to go. My mom's extended family and friends had drifted away somewhat because of my dad's behaviour, so they didn't come to visit very much if at all, and it was so long since Mom had worked—seventeen years—that the idea of having a job intimidated her. Her husband really was her whole world now—a small, uncertain world quaking with unnatural disasters.

One weekend just before the end of my second semester, my mom asked me to join her outside on the deck. She routinely confided in me in private. This time, though, the raw tension in her voice told me something big and awful had occurred.

She tapped her slippers on the deck, trying to work up the strength to speak. Finally, she said, "The College of Physicians called your father's colour this week."

I let out an exasperated breath. She nodded, confirming my fears that Dad had failed his urine test.

My dad had skipped a urine test a few weeks before, telling the college he was too busy that morning; he got a written warning for it. But I didn't know he was playing the odds with his tests.

"Every time his colour came up," said my mom, "he'd go have a drink to celebrate. 'Harmeet, they won't call it again two days in a row.'" She shook her head, disappointed and downbeat.

"You can't stop him," I said. "Did he lose his licence?"

"No, thank God. But now he has to do a screening test every morning, and before he can practise again, he has to go to rehab again." He had tried rehab before, and it hadn't worked.

I looked up at their bedroom window; his beastly grunts were slightly audible. I pictured my dad tangled in the bedsheets and pillows, lifting himself only to reach the Russian Prince bottle almost certainly on the bedside table. "He really needs the help. Hopefully this time rehab will make the difference."

My mom looked at me doubtfully.

Arrangements were made and there was an opening at Homewood Centre, a rehabilitation centre in Guelph, Ontario. It was the same rehab centre my dad had successfully attended in the past, so my dad took the first available admission.

He was accepted for the following weekend. The plan was that when I visited then, I would take him to Guelph on Sunday and then head back to school in London. We left Sunday morning for Homewood. My dad sat in the passenger seat, sluggish but surprisingly wide-eyed and optimistic.

"I'll be back on my feet right away," he said. "My son, my boy, don't you worry. This is just a slip-up."

"It's not me I'm worried about," I said. "It's Mom."

"Don't worry. I'll be back to work next month."

"No, you're not listening," I said. "Mom has been really patient with you, but she's breaking down."

"I know."

"It's happening regularly now."

"I know."

"You need to be better to her."

"I will."

"And a better dad to Manjot and Gurratan."

"I promise."

I don't know when we got comfortable with this role reversal, but every now and then I would catch my parental tone and think, *This isn't normal.* He should be the one reprimanding me for not calling home enough, for spending too much money, or for clubbing too much and not studying enough. I still loved my dad, but somewhere along the way, he'd lost his role as a parent.

The role reversal became even clearer when we arrived at Homewood. The place felt a bit like a university. The bedrooms resembled a cross between a dorm room and a hotel room, and there were classrooms for programming, and meeting rooms, and a gym. As we began to unpack the car, I was reminded of parents dropping their kids off at university during frosh week.

Except, in my case, the kid was my dad, and university was a rehab centre.

Still, I couldn't help but feel a small flicker of hope as I helped him carry the last of his boxes of clothes and books into the residence. We hugged each other like brothers, punctuated with a couple of hearty pats on the shoulders. I turned back onto the highway, drove west to London, and returned to my dorm.

Nobody on campus knew about my personal issues. Mike, as always, filled me in on his weekend and everything I'd missed: the rumours of student residence drama, the latest pranks, who was dating who. It was carefree teen stuff from a different universe.

"How's your family?" Mike finally asked.

"Great," I said. "It was a chill weekend."

—⚊—

Within a few months of being discharged from rehab, my dad returned to work. He made it without issue until my second year at university. By that point, I'd moved into Essex Hall residence. I lived in a four-bedroom suite with three of my friends and one freshman we didn't know. A couple of months into that year, my dad failed another screening test. He had one more chance to get sober, stay sober, and continue practising.

Rather than try Homewood for a third time, my dad decided to try a different rehab facility. Homewood had worked before, but he felt he needed something new. He didn't want to leave any option untried. He asked around for advice and received a recommendation for an elite centre in Atlanta, Georgia. After confirming that his insurance would cover it, he started making plans to get admitted. My mom and I wanted him to stay in

Canada so he could be closer to home, but when it came down to it, I didn't care where he went. I just wanted him to get better.

He stayed in Atlanta for almost two months. Then he came home and began to work again a few months later. The morning screening tests continued. He kept passing, aided by prescribed anti-alcohol pills that made him gag and vomit at the first sip.

My dad felt the pressure. He understood that his job, reputation, and his family's well-being were on the line. But he also begrudged the pills and check-ins. He seemed offended that he couldn't be trusted anymore, or maybe he was offended by his own self, knowing he'd lost all credibility. The first time he'd gotten sober, he'd turned into a lighthearted jokester, a delight to be around. This time, he became an even more miserable presence.

I'm ashamed of what this brought out in me. One weekend when I was back home, my mom told me she thought my dad was only pretending to take his pills. I stormed into the bathroom, grabbed the medicine bottle, and crushed up a pill and stirred it in a glass of water. I brought it to him in the living room and slammed it on the coffee table.

"Drink," I said, glaring at him the way I used to stare down someone in a street fight, right before the first fist was thrown.

He swallowed the lump in his throat, took a sip, and put the glass back on the table.

"All of it," I said.

He closed his eyes, shook his head, and chugged the whole thing, his eyes never leaving mine. He exhaled triumphantly, and then coughed into his hands uncontrollably. He started gagging and hurried to the toilet. I sighed as he fled the room, wondering how much longer this could go on.

People are bonded by trauma. It syncs them in such a way that they can read the minds of others with just a glance. While my dad was trying to find his path again, I did what I could to make sure my family had what they needed. Manjot was incredible about watching out for Gurratan during the week. The two of them had bonded while I was away, and I wanted to make sure I was helping by paying my own knowledge forward every chance I got.

So, one weekend visit, I came home and handed two sets of black cloth to Gurratan, who was watching TV in the living room.

"What's this?" he asked.

"It's time you started tying a turban," I said.

"Why?"

"A turban would look much better on you. And besides, your beard is starting to grow in a little," I said.

"Really?"

"It's time, bro."

He patted his head curiously, anxious about the change. The *patkas* he wore as a kid were fast and easy to do, with little room for error. Tying a turban, well, that was going to take some practice.

"Relax. It's not a big deal," I said. "Once you start tying a turban, you're going to notice it's more comfortable, and it will suit your face a lot better. Trust me, okay?"

He hesitated. "Okay," he said finally.

"Cool, let's find a mirror."

We went to the bathroom. "Hold it lengthwise," I said, pinching the sides of one cloth and guiding his arms away from his body.

I coached him as he wrapped the cloth clockwise, smoothing the edges just like my dad had taught me in better times, slowly building up the fabric into a stylized dome.

We practised until Gurratan got the hang of it. It wasn't perfect—but he had a knack for tying it and it was more grown-up than the *patkas* he wore.

"Good enough," I said.

"You think this looks cool?" he asked.

"It looks really good, actually," I said.

"Thanks, bro."

"When are you going to start tying it?"

"On the weekends. I think I'll ease into it."

"That makes sense," I said.

He wore his turban the rest of that weekend, practising again each morning and retying it whenever it fell apart. On Monday, when I was back in London, I got a panicked call from him at 7:30 in the morning.

"What'd you do with my *patkas*?" Gurratan asked.

"I threw them away," I said. "You don't need them anymore."

"What? I'm not ready to wear a turban to school, man. It's going to make me late! It might fall apart!"

"Just tie the turban, Gurratan. You know what to do, and you'll be fine. Talk to you later," I said.

Was I a bit hard on him? Maybe. But the next weekend, when I went home, my little brother was carrying himself a little taller with a beautiful turban I could tell he was proud of.

—◆—

As my second year of university wrapped up, I struggled to study for my finals. No matter how hard I tried to focus on the notes and texts before me, my mind zipped west across the 401 highway to my family. Manjot was wrapping up twelfth grade, and she had already been admitted to Western and registered for a dorm. I was excited to have a sibling near me in London, but I feared for Gurratan alone in Windsor without either of us to take care of him. The three of us had always felt like a team in the struggle against my dad's worst tendencies. Now the youngest member would be left to fend for himself.

I had reason to be worried. My brother called me one evening, and as soon as I heard his voice, my stomach sank.

"Dad just called the cops on me," Gurratan said, voice laced with adrenaline. He spoke so fast I asked him to repeat himself. "Dad. Called. The. Cops." he said.

I jumped to my feet. The notebook on my lap went flying, startling my roommate, Shoab, who looked at me concerned. "Everything okay?" he mouthed.

I flashed him a thumbs-up and took the phone to my bedroom. "What happened?" I asked my brother.

Gurratan had been reading in the living room, an area sectioned off from the rest of the house by a glass door, when he heard my dad moaning and yelling. That wasn't unusual—the sounds my dad made when he was inebriated often made him sound like a man possessed. Gurratan thought he was safe because the sounds were coming from the bedroom upstairs. But a few minutes later, my dad emerged from his bedroom in a stupor and stumbled toward the living room.

Having seen my dad in that state countless times, I understood why my brother then slammed the door on him. "Go back to your room," Gurratan said as he returned to the couch.

My dad freaked out and tried to force open the door. Gurratan used his body to keep it shut, while my dad pounded on the glass and screamed at him.

My dad wouldn't give up, so Gurratan, in a panic, grabbed an ornamental spear off the wall, shaking it at my dad on the other side of the glass door.

"Stay away," Gurratan yelled. "I said leave me alone!"

More confused than anything, my dad returned upstairs without another word. Gurratan slumped onto the couch. His heart pounding, he kept the spear across his lap in case my dad returned. Minutes passed. Just as Gurratan thought the event had simmered down, he looked out the window to see a police cruiser turning onto our driveway.

Gurratan sprinted upstairs to the meditation room directly above the front entrance. He watched two cops exit the car and walk up the stoop. The doorbell rang. As my dad descended the stairs and walked to the door, Gurratan cranked open the window.

"Tell us what happened, Dr. Dhaliwal," an officer said. Many officers in Windsor knew my dad; there weren't many psychiatrists in the city. They might admit someone in custody to the hospital while he was on call, or subpoena him to testify in court. They'd developed a chummy relationship with him over the years, but they'd never seen him like this.

"My son tried to attack me," my dad said, slurring and holding himself up by the door handle.

"How?"

"He tried to attack me," my dad repeated.

Gurratan called out the window: "It's because he's drunk."

The officers' heads shot up, trying to make out the voice coming from upstairs.

"He's going to hurt me," my dad said.

"I told you to leave me alone," Gurratan said.

"Son," said an officer, "can you come down? We want to talk to you."

"No way, I'm not going near him."

My mom, who up until then had been nervously trying to keep to herself in the living room, came to the door and tried to calm the situation. "There is no problem here, officers, everything is fine." Somehow, my mom convinced them it was all a big misunderstanding.

"Just be careful, okay?" one of the officers called up to my brother. They didn't know what to make of the situation. "Don't scare your dad." Before the cops returned to the cruiser, my dad quietly asked them not to make a report. "I'm afraid we can't do that, Dr. Dhaliwal," one responded. "We have to report this—it's an official call."

As my brother recounted the story to me over the phone, I felt a mix of anger at both my parents and the cops. It's hard to know what police should do in domestic situations with three conflicting stories, but I felt they could've done better than to solely lay the blame on my brother. "That's not cool," I told him over the phone. "Put Mom on."

My brother called out to her to pick up the landline in another room. I heard a click and before she could say hello, I started yelling. "This isn't right. Dad called the police on a little kid—that's traumatic. What if they charged Gurratan with something? What if Dad lied and said, 'He hit me'?"

My mom tried to speak, but her voice cracked, and she dissolved into tears. I immediately felt regretful. "I'm sorry for lashing out," I said. "It's not your fault, I know you can't control him. But this is messed up. There's no way we can leave Gurratan at home with Dad. That isn't going to end well for anyone."

"What can we do?" asked my mom.

"Let me think about it," I said.

I had an idea, but I wanted to talk it over with Manjot first.

"I don't think it's safe for Gurratan to stay in Windsor with both of us gone," she said when we sat down to talk about it.

"You're right," I said. "Mom has her hands full with Dad. With you at university, Gurratan will be on his own."

So, on my next trip back home, I took my mom aside and levelled with her.

"Gurratan needs to live with me," I said. "He can't stay in Windsor; it's not safe, and he's not going to be able to succeed in this environment if he's scared all the time. He needs somewhere where he can just be a regular high school student."

My mom didn't speak. I knew how terrible what I'd said must have sounded to her, but I had to say it. Gurratan was my mom's baby, and the thought that she couldn't protect him made her feel like a failed mother. Still, she didn't protest the idea.

With my mom and Manjot on board, I sat Gurratan down and outlined the plan.

"Gurratan, you're going to live with me in London," I said. "We'll find you an awesome school, and we'll have a nice place. Manjot will be there, too, and she and I will be able to take care of you. You won't have to worry about Dad."

I could see the immediate relief on my brother's face. He hadn't said anything, but it was clear that he must have been dreading the thought of being alone at home.

But then, just as suddenly as it had arrived, the happiness left his face.

"What about Jugnu?" he asked.

Nobody could predict the condition of our dad on any given day. But one thing we could always count on was that Jugnu would want to go for runs, play catch, or slobber our faces with kisses. Jugnu was a source of stability and comfort for all of us, but Gurratan most of all. "We'll bring him with us," I said. "We'll find a place that allows dogs."

As the words left my mouth, a flicker of doubt entered my mind. *What am I getting myself into?* I thought. But the look of relief Gurratan gave me said it all, and I knew we were making the right decision.

My mom and I had been toying with the idea of buying a condo in London for me and my sister, but when Manjot made it clear she wanted her independence, we put the idea aside. I told my mom that I'd find an affordable two-bedroom condo near the university and a decent high school for Gurratan to attend. Thinking back, it was pretty incredible what I was able to buy for a very affordable price in London.

I was twenty years old, had not even finished my second year of university, and I'd just made the decision to take in my kid brother. Feed him, care for him, enroll him in school—all of which was more than a little daunting. What did I know about being a parent? Not much. Like anything else that challenged me in life, I'd just have to find my confidence and learn on the fly.

Part Three

Chapter Eleven

BOND BETWEEN BROTHERS

Gurratan and I must have made quite the pair when we went to register him for his new high school. We rolled up in one car, a black Mercedes. I had a goatee, and I was steadily adopting an early 2000s hip hop–inspired style, complete with Dead Prez blaring out of my car speakers, slightly baggy track pants, and a fitted grey T-shirt. Gurratan was coming into his own identity, developing a style probably inspired by me, but he was a lot more confident with it than I was at his age. But the age gap between us probably didn't make a lot of sense to anyone paying attention. We stepped out of the car. I walked toward the steel-blue doors trying to project confidence.

Gurratan looked over at me skeptically. "Do you know what you're doing?"

"How hard can it be to register someone in school?" I said.

We climbed the stairs, walked down hallways decorated with bubble letters that spelled out school-spirit chants. We came to an open door under an OFFICE sign. I looked over at my brother and saw how at ease and excited he was—he was clearly looking forward to a fresh start—and I smiled at the thought of him thriving.

"Jagmeet Singh Dhaliwal," I said, introducing myself to the administrator. "This is my brother, Gurratan."

The office administrator looked at me, then him, then back to me. "Nice to meet you both," she said. "Are you former students, Goo . . . I'm sorry, your names again?"

"*Gur-ruh-tun*," he said.

"And Jagmeet. It's pronounced *Jug-meet*," I said. "Gurratan is fifteen, just moved here from Windsor. I would like to register him for eleventh grade this September."

She printed out a form and stuck it to a clipboard for me to fill out with Gurratan's name, social insurance number, and the rest of it. To my brother's surprise, I had actually come prepared. I signed my name on the line above GUARDIAN.

As we drove back to the apartment, I went over our arrangement.

"We've got you in school," I said. "That's one thing off the to-do list."

"What else is on that list?"

"I promised Mom I would make sure that you do your homework, actually go to school, are well fed, and do well in school."

"For now, let's focus on the keeping me fed part," Gurratan said. "I'm starving."

When we got home, I set out lunch on the kitchen island in serving dishes. Gurratan pulled up a stool and helped himself, scooping dal, roti, and rice onto his plate in big spoonfuls.

Another item checked off the list, I thought, savouring the sense of accomplishment. *This is going to be easy.*

"Is there any more to eat?" Gurratan asked, his plate empty.

I snapped back to reality. "Are you serious?"

First lesson of being a guardian: nothing can prepare you for looking after a teenager in the middle of a growth spurt. Gurratan was insatiable. I called my mom constantly to talk through recipes. I'd follow her directions and cook huge stir-fries that looked like mountains in the skillet, only to watch Gurratan go to town on them. He left nothing to pack for lunch the day after, and after most meals, he still needed to scour the pantry for something to top off his appetite.

Eventually, my biology education kicked in, and I figured out an answer: pasta. But not just any pasta—the richest, most carb- and protein-heavy pasta imaginable. Whole wheat rigatoni, tofu chunks, blocks of butter. I'd melt mozzarella directly into the tomato sauce, throw in sautéed onions and garlic, and then top off each serving with another mound of mozzarella. It practically knocked him out.

Thankfully, we soon got lots of support from Mom. She visited us every couple of weeks, just to check in, so the freezer was full of meals that she would leave behind for us. Once, we got some help from one of Gurratan's friends' grandmother, a sympathetic, elderly Polish woman who made us what seemed like a year's worth of perogies for a very reasonable price. And some of Gurratan's Panjabi friends would send over dishes to eat, which we would keep in the fridge. Manjot lived in London now, too, and she helped me look after Gurratan, but she deserved space to discover herself and enjoy her independence, the same as I'd had. Ultimately, I felt it was my responsibility, as the eldest, to take care of my brother.

Panjabi has a word to express the sentiment of the saying "You are the company you keep." That word is *sangat*. The thinking is that you become your *sangat*. Thankfully, Gurratan had solid *sangat*, a crew of classmates who had good heads on their shoulders. They'd go out and have fun, often end up back at our place, but they never got up to anything that gave me concern. Gurratan was always welcome to crash at his friends' places, too, where their parents happily doted on him like their own son.

Gurratan was easy to trust, so I might have given him too much freedom. But that was how I was raised. I knew Gurratan had the right values and I was confident I could trust him, so I was pretty relaxed about the situation. Maybe a little too much so when it came to school, though.

I remember waking up at eleven in the morning once and walking out into the living room to find Gurratan eating cereal in front of the TV.

"Yo, what are you still doing here?" I asked.

"I don't feel like going to school," he said.

"Are you sick?"

"No, I just don't feel like going."

"You sure?"

"Yeah," he said.

I paused, trying to consider how to respond. I hadn't exactly set a great model—I wasn't the best about attending my own classes, particularly my morning ones.

"Okay," I said finally, "but make sure you're on top of any assignments or tests coming up."

My relaxed attitude was partly a result of my "parenting style" and partly because Gurratan had been through so much crap in Windsor that I wanted him to have a good time.

My nonconventional parenting also included exposure to my friends, who regularly came over to our condo. My friends were studying in a range of fields—some, human biology in pre-med; others were engineers, computer programmers, or philosophy majors. We'd often sit around and talk about whatever topic interested us, and Gurratan would soak it all in. Later, when he was in university, all of that training would come back to bite me—to this day, our quarrels over semantics, logical fallacies, and hypothetical arguments can quickly clear out a room.

Despite a few lapses and sleep-ins, I committed myself to teaching Gurratan healthy habits and shaping him into becoming a confident young man. I taught him self-defence moves in our parking lot and showed him how to lift weights. I took him shopping to make sure his outward appearance mirrored his inner confidence, and I showed him how to tie up his hair for sports. I loved being able to share my passions with my little brother; each day brought us closer together as siblings. Some things, though, were trickier to teach.

"So, I've got a school dance coming up next week," Gurratan said one evening.

"Sounds fun," I said. Gurratan kept looking at me silently until my realization set in. "Wait, Gurratan, do you know how to dance?"

"Not really," he said.

"What kind of dance is this?"

"The kind where I might be dancing by myself or maybe with others."

"What kind of dancing with others?"

"The slow kind," he said shyly.

"Oh," I said, smiling. "I guess we better teach you how to slow dance."

We moved the coffee table aside to open up the living room floor, and I put on a Mary J. Blige song.

"I'll show you how to lead," I said. I hesitantly touched Gurratan's hips and told him to grab my shoulders. We shuffled into an uneasy two-step.

"Stop looking at your feet," I said.

"I can't," he said.

"Look at me," I said. He lifted his head. For a brief moment, we looked into each other's eyes—then laughed. There was no way he would take this seriously while looking into my eyes. "Maybe not, actually. Look at the wall, but still try to feel the rhythm. Let me lead so you get a feel for it, and the next song you'll lead."

"I don't think I can make it through another song."

Our arms dropped at the same moment, and we laughed.

"This isn't working," I said.

"Not really," Gurratan said.

"I have an idea." I picked up the phone.

"Who are you calling?" he asked.

"An expert," I said.

A couple of hours later, my friend from university came to the rescue. My brother knew her, so he was comfortable around her, and as an added bonus, she was a great dancer. I left the house with Jugnu, ran a few errands, and grabbed some take-out. When I returned home, Gurratan was leading the two-step like he damned well invented it. He flashed me a thumbs-up in mid-dance.

I relied on the charity of many friends who pitched in and looked out for Gurratan like he was their little brother. No matter what he needed—a ride to class, help with homework—I knew I could call on any friend and someone from our crew would be there for us. Our apartment itself was a bit of a clubhouse for young people. Cell phones weren't common yet, so most of the time, our friends stopped by unannounced and, too lazy to walk around to the buzzer on the other side of the building, stood under the balcony and yelled our names to let them in through the back door.

One visitor was Amneet Singh, a close friend of my brother's and a sharp but unintentionally funny fourteen-year-old. I'll never forget the day I met him at his family's house in London in my first year, a couple of years before I brought Gurratan to live with me.

"What's your vertical?" he asked me as I took my shoes off.

I looked at him, this kid whose *patka* barely reached my chin, staring at me with the most earnest expression. "Sorry?"

"How high can you jump?" he asked.

"Why are you asking?"

"You play ball?" Amneet said.

"Sometimes," I said.

"Cool," he said and walked away.

I never would've guessed this kid would one day drive me into politics and become my first campaign advisor. Back then, I never would've guessed I'd be a politician. I didn't know what I wanted to do anymore.

As the clock counted down on the twentieth century, my career path felt far away. For most of my life, I had planned on becoming a doctor but now I wasn't so sure. I still found the human body and healing fascinating, but now, in my final year of a bachelor's degree, I had to make a decision about my career path. But I didn't let that stress me out. There was so much more on my mind than school and a career.

—⟶⟶—

A couple of months later, my brother, my sister, and I rang in the new millennium with family in Brampton. We were gathered at my cousin Sharanjeet's house.

Sharanjeet's dad—my *mama-ji*, or maternal uncle, Baljinder Singh—arrived early in the evening for dinner. Baljinder was a taxi driver, and like a lot of other recent immigrants who turned to driving to make a living, it was hard to get him away from his job. Every passing hour with the meter off was an hour without pay. That night, he quickly became restless after the plates were cleared. Not long after, he announced that he was going to look for passengers.

His younger brother, Satnam, barked at him. "There's no business today—everybody is at home resting. Relax."

"There's always business," said Baljinder. He threw his coat on and left in his taxi.

When the phone rang a few hours later, Satnam left the room to answer it. He returned to the living room looking sickly pale. "Baljinder is hurt," he said.

Sharanjeet jumped to his feet. "What happened?"

"Someone robbed him," said Satnam. "They're taking him to the hospital."

We all immediately jumped in our cars and rushed to the hospital. By the time we arrived, my uncle—a devoted husband, and father of two boys—was dead.

Over the next few hours, we learned the horrifying details. Baljinder wasn't just robbed. Not long after he left the house, he picked up two passengers—eighteen- and nineteen-year-old men—and was repeatedly stabbed in the neck and shoulders after being robbed of every dollar he had. It probably wasn't more than $100; it could have been as little as $25. For that, he was left to bleed to death in a deserted part of the city. Baljinder managed to pull himself back into the car, step on the gas, and drive to a pizzeria, where he alerted passersby. But it was too late.

Earlier that week, in an unrelated incident, an Afghan immigrant—a former doctor supporting his family in Canada by driving a taxi—had his throat slashed and bled to death in his car. The violence was all too relatable for the dozens of cab drivers at my uncle's funeral, many of whom took the microphone to condemn the many, many attacks against them that were rarely acknowledged. The drivers' English was imperfect, but their outrage was immutable. They were sick and tired of police and the general public treating the violence against cab drivers like a routine work hazard. There was a sentiment that, as brown people, as immigrants, their lives were less valuable.

The night my uncle was killed, Gurratan, Manjot, and I all slept in the basement at Sharanjeet's house to console our cousin and his family. We were in a state of disbelief. We were all struggling with the idea that he was gone, and the horribly violent way in which he was taken only amplified our disbelief.

Before the actual funeral, my uncles and I all went to the

funeral home to wash the body, one of the final rites in the Sikh tradition. Sharanjeet didn't want to go, nor did his brother, so my uncles asked me to go with them to help take care of things.

When we arrived, the funeral parlour staff told us what to do. I picked up the washcloth, dipped it in the soapy water, and began cleaning my uncle's body. One of my uncles reached out to touch the body, and when he did, he cried out, shocked by the cold touch. Washing my uncle Baljinder's body was a surreal experience. It was my first experience so close to death, and it made me consider my own mortality. The neck wound stitches were visible, and the sight of them filled me with anger at the violent senselessness of his death.

My uncles were similarly in shock. They were particularly upset that someone at the hospital had shaved my uncle's beard to treat his neck wounds. It had been necessary at the time, but my uncle Baljinder had only recently turned to Sikhi. Seeing him lose the symbol of his hard-earned faith only added insult to injury.

After we cleaned the body, we dressed him in the five Ks and a turban. Wearing a turban made the absence of his beard even more glaring, so one of my uncles wrapped a cloth around his neck like a scarf to cover it up.

My parents came to Brampton for the funeral rites, which lasted three days. When I saw my dad, I almost wished he hadn't come. My dad was unpredictable, and his presence added another stress to an already difficult time. Despite my misgivings, though, he seemed all right when he arrived, so I was hopeful the funeral would pass without incident.

We went to the *Gurdwara* to complete the last rites with meditations and prayers. As we sat cross-legged on the carpet, I glanced over at my parents to make sure they were all right, and I noticed my dad's hands shaking. Before I could react, his eyes rolled back, his body went limp, and he slumped sideways onto the floor. He quickly got back up and played it off as if nothing had happened.

After the service, one of my uncles who had seen what happened approached my parents and suggested that they go to the hospital. My mom took my dad there, and when they got back, I asked her, "What's going on?"

"Withdrawal," she said. From her matter-of-fact tone, I could tell this wasn't the first time she'd seen these symptoms. I knew things were bad at home, but I hadn't realized they were this bad. Why hadn't she told me? How much longer could my dad function when his chemical dependency to alcohol was so strong that his body couldn't go three days without it?

As a condition of failing his random screening test, my dad had to attend monthly meetings in London for doctors. He usually dropped by my condo before taking the bus back to Windsor. Gurratan made sure to leave the house before he arrived. My brother hadn't talked to my dad since the day of the police report.

My dad was struggling. His addiction was all-consuming. The meetings, with their attempts at motivational messages or coping strategies, weren't working. It seemed inevitable, then, when the College of Physicians and Surgeons suspended my dad's licence in July 2000 after he failed a test for alcohol for the second time.

My mom called me the next day to explain the situation.

"Jagmeet, *beta*, your dad failed another test."

"What happened, *bebey-ji*?"

"He tested positive and now they've suspended his licence to practise."

My heart sank. "For how long?" I asked.

"It's indefinite. He needs to prove that he is sober before they'll consider lifting the suspension."

Her words hit me like a ton of bricks. I thought about all my dad's struggles—the year of exams and prep courses across Canada and the States, studying all day and then working as a security guard by night. I knew how proud he was when he finally gained entrance into a Canadian medical school, and the sense of accomplishment his work gave him. He had achieved so much and now it was gone. I struggled to imagine the sense of loss he must have felt.

It also meant that things were not going to suddenly improve. I had always secretly hoped against all odds that my dad would get better. We had seen glimpses of it over the years, but he had never really managed to turn things around. I had never given up on him, but things were bleak.

"*Beta*, we won't be able to send you any more money," my mom said, a little embarrassed.

"Don't worry about that, I'll get a job," I said. "I can take care of myself and Gurratan, and I can help Manjot out with anything she needs as well."

"But how are we going to pay all your bills?" I asked. I knew our finances were overextended since my dad had built the new house, and the past couple of years hadn't been the best because of how irregularly he was working.

"We might have to start taking out money from our RRSPs,

but we have a line of credit we can use for the short term to get us through."

"How much do we owe?" I asked.

"I'm not sure. Your father dealt with the money, not me."

I crunched the numbers in my head. I knew the condo and Santo Drive house were paid off, but we had a big loan on the Disputed Road house. We had another significant loan on my dad's office building in downtown Windsor, which my dad had just refinanced to renovate. Even if my parents sold everything they owned, they would still be in massive debt. Then there were all the other expenses, utilities, credit card interest, and who knows what else. I knew we needed to start trying to get rid of all this debt.

"To start, we've got to sell the downtown office as soon as possible," I said. "We're going to be okay, *bebey-ji*, don't worry. I'll take care of it."

I didn't want to dictate what would happen, but I was comfortable being my family's decision maker. My mom hadn't given up—she still had fight in her—but her decision-making abilities were drained from all the stress she was going through.

I opened the résumé file that I'd been building since the age of seventeen. I'd worked a variety of jobs over the summers—roguing corn, stocking shelves, working cash registers, climbing telephone poles to install internet connections, promoting health issues for a community health centre. I updated the résumé, printed it, and dispersed copies to local businesses in London like it was a flyer. After one week, I'd accepted the first three part-time positions offered to me, not thinking through the complicated mess of trying to piece together a schedule from that.

I quickly realized I'd panicked and overreacted, and that balancing three jobs while taking care of Gurratan wasn't tenable. I got my work schedule down to two retail jobs: one at the clothing store Bluenotes and the other at Aldo, a shoe store. Both were in Masonville Mall, close to our apartment and the Western campus. Before long, Aldo offered me a full-time position and gave me more hours—so many that, during the summer, I was working back-to-back shifts, from nine to nine, six days a week, and then from ten to five on Sundays.

Still, without my parents' support, I found it hard to make sure I was taking care of Gurratan properly. Before, I could go out to a restaurant or pick up a new pair of jeans any time I wanted. Now, I had to think twice about every expense. We were just barely making ends meet, but we were fortunate to have help from friends who offered to feed us.

Despite the new difficulties, we were lucky in many important ways. We were tight on money, but we were safe and healthy and remained far away from the trauma. I could have packed up, sold the condo, moved back to Windsor to save money, and found the same low-paying jobs there. But I didn't want to disrupt Gurratan's life. Despite our parents' turmoil, the loss of our uncle to a senseless murder, and our financial problems, my brother had just lived the best year of his life. Could I really take that away from him? No way. I decided we would stay in London until he graduated high school. Instead of talking things over with my mom, who had enough to worry about, I sought Manjot's advice and talked things over with her. We agreed that keeping Gurratan in London made the most sense for him.

With that solved, I turned to my other dilemma. I'd just

finished my bachelor's degree after three years, but I had no clue what to do next. If my dad remained unemployable, that would leave me, as the eldest son, to be the breadwinner. My job at Aldo was paying the bills, but obviously it wasn't going to cut it for the long term. I had pulled a lot of overtime throughout the summer, so I had a little bit saved up to help get through the school year. My mom and I had some extra money to supplement what I had earned over the summer as well. That addressed the short term, but I still needed to figure out what I was going to do in the long term. I gave notice to Aldo that I would be going back to school in September. When September rolled around, I registered at Western for some science courses and philosophy courses, as I wanted to bump up my average.

I was still considering writing my MCAT and applying for medical school. But when I thought about how long it would take, and how much it would cost for me to reach the point where I could support my family, I knew I needed something quicker. But I still didn't know what that was.

It was a philosophy of law elective that unexpectedly opened up a new career path. The professor offered to meet with each student to discuss our most recent paper and ways to improve for the next. I took up the offer and scheduled a meeting in his office.

We started by chatting about my course load.

"Are you pursuing a degree in philosophy?" he asked.

"No, I've just finished up my science degree. This year I'm taking some courses to upgrade my marks and cover off a couple of prerequisites to keep my options open for grad school."

I felt a little embarrassed about mentioning grad school specifically.

"But I'm also taking a couple of philosophy courses as electives," I said.

"Have you ever considered law?"

A career as a lawyer was probably the last thing I ever imagined.

"Not really," I said. "But I do enjoy your philosophy of law class."

"I can tell," he said. He rested his chin on his knuckles and leaned in intently. "Why do you like my class?" he asked.

I thought for a moment. "I suppose because laws make up some of the bonds that hold us together," I said. "Good laws can hold us together while bad laws can tear us apart. I like exploring how we form bonds with each other to build a framework for cooperation, but I've never thought about practising law."

He handed back my past paper, with 90 per cent on it. "You should consider it," he said.

—ɷ—

At the end of my fourth year, I still wasn't sold on law school, so after a lot of reflecting, and seeing the rapid growth of the digital sector, I enrolled in summer school to complete the first-year computer science prerequisites. I decided I would start my second year of computer science in September 2001, convinced it would be the fastest path to stability. That summer, when I wasn't in classes, I worked at a call centre for TD Bank. It was the first time I worked full time and went to school full time as well. And it was brutal. I still managed to score decent marks in my classes, but I learned that cramming a year of computer science prerequisites into a couple of months doesn't work well with evening and night shift work.

In quieter moments, I felt a shadow of doubt. Ever since I was a kid, I'd believed that becoming a doctor was my future. The path had always seemed clear. Now I had no direction, and limited time and money to figure things out. Would this new route actually be the quickest and best path to providing security for my family?

We weren't having any luck selling the downtown office so we finally accepted an offer far lower than we should have, which meant we were still carrying a big chunk of debt from it.

"Okay," I told my mom, "now we're going to sell the house."

"Thank God," she said.

I gave the renters at the Santo Drive house their notice and prepared to move my parents back to our childhood home. But, again, the market quickly punctured any sense of relief we might have had. Not many jobs in Windsor were recession-proof except, ironically, those of doctors, so there was little interest in an upper-market property.

We'd learned from our failed first attempt to sell the farmhouse in 1997, shortly after we'd moved in, not to set our asking price too high. But even with our lowered expectations, we were disappointed. With Windsor in a full-on recession, the highest offer we got wasn't even enough to make back the mortgage. But what choice did we have? It was a fantasy to hold on a little longer, thinking the city could go back to being a boom town overnight.

So we did what was necessary. We sold the house on Disputed Road. On the day we moved my parents out, I thought about how the farmhouse was supposed to have been our family's dream home. It had never lived up to that ideal—for Gurratan, it was more of a nightmare. Leaving wasn't hard at all. I had lost any notion of happiness coming from the size or beauty of the house. I knew that happiness comes only when you feel peace and security in your home. Manjot, Gurratan, and I were experiencing what that meant. I hoped that one day my mom could as well.

Chapter Twelve

A NEED FOR JUSTICE

The World Trade Center attacks were horrific, and on that day and every one that followed, our thoughts and sympathy went to the victims and their families. Closer to home, the attacks also ramped up the racism of my youth all over again. The racism my brother, friends, and I confronted after September 11, 2001, made all the "Paki," "diaper head," and "dirty" insults of our youth seem innocent by comparison. Still, I often preferred the physical assaults to the laughter and mocking. I could block their blows, but their laughter always cut through my defences.

Shortly after the Twin Towers were destroyed, I saw a picture of Osama bin Laden on TV and the first thought that popped in my head was, *I will never be able to wear a white turban again.*

Of course, avoiding white head wraps wasn't deterrent enough. The image repeated regularly in the media was *brown skin, young male + beard + turban = terrorist.* No one seemed to understand that I hated al-Qaeda as much as them—the crimes and violence committed by them were horrible, and they should rightly be condemned and denounced. I often heard "Osama" or "terrorist" yelled at me with hatred from passing cars. Other times, people simply walked up to me and said "*Boom!*" before walking away. It happened wherever I went—no place was immune to the power of indiscriminate hate.

Later that school term, while Walid was visiting me in London, we were standing at an intersection, waiting for the light to change, when a truck pulled up beside us. The truck's passenger window was rolled down, and I could see the people staring at me. Walid and I kept chatting, trying to ignore their looks, but I had a feeling something was going to happen. They were looking toward me and laughing. When the light turned green, the passenger yelled, "Watch out, Osama has a bomb!"

I gestured with my arms, challenging them to stop their vehicle, but they sped by, shrieking with laughter.

"That's ridiculous," said Walid, wide-eyed with disbelief. "I can't believe you're being harassed for being a Muslim. *I'm the Muslim.*"

"Some things never change," I said with a forced laugh, trying to lighten the mood. "It's been getting worse since 9/11."

Walid was right—it was ridiculous. But it was reality for me and countless others. Throughout my life I had learned what it was like to feel like I didn't belong, but I was also learning that I wasn't alone in that feeling. The more I looked around me, the more I saw all sorts of people who were being made to feel they didn't have a place in society, whether that was because of the way they looked or how much they earned or where they were from. But at the time, I didn't have the language to express my concerns. That changed when I met Anton Allahar.

In my last year of university, Manjot and I had registered for Anton Allahar's class the Sociology of Minority Groups. I could tell immediately this wasn't going to be like any other course I had taken. Professor Allahar walked into class with a mixture of confidence, style, and a little bravado. He was West Indian, from Trinidad, and dressed sharply. I liked him immediately.

He introduced himself and posed a question.

"What is the largest minority group in Canada?" he asked.

I smiled because I'd done my research. The week before class, I brainstormed what groups we would talk about. I knew there was a large South Asian minority group in Canada, but I figured that recent immigration from Hong Kong and mainland China probably tipped the scales. I raised my hand and he signalled for me to respond.

"The Chinese are the largest minority group," I said.

"Nope."

Others answered: South Asian? Caribbean? Black?

To each answer, Professor Allahar simply said, "No."

Finally, when we lapsed into silence, he said, "The largest minority group in Canada is women."

I was confused. Women weren't a minority group, were they? Based on what definition, I wondered, because it can't be based on population.

Women, Allahar explained, were not a minority in terms of numbers, but they were in terms of power. He cited economic and political representation disparities as evidence to support his claim.

As Allahar spoke, I saw the paradigm from a lens I hadn't considered. As the understanding began to dawn on me, I thought about my mom. I sent her a silent thank you. She'd always said we were all connected, and even in this, I saw that she was right. I was part of a minority group, but right in front of my eyes was an enormous group—women—who were a minority group still fighting for equal rights. *We are all truly one,* I heard my mom say.

—⚭—

I thought a lot about my law professor's suggestion. I needed to decide about how I was going to support my family long-term, and a career as a lawyer certainly presented a degree of much-needed stability. Our family funds were dwindling. My parents were settled back in our childhood home now, but without my dad's salary, they could barely pay the bills. I was hardly making enough to support myself, let alone Gurratan. There was only so much time left before I'd have to earn real money. Each week, I watched our family funds wither away a little more as we tried to pay off our debts. As our bank account grew steadily smaller, I reflected more seriously on law school.

The October 31 midnight deadline to apply was fast approaching. I was so unprepared that I hadn't even written my LSAT. Nobody applies to law school without knowing their LSAT score—that's crazy. Without one, your application is incomplete. If I had any sliver of a plan, I'd have already taken the test and hopefully earned an impressive score. But I'd already missed my chances to write the exam in the summer. The next round of tests was in December.

Halloween arrived, and I was ready to let the application

deadline pass. All my friends were making plans for parties. Halloween has always been one of my favourite times of the year. I loved dressing up. I even saw Gurratan walking around the condo trying out different costumes. One of my friends called up and said they knew about the best party for Halloween.

"So are you in?" he asked.

"Obviously, I'm always down for a Halloween party."

As I sat there figuring out what my costume would be, my thoughts drifted back to my law professor. If I was being honest with myself, I couldn't really see myself as a computer programmer. I wanted to become another kind of professional. I needed some job security and the ability to earn a good salary to support my family.

My family had fallen way behind financially, paying less than half of what we owed each month. My mom routinely fielded calls from creditors, and the pressure stressed her out. I couldn't ignore my duty to her any longer.

On a whim I decided to do it. I called up my friend. "Hey, man, sorry but you have to count me out for the party."

"Oh no, why?"

"I'm going to fill out an application."

"No way! That's awesome, so you're going to do it?"

"Yeah, man."

"Okay, brother. Do your thing."

"Thanks, have fun!"

I opened up the link to a law school application only to receive a 404 error.

"Weird," I muttered to myself. I tried to find the application page a few different ways, but every time, the site blocked me. It dawned on me that I'd missed the online deadline. The only way I could still apply on time was to get a hard copy of my application to an office in Guelph before midnight. But it was too late to call a courier. If I was going to meet this deadline—the last one until next year—I'd have to fill out and drop off my paperwork in person at a location an hour away.

I printed the form and filled it out as quickly as possible, checking "n/a" next to anything referencing the LSAT. I paper-clipped the form to my university transcript, jammed it in an envelope, and raced to the car.

It was close, but I managed to get the application to the office before midnight. Now all I had to do was write the LSAT, and I had six weeks to do it. *No big deal*, I thought on the drive home, congratulating myself on a job well done.

I bought a used LSAT prep book and scheduled my test date in December. Over the next few weeks, I casually flipped through the book. My overconfidence didn't serve me well. The day before the exam, I woke up and wandered downstairs to grab breakfast, telling myself I'd read through the book that afternoon. As I was walking down the stairs, though, I suddenly realized that it wasn't the day before the exam—it was *the day of* the exam.

I ran out the door without a jacket, jumped in the car, and rushed to the examination room at Western. I sprinted to the entrance, snow clouding around my feet as I threw open the main doors, and ran up and down the hallways looking for the right room. I finally entered, panting and covered in snow from the knees down. I noted the eyes of two dozen aspiring lawyers staring at me.

The exam facilitator approached me as quietly as possible. "Can I help you?" she asked.

"I'm here . . . to write my L . . . SAT," I said between breaths.

"Are you Jayg-meet?" she asked. "I'm sorry, but it's a timed test. You'll have to reschedule."

"That's okay, you can just deduct my time. I'm okay."

She had to suppress her laughter. "It doesn't work that way. I'm sorry."

The next available date was February, long after the acceptance letters would go out. I had no choice but to reschedule my LSAT for two months later.

When I got home, the first thing I did was circle the date on my calendar. Then I wrote out the date in big letters and taped it to my bedroom door. This time I actually studied. I read the prep book and did one practice test. The day of the test, I made sure to wake up hours before the real thing and work out, psyching myself up for the LSAT like I was Rocky Balboa facing Apollo Creed.

Unlike Rocky, I walked out of the exam room victoriously. I knew they couldn't turn me down.

My fifth year at Western was also my brother's last year at high school. I helped Gurratan apply to universities. He applied to a number of schools across Ontario. He wasn't sure where he wanted to go, but he definitely didn't want to go to Western. Not that he didn't like Western or London. In fact, it was the opposite. Those three years in London were some of my brother's best years of his life. In fairness, they were some of my best years, too.

To this day, my brother and I reminisce about the good times we had. The stability and comfort of our condo in London was better than the years in the farmhouse or even the times in our home on Santo. The fun and relaxed vibe was a stark contrast to the painful trauma of living at home with my dad. Those three years included endless summers of weekend beach getaways to Grand Bend on Lake Huron, barbeques with friends, and walks along the Thames River in the "Forest City," as London is often called. Gurratan had hung out with me at Western so often that everyone knew him as my little brother. Now, Gurratan wanted to spread his wings a little and make a name for himself, a name other than "Jagmeet's little brother."

Gurratan quickly decided on McMaster University in Hamilton. We packed up our place in London so that I could rent it out for some income. He was going to be starting school in September and was planning on living on campus in a dorm. I had my fingers crossed that I would get into law school.

I had finished writing my last exams during the middle of April. So for the past two and a half months I was basically in limbo waiting to see if I was accepted to law school. If I wasn't accepted, I had no idea what I was going to do in September.

I finally received a letter from Osgoode Hall in the beginning of July. I was nearly overcome with anticipation and fear. I opened it. It took me a while to register what it meant. I was accepted! I was elated and filled with a sense of purpose.

After that, my brother and I moved back to Windsor. Gurratan was going to McMaster and I was going to law school. I spent that summer preparing for law school and applying for student loans.

I had been training in muay thai and jiu-jitsu pretty regularly in my last couple of years at Western, and I was really enjoying it. I figured I'd continue the training in Windsor.

I opened the phone book to search for a new gym in Windsor. I flipped to the martial arts section. My finger ran down the listings in the yellow pages, past aikido, boxing, judo, and kickboxing.

My finger stopped at muay thai. I continued reading the ad and stopped dead at the name of the instructor. There, staring back at me, was a name I knew from more than a decade earlier. That name was Mr. Reginald Neilson.

There's no way it's the same Mr. Neilson, I thought to myself. *This is just a coincidence. There's no way he's still teaching. He may not even be alive anymore.*

I don't know why, but I picked up the phone and started dialing the number listed. I didn't have a plan in mind. I just dialed it. Someone answered and said "Hello?"

It was him. I slammed down the receiver.

I felt a sickening sense of nausea as a decade of pent-up shame bubbled to the surface. Instantly, I was assaulted with memories, some of which were familiar and some that I had buried so deep that I'd almost forgotten them. The cloying smell of Old Spice overpowered me. It's as though he had purposefully applied it to mask a stench. His severe shaved face came back to me in crystal-clear focus; I heard his gravelly, coarse voice training me, telling me what to do all those years ago.

It triggered a flood. For a moment, I was reduced to my ten-year-old self, awash with shame and guilt. I remembered the "special program" he'd put me through, the way he manipulated me. I tried to fight the memories, to push them down again by using my mantra: *Don't think about it. Just don't think about it.* But it didn't work. I couldn't stop thinking about it.

I had to face the familiar feelings of guilt and self-blame all over again. *I should have known better. I should have seen through the program. How could I have let this happen?* The shame came back, too, alongside the fear of people finding out. *Who would believe the elaborate point system that he used and the pseudo-science he plied me with? Who would ever believe me?*

I slumped down into the kitchen chair, the weight of all these thoughts too much for me to bear. My next thoughts turned violent. *I want revenge for what he did to me.* I quickly shot that idea down. He was an old man—where would the honour be in that? Next, I thought about bringing him to justice. Maybe if I told someone, I could prevent him from abusing someone else. Sadly, I still didn't have the courage to do that.

Gurratan appeared by my side. "Hey, brother, is everything okay?"

"Yeah," I said. "Everything's cool. I gotta use the washroom, and I'm just being lazy."

He chuckled a little as I went upstairs.

I walked into the washroom and locked the door behind me. I sat on the edge of the tub with my face in my hands and I cried.

In all those years, I don't think I'd ever let myself cry about what I'd endured. I slid off the edge of the tub and sat on the floor, hugging myself. *It's not your fault. You were a little kid. It's not your fault, because an adult manipulated and assaulted you. Don't blame yourself for this.*

These were the powerful thoughts that at last soothed me. Later that year, another human being would say these words to me out loud, and those words are ones for which I remain eternally grateful.

But in that moment, alone on the floor of the washroom, I began to shed a little of the shame and guilt. In that moment I realized how important it is not only to love the people around you but to love yourself.

I didn't have the courage to bring Mr. Neilson to justice then, and I regret that. I recently learned that he apparently died years ago. Now I do have the will to share my story. I hope that other victims of abuse who read this will feel safer than I did to speak out about what happened to them. I hope that they will have the courage to love themselves and to forgive themselves, because they were never to blame.

Chapter Thirteen

A DIFFERENT KIND OF FIGHT

Eventually, I found a reputable club in Windsor, Furukawa Judo, where I could practise Brazilian jiu-jitsu, boxing, kickboxing, and judo. I loved that I could train a bunch of different styles with the team there. I continued competing in tournaments again throughout my time in law school. Back in Toronto I would train with different gyms and back in Windsor I kept training with the guys from Furukawa. My winning streak continued, and I slowly started making a name for myself in mixed martial arts circles as a good sparring partner.

I ended up training with a couple of fighters who went on to compete in professional muay thai and MMA matches. One of my sparring partners was Jacob Conliffe. He fought heavyweight. He was a couple of weight classes heavier than me, but I held my own with him. He would get the better of me in striking, but I had a slight edge in grappling.

Our coach at the time was Mike Nomikos. He was a skilled

judoka in his own right, a black belt who competed regularly in submission grappling tournaments.

One day after training, he said to me, "You know, you could probably fight professionally if you wanted."

"You think so? I mean, I like submission grappling tournaments and helping the guys out as a sparring partner, but I don't know about fighting professionally."

"Well, you can hold your own with guys heavier than you who fight professionally. You can strike, grapple, and have cardio for days."

"Thanks, Mike," I said, warmed by the compliment but not totally convinced.

I loved martial arts. I found the practice and training incredibly rewarding. While I was interested in challenging myself and I was intrigued by the idea of taking it to the next level, I had bigger responsibilities to consider, so I couldn't entertain the idea. I didn't know it then, but a different kind of fight awaited me.

—⁓—

For the first three months of law school, I lived in Scarborough with my aunt and uncle, the relatives who'd supported my parents when they first arrived in Canada twenty-six years earlier. I shared a room with their nephew, my cousin, who'd just arrived from Panjab for his university education. Sleeping in the room my parents once lived in, I felt like I'd stumbled into their footsteps.

It didn't take long for me to realize that the professor who first suggested I study law was clearly onto something—it felt like the right path for me. After my first year of mandatory subjects, instead of focusing on one particular field, I took a range of different courses—from refugee and immigration law, which appealed to my social justice passions, to patent and trademark law, which spoke to my science background.

I found something interesting about every course I took. I was particularly fascinated with how laws keep society together, how they form links between all people. Sometimes these connections advance justice and sometimes they maintain inequality. Understanding how the law works gave me another frame in which to consider how we build a fairer society.

One class struck me in a personal way. During a first-year criminal law course, our professor, Sonia Lawrence, lectured on manslaughter and fighting.

"Can you consent to a non-professional fight?" she asked the class.

"Of course," I said, not so much sitting in my desk as slouching in my velour track suit.

"Even if it leaves you with a serious head injury?"

"Yes."

"Why's that?" she asked.

"When two guys 'take it outside,' there's a certain amount of harm that they're agreeing to," I said with full confidence. "Obviously, nobody is consenting to being maimed. If someone pulls out a knife and stabs the other guy, he didn't consent to that. But both of them are consenting to the risk of injury."

"What if that injury leaves him brain-dead? What if it kills him? One could argue that's manslaughter." Professor Lawrence recalled a case study involving two men in a street fight. The first punch that was thrown dropped one guy. His head hit a curb and he died. "Sure, he agreed to the fight," she said, "and there was no excessive force, there was no intention to kill. But that one punch resulted in a manslaughter charge."

"Was he convicted?" I asked.

"He was," she said. "You can't consent to a fight that ends in death, but there's no way to know it'll end that way until it does."

I felt like I'd been hit with a thunderbolt. With just a few words, Professor Lawrence made me realize that I had never truly considered the repercussions of the violence. Even if you're defending yourself, I realized, you can't control the outcome. Life is so fragile and violence so unpredictable. I told myself I would find ways to project confidence without aggression, power without peril. Violence is no path to solving a problem.

The answer didn't come to me suddenly, but as I looked down at my track suit, I knew one place where I could start: my clothes. In my dad's better days, I had seen how his tailored suits, slim trousers, vests, pocket squares, and English brogues elevated him above the stereotypes others might have of a brown-skinned immigrant.

As a kid, I hadn't understood the subtle power his clothing had.

After I graduated from law school and started articling, people stared when I walked into court. If people were going to stare at me, I might as well give them something to look at. I started spending time in tailor shops, asking questions and getting a feel for fabrics. I learned the different cuts of suits and what they communicated. I paid close attention to fit, lapel width, and button placement. Each element of the suit communicated something. Taken in total, a suit could convey casual confidence or boardroom power.

I began to trade loose T-shirts for fitted white dress shirts, and hoodies for blazers. Style and fashion became my new social armour, shielding me from stereotypes, disarming prejudices, communicating my dignity, and projecting my confidence even when I didn't have much. I knew that I'd continue to get hit with stereotypes, myths, preconceived notions, and biases both conscious and unconscious. If my clothing could deflect some of that negativity, I'd use it to my advantage. If people were going to stare at me, I might as well give them something to stare at.

Many years later, on King Street in downtown Toronto, I stepped out of the driver's side of a car and heard someone shout my name. It was an MMA fighter I'd trained with and who I'd recently read about in sports news.

"I saw your last fight on TV—congratulations!" I said, slapping him a handshake and pulling him in for a hug.

"Thanks, man," he said. "How've you been?"

"I'm good," I said with a smile.

He pointed at my car. "Yeah, man, it looks like you're doing *really* good. What happened?"

"I'm a lawyer now," I said. "But I miss the fight game."

"Don't worry about the fight game," he said. "You're doing better than I ever could. You're way ahead." We were looking at each other as though we'd both made it—each with a little envy of the other's success.

Back during my first year of law school, though, I was nowhere near living anyone's dreams. Sports cars and tailored suits felt like a distant, if not impossible, future. My family still lived under a mountain of debt, and it was ready to avalanche.

Chapter Fourteen

A PLACE TO CALL HOME

Another thing I admired about my dad besides his big-hearted generosity was his resilient optimism. Even when the odds were against him, he still believed he could bounce back. It was that optimism that gave me hope that he could beat his illness.

While my siblings had effectively ended communication with my dad, I tried my best to check in on him.

"How's it going, Dad?" I asked during a visit to Windsor.

"Much, much better. I feel one hundred per cent, like a new man."

"That's really good," I said with reserved encouragement. As much as my logical mind kept recounting the countless times he said this in the past, I couldn't help but feel a little hopeful.

My dad didn't betray a hint of defeatism—he never did when he was sober. I'd heard every variation of his positive assurances countless times before: "I'll be fine." "I'll be back on my feet." "I promise not to drink anymore." "I'll get back to work." All of his statements were uttered with intensity and energy. I felt like an elderly man sitting with an old friend, affectionately listening to the same story as if it were new.

"Dad, you really have to stop drinking. It's obviously going to take a toll on your health. It also really takes a toll on Mom."

He closed his eyes, overcome with shame. "I don't always remember what happens when I drink," he said with tears forming in his eyes. He quickly blinked them away.

In sharp contrast, I couldn't help but remember everything he did and said when he was drunk. Each memory was etched into my mind. Perhaps his mind had shut out fifteen years of trauma, a condition of brain atrophy or blacking out. But in these more tender moments with my dad, I saw his caring and thoughtful side, the father who had always tried to give his family everything, the man who was generous to a fault, with an intense ambition and will to succeed.

"I'm really enjoying law school," I said. "The classes are great, and I've got my own place in the student residence. I think law is going to work out for me."

"That makes me happy," he said. "How are your brother and sister?"

"Manjot is doing well. And Gurratan loves McMaster. He's getting into activism, so he's busy, but he wishes Jugnu could live with him instead of here in Windsor."

"I'm glad," my dad said. He paused and looked at his hands. "Do you have enough money?"

I caught my breath. He and I both knew that we were hard-pressed to make ends meet, but neither of us wanted to say it out loud. "I'm on top of it," I said.

The truth was, there was only so much I could do to help with my parents' financial situation. I had made a deal with my parents' creditors to have them pay a certain monthly amount, but it was still more than my parents could afford. The calls demanding repayment had become more threatening, and because my mom couldn't bring herself to answer the calls, I often bore the brunt of them. I tried not letting it get to me but every time UNKNOWN CALLER appeared on my cell display, I thought twice about answering.

"We know what you're doing with your finances—we know you have money," one creditor said.

"We just need some more time," I said. "We'll get the rest of the payment sorted out."

"We know the value of your house. If you keep defaulting, we're coming for it."

Even though it was just a voice on the phone, I was filled with fear and anxiety as I hung up. I wasn't sure if the creditors could actually make good on those threats, but I didn't want to take chances.

I needed some expert advice. There was no way we could continue the way we were going. We were slowly bleeding dry. I took a hard look at our situation and made a call to a bankruptcy trustee. I asked if I could get some preliminary advice on the phone. The trustee agreed and started asking some questions.

"How much is the debt?" he asked.

"Between a line of credit and the remaining mortgages, it's substantial."

"And your monthly payments?" he asked. When I told him the number, he agreed that was completely unsustainable. "What do you have in terms of assets?"

"My parents have their RRSPs and a house they live in," I said.

"My suggestion? Sell the house, cash the savings, and pay off your debt," he said.

"Are you serious?" I asked. "Then my parents will have no money *and* no place to live. Why would they do that?"

"I know maybe it's not what you want to hear. But if you do all of that, you'll be able to pay your debts. That's the best advice I can give you."

I was just twenty-four, and I was scared of mismanaging the family finances. I honestly didn't know what to do, but I also knew my mom was similarly lost and my dad wasn't in a state to help. There was no one else to pass these decisions on to—I had to figure it out.

—⁊⁊⁊—

Near the end of one of my semesters, my mom called me in distress. My dad was back at home from rehab, but he wasn't well. Things had gotten much worse. He was at an all-time low.

"He's unpredictable," my mom said.

"That's not a healthy environment," I told her. I knew I wouldn't be able to focus on my finals if I was constantly worried about my mom, so I proposed a wild idea.

"I'll bring Dad to live with me in my apartment," I said.

I hung up and looked around my place, a bachelor suite in York University's graduate student residence: a kitchenette and bathroom on one side, one open space with a coffee table and some padded seating, and a twin-size futon crammed in the opposite corner. It would be a tight fit with the two of us in my apartment, but it was better than my dad being at home, and there was nowhere else for him to go.

I picked him up the following Friday and brought him back to the apartment. That first night, knowing my mom finally had some peace at home, I slept better on the floor cushions than I had for weeks beforehand in my bed. But my dad quickly became distracting. I had to keep my eye on him constantly, to keep him from walking to a liquor store, to keep him from going to a bar. I prepared heavy meals—my epic pastas—to fill him and struck up random conversations to prevent him from getting bored. I couldn't give him any excuse to leave. But, of course, I couldn't always stay by his side.

On the fifth day, I came home from class and knew at a glance that he'd been drinking. Everything about him was slightly off: his eyes were glassy, his voice was a bit slurred, and he was slow to look me in the eye.

"You're drinking," I said.

"No, I promise—"

"I'm not asking you." My voice was cold and hard; I didn't raise my voice but I didn't need to. "How could you do this to me? I'm in law school now, I'm trying to get my life started—don't you realize you're messing with that?"

He apologized remorsefully, shamefully. I went to sleep frustrated and upset. The next day, I returned from class to study and he was sitting quietly on the couch. I could tell he was still feeling bad about the day before. He still didn't seem totally with it, but I let it slide. *Better me than Mom*, I thought.

The next day, when I returned home, my dad was gone. I figured he was out for a walk, so at first I was grateful for the break. But then I started to fear what condition he might return in. As the hours ticked by, I wondered if I should go looking for him, but I had no clue where to start. Just before I was about to leave and start searching, my cell rang. It was my mom.

"Your dad's in Windsor," she said. "He took a taxi to his friend's house and made him pay for it. We owe him $400."

Angry as I was, I couldn't stop myself from laughing at the insanity of my life. "I can't believe I thought I could handle him," I said. "Is he still at his friend's place?"

"Yes, his friend offered to let him sleep there for a few days, thank God."

I assume my dad wore his friend down quickly, because my dad was back at home within a couple of days and the cycle of chaos continued.

"It doesn't look like he's going to stop, and I can't keep an eye on him," I said to my mom. "I'm worried about you."

"It will be okay. Don't worry about it, *beta*," my mom said. I finished off my first year and came back to Windsor for the summer.

—⟋⟍⟍—

In my second year of law school, my mom called me in panic. My dad was getting worse. My sister was back in town. Both my mom and sister were afraid. I had been struggling with this decision for a while, and I finally decided enough was enough. There was no other option.

"We have to do something. This isn't fair to anyone." I sat back and sighed as I thought things through. "If we can find a separate apartment for him for cheap, it probably wouldn't make much difference to our financials."

"Are you sure?" my mom asked.

"It would be worth every cent in the peace of mind it would bring us," I said. We talked through a solution over a few days.

"I don't want to be the one to tell him," she said.

"I would never put that on you. I'll explain the situation to him."

The next weekend, I drove back to Windsor. I tried to stay calm as I prepared for what I had to do. I found my dad in the living room, and I told him we needed to talk. He could tell it was something serious, so he was more coherent than usual. We went upstairs and sat down in his bedroom. I looked around the room and thought about how many times my siblings and I had run to that same bedroom when we had nightmares or just wanted the company of our parents. It was ironic and tragic all at once.

"Dad," I said gently, "you need to leave. You can't live here with Mom anymore."

"I'll stop now, I promise," he said. "Please, my son, don't do this to me."

"I hope that you do stop," I said, placing a hand on his shoulder. "But I don't believe that's going to happen right now. You can't put Manjot and Mom through this and then leave us wondering whether or not you'll stop."

"I'll get better, I promise."

"If you get better, we'll figure it out. But, for right now, it's not fair and it's not healthy for you to be here."

He looked at me in disbelief. I couldn't tell if he was so hurt because he was being asked to leave or because things had gotten to the point where we had to choose between life with him and life without, and that we'd chosen the latter. Making that decision, I had to finally fully admit to myself that my dad's illness had hurt us all. Not just in that moment—it had been painful for years. Seeing my dad so lost and alone cut me to my core.

I kept explaining to him that his decisions made people unsafe. Eventually, he resigned himself to leaving. Over the next few days, I tried to make him feel involved with the apartment search, but he couldn't bring himself to care. My mom, ever the frugal one, found a suitable apartment building. The building's demographics included a mix of new immigrants trying to make it and other folks facing difficult times. My dad had started his life in Canada in the first category and he'd prospered beyond anyone's imagination. Now, twenty years later, he'd fallen into the second category from ten thousand feet above.

The day he got the lease, my mom and I filled the back of a borrowed truck with leftover furniture from the basement, mismatched and old but sturdy. He would hang nothing on his walls. No family pictures, no Sikhi inspiration, not even a calendar to keep track of time.

"The apartment has a lot of natural light, doesn't it," I said.

My dad shrugged his shoulders, unable to look me in the eye.

I looked out the window. "You've got a pretty nice view from here. And a balcony, too. That's nice."

My dad smiled ever so slightly, trying to humour my attempts to make conversation.

I pointed out a few more obvious things to try to lighten the conversation and distract us from the weight of the moment. There was no way around it, though—the apartment, my dad, and the day were all sad.

Initially, my dad seemed okay. He maintained some pride in

232

his appearance and enough coherent hours each day to make a network of friends from the building. A Polish neighbour visited often. Another Eastern European woman brought him leftovers, though he rarely had an appetite anymore.

Still, the apartment was depressing, and he soon got anxious living by himself. A few weeks after the move, my mom called me to say he'd come back home—just walked through the door with his house key—and was refusing to leave. She put him on the phone. I told him to go back to his apartment, hung up, and called a cab for him. He went back without a fuss, so I hoped it was just a one-time thing.

But a few days later, he was back.

"That's it," I said when my mom told me.

I stopped what I was doing and immediately got in the car to drive the three hours back from York. When I arrived at my mom's house, I found my dad seated on the couch.

"You have to go," I said. "You cannot stay here. Do not come back here."

Our first discussion had been rational, logical, a discussion of fairness between two men. This was different—I was issuing a decree.

"You are not welcome here," I told him. "Get out."

Despite everything we had gone through and all the pain his illness had caused, when I looked at my dad, I still felt deep love. Seeing the look on my dad's face as I ordered him to leave, something inside of me broke. I hated knowing that my words and actions were causing pain to someone I loved. But I remained steadfast. Eventually, my dad left. He didn't have much of a choice. Soon his apartment would be the only place in Windsor to call home.

In spring 2004, my mom got a knee replacement, and I moved back in to take care of her before my third year of law school. She was afraid to be in the house by herself, so it was incumbent on me to help her dress, cook her meals, and sometimes help her in the washroom. As fall semester and my return to York inched closer, I worried that she'd hurt herself climbing stairs or walking Jugnu after I left.

But there was a bigger problem. Though my parents owned the Santo house, they were deep in debt and the creditors were closing in. Even if they sold the house and used it to pay off some of their debt, my parents would still be behind. But there was no choice. They had to sell the house. There's a difference between selling your house because you want to and being forced to sell because you are in massive debt. In this case, it felt less like selling the house and more like losing the house.

We put the property up for sale and started calling relatives, asking if we could stay with them for a bit. It was a tense time. We'd already agreed that, with me at school in York and Gurratan at McMaster, it made sense to find a place in the Greater Toronto Area so that the two of us could look after Mom. We had already given up my apartment at York. And I wanted to buy a place, if I could. But I wasn't sure I could. I was still in law school, didn't have an income or anyone to co-sign a mortgage with me. On top of that I hadn't been able to find a place within the modest budget I had. I was afraid we were not going to have a home.

It took a while for our home to sell, and when it eventually did, we were confronted with a problem. We didn't have anywhere to go yet. We negotiated a little time on the closing. This gave us some time to empty out the house and figure out the next steps. Luckily, one of our relatives agreed to let us stay with them for a bit until we figured out our next move.

Meanwhile, an uncle helped find a place within my budget, a modest two-storey house in Mississauga. But I wasn't sure how I was going to secure a mortgage. I emptied out my personal savings. I tried the banks but was immediately refused because I was still a student. I confided in one of my friends and he told me about a mortgage broker who had some experience working with young professionals. I spoke with him and he said the only way he could secure a mortgage given my situation was if someone with sufficient proof of income co-signed the mortgage. I asked around to no avail. Finally, after some persuasion, an uncle agreed to help me as long as I promised to take his name off the loan as soon as I started practising as a lawyer. At long last, I was approved and I closed the deal on the house.

Next, my uncle, Gurratan, and I spent a weekend emptying out the house in Windsor. It was bittersweet for Gurratan and me. We had some fond memories there—warming up in front of the fireplace and hanging with friends by the pool. But we had horrible memories, too, like hiding from my dad in the basement, trying to drown out the screaming and crashing noises with pillows, and picking up after Dad the next morning.

As anticipated, selling the family home put only a small dent in the debt my parents owed. "It doesn't make sense for you to keep paying these interest fees," I told my mom. "You're spending too much."

"Your dad's not well and there are no guarantees he's going to get better any time soon. What do we do, then?"

"I hate to say it, Mom, but I think you just have to stop pay-ing the amount you and Dad owe. I think I should help you file for bankruptcy."

I'd taken a bankruptcy law course earlier that year, so I knew the procedure was more complicated than filling out a form. On their behalf, I'd need to argue for a full discharge, and there was a risk of applying for bankruptcy and the judge not actually granting it.

"We can't afford a lawyer," my mom said.

"You don't have to do anything right away," I said. "And be-sides, you don't need to hire a lawyer. You already have one."

I had a basic understanding of the bankruptcy process, but I wasn't an expert. I was still in law school, but I knew the filing process and challenges could drag on. It was likely that I'd be out of law school by the time the case actually went to court. When that time came, I'd be ready to represent my parents. I hadn't yet worked so much as an articling job, but I had fought for my family in every arena so far. The courtroom was next.

Chapter Fifteen

TO WALK A BETTER PATH

One day, in June 2005, Jugnu stood by the back door and whined for my mom to let him inside. He was twelve years old by then, an old man whose age was catching up to him. While he still loved going for walks and his tail still wagged every time I came in the door for a visit, he was definitely slowing down—sometimes, a sore hip would cause his back leg to give out during a walk. Thankfully, Jugnu's more mellow nature had grown on my mom, and she spent more time with him.

When she heard his whine, my mom slowly made her way to the back door to let him in. He settled down for a while, but then started whining at the door again. My mom thought his behaviour was odd, but didn't think much of it. The next morning, though, Gurratan came downstairs and found Jugnu lying in front of the door, not breathing.

Gurratan called me at school to break the news. I blinked back my tears, thinking about how Jugnu's companionship had helped me through some of the most difficult periods of my life. He had protected me from bullies and listened to me when I was too ashamed to talk to anyone else. He had provided comfort and companionship to my brother. In fairness, Jugnu was often the only one in the house who would spend time with my dad.

That evening, along with Manjot, Gurratan, and my mom, we said our own tearful goodbyes. Finally, Gurratan and I wrapped Jugnu in a cloth and brought him to an animal clinic for cremation. I comforted myself with the knowledge that he had lived a good life. I was sad, but not overwhelmed by it—it was the sort of sadness that comes from knowing that you've loved and lost.

I was trying to channel that resilience and direction in all areas of my life. I was enjoying law school, and although I knew that I would enjoy a career in law, I didn't know what type of law I wanted to practise.

At the time, I would have been happy to practise any of them, just so long as I got to work. After my first year, my grades weren't good enough for a summer job in law. Without work experience, I began to fall behind some of my classmates. Nobody hired me the summer after my second year, either, so I fell further behind. I should have been stressed, but I wasn't. I continued to work as hard as I could, and I honed the *chardi kala* spirit my mom had taught me about so many years ago.

In June 2005, after I graduated from my third year of law school, the bar admissions classes and exams began. I saw my classmates again after a couple of months' break at Ryerson University, where the classes were taking place. As we mingled outside the classroom, waiting for the doors to open, surrounded by a thousand future barristers and solicitors from other law schools, we did what all graduating law school students do: we talked about articling.

"Jagmeet, where are you doing your articles?" one person asked.

"I don't have a position yet," I said.

"Oh," they responded, and the group fell silent. It was as if I'd just told them I had a terminal illness.

"It's all good, I'm sure I'll figure out something soon," I said.

"Well, it was nice seeing you," they said before turning away, no doubt thinking, *How is that even possible?*

After I finished the bar admission courses and passed all my exams, I put all my energy into transforming that faith in my future into reality. I started by making regular trips to the courts nearby. Our house in Mississauga was located just a few minutes away from the A. Grenville and William Davis Courthouse, one of the busiest in Canada. I thought if I saw some court cases, maybe I could figure out what type of law I wanted to practise. So I started going to the courthouse whenever I could.

One day, I watched a lawyer named Richard O'Brien cross-examine a police officer. O'Brien's client was a young black man facing serious drug charges, and O'Brien was arguing that his client should be released on bail. The officer on the stand testified that he believed the young man would not return to court when required and that he was at risk to commit further offences. O'Brien proceeded to systematically destroy each of those arguments.

He revealed that police had stopped the same young man multiple times, going back years to when he was a young teen—he'd been carded and questioned aggressively all his young-adult life. There were no grounds for any of it. Through his cross-examination, O'Brien tore apart the officer's alleged reasons for detaining the young man, and step by step, he deconstructed the officer's bias.

I was captivated by the cross-examination. As I watched O'Brien eviscerate the witness—every razor-sharp question intended to challenge and hold accountable the power of government—I thought back to all the times I'd been harassed by the police since I was a teenager; at least eleven, from what I could recall. And the carding incidents I experienced in Windsor and then in London had continued after I moved to Toronto.

I remembered an incident that happened when I was in my third year of law school. I was visiting a friend who lived near Casa Loma in Toronto. I drove to the castle and parked in the public lot. It was a beautiful day and my friend was running late, so I got out and walked around. I sat on the low concrete barrier surrounding the castle property, my legs dangling over the edge, and took in the scene. There were kids screaming and running around a large, ornate fountain. Tourists were posing in front of the castle, and a bridal party was capturing their special moment.

Then, out of the corner of my eye, I saw two police officers pedalling up the steep hill. I started staring for a couple of reasons. For one, they were biking up an incredibly steep hill, so I was curious to see if they could make it. And secondly, my experiences had also trained me to pay close attention to what nearby police were doing.

I watched them bike up the incline, and then I lost sight of them as they rounded a corner. Then I called my friend to let her know where I was waiting.

"I'll be right out, just need a couple more minutes," she said.

"No worries," I said. "I'll wait by the castle."

All of a sudden, I looked up and noticed the two bike officers had stopped a few feet from me.

I switched to Panjabi. *The police are here.*

"What happened?" she asked in alarm.

"Nothing," I continued in Panjabi. "I'm just sitting here at the castle."

"Do you need to deal with this? Should I let you go?"

"No," I said. "Stay on the line a little longer and let's see what happens."

"Okay," she said with a touch of concern. "Don't do anything stupid."

I laughed. "When do I ever do anything stupid?"

We chatted for a couple more minutes, and all the while I felt the intense stares of the police officers on me.

Finally, my friend said, "Listen, I'm just about ready. I'm going to hang up and walk over."

"Okay."

I flipped my phone closed and looked up to see if the officers were still watching me.

"Is there a problem?" one officer asked sternly as soon as we made eye contact.

"No, no problem," I responded.

"You sure were staring at us like you had a problem," he said.

"I didn't think that the direction of my gaze was an issue."

The other officer stepped closer. "We're going to need to see some identification," he said.

I thought for a moment. I didn't have to provide identification unless I was under arrest. I had been learning about the basic rights of citizens for three years in law school, and I strongly believed that it was just as important to exercise those rights as it was to study them. So I made a choice.

"Sorry, officer, but I'm not going to provide you with my identification," I said.

I could instantly see their body language change. Both officers stepped closer.

"Sir, we need to see your identification right now. We need to know what you're doing here and whether or not you live in the area. You need to provide some ID and answer our questions right now!" The officer raised his voice until he was basically issuing commands at me. I knew I could just give in to the aggression and answer their questions. I had nothing to hide. But I knew my rights.

I stood up and looked the officer squarely in the eye. *Here goes nothing*, I thought.

"Officer, I am not going to provide you with identification, and I'm not going to answer any of your questions. This conversation is over," I said.

I turned away and started walking. With each step I took, I imagined that I was going to get tackled to the ground. I started planning out how I would break my fall with the tumbling exercises I had learned in aikido. I imagined being struck by the police and how I could protect my head. But nothing happened. I got to my car safely, turned the ignition, and started driving toward the exit. Then I saw that the police officers had blocked the driveway with their bikes.

"You seem to know a lot about your rights," one officer said. "So I'm sure you'll know that, since you're operating a motor vehicle, under the Highway Traffic Act, you must provide us with identification, as well as proof of insurance and registration."

Damn it, I thought. *They're right.*

I waited while the officer ran my information in the system. While I sat there, a cruiser pulled up. *Why did they call for backup?* I wondered. To my surprise, out of the car stepped a turbaned, bearded Sikh police officer. He spoke with the two bicycle officers and then came over to my window.

"Here are your documents," he said, handing me my licence, registration, and insurance.

"Thanks," I said.

"I just wanted you to know that this wasn't racial profiling. It was just a routine stop. You're free to go—take care now."

My jaw dropped. I couldn't believe the bicycle police officers had called a racialized officer to tell me that their stop wasn't racially motivated. Even if I hadn't already interpreted the stop that way, the fact that he said it wasn't only confirmed it was.

I said as much to the officer.

"If I didn't think it was racial profiling before (and I did), the fact that you had to come here and say it wasn't only highlights how much it really was," I said.

The cops went on their way. My friend, who had been observing everything from a little distance away, finally got in the car and we headed out. As we drove away, I thought about how I'd worked hard through my undergrad, hustled to get into law school; was about to become an attorney, a professional; and despite that, the police treated me like the same kid in Windsor who got pulled over for nothing. Always just "a routine procedure."

After leaving the courtroom, I kept thinking about how O'Brien revealed the officer's abuse of power by peeling away at the truth. As I drove home, I wondered how many other people were regularly pulled over, people who didn't know their rights—who maybe didn't have access to law, or didn't really *understand* the law. How many of them had to put up with this? How much more intimidating was it for them? Did they ever feel, as I sometimes did, like they didn't belong? I wanted to speak for them the way that defence lawyer spoke for that young black man.

I finally knew what type of law I wanted to practise: criminal law. I visited the Law Society of Upper Canada website and found a link to all of the recognized criminal law specialists in the province. I started making calls to every name on the list, asking for a meeting. I had dreams of working at a big law firm and learning from the country's greatest criminal law minds, and I hoped that my outreach might lead to an articling opportunity. But I was willing to start with anything that helped me get a foot in the door.

I didn't get a big break, but I did get a couple of calls back. One in particular stood out for his warmth and willingness to meet: Thomas Carey.

Thomas—or Tom, as he preferred—was a gregarious Irishman, tall and balding, with a grey moustache. We met up for lunch near the Peel Courthouse.

"I've always thought there was a missing link between Irish and Panjabi people," he said. "Why else do we share so many last names? Gill, Dillon—"

"Mohan," I added.

"That's right!" he exclaimed. "Somewhere down the line, I'm sure you and I have a distant cousin or two."

Though Tom wasn't able to take on an articling student, he let me shadow him for a couple of weeks. His hustle amazed me. Even though he was quite experienced, he worked as defence counsel and per diem prosecution for public services, as well as being a part-time small claims court judge on civil matters. I thought it was pretty impressive that he worked all three positions—defence, prosecution, and judge.

After one of the days when I was shadowing him, Tom invited me to a get-together at the office of Carey and Associates. The other associates at the office, their friends and partners, and the administrative staff made an intimate group.

As we sat around the table chatting, Tom turned to me and said the words I'd been dying to hear. "I have a case tomorrow, and I don't think I can make it. Would you be able to go for me?"

"Absolutely," I said.

He laughed. "I haven't even told you about the case."

"Doesn't matter, I'll do it."

"It's a guilty plea for a conditional discharge. It's already been arranged for my client," Tom said. "You just have to confirm the client is entering into the plea voluntarily and that he understands he's giving up a right to a trial. The judge will then have the final say on the sentence. It's very simple. You'll be fine."

The next morning, I drove to court wearing my favourite suit. I got there hours early so that I could observe how other, more experienced lawyers made guilty pleas on their clients' behalf. I didn't want to be caught off guard, and even though my instructions from Tom were clear, I felt a responsibility to ensure I was doing everything I could for our client.

After a couple of hours of watching how other lawyers had played their hands, I had an idea. I approached the Crown during an intermission between cases.

"I understand the agreement for your client is a conditional discharge," the Crown said, barely looking up from their papers.

"That's correct," I said. "But I would like to have the judge consider an absolute discharge. Do you have any concerns with that?"

The prosecutor thought about it for a few seconds and shrugged. "No, that's fine. We'll be asking for a conditional discharge, but you're free to argue for the absolute—it's the judge's decision at the end of the day."

I found my client in the pews. "We're ready to go," I said, and walked him to the front table.

Listening to other lawyers in the court, I had concluded that this judge was open to considering lighter sentences if the details of the case merited it. The judge seemed to have a strong inclination toward giving first-time offenders a break, especially if they had the potential to return to work.

After entering the plea, I made my argument.

"Your honour, you'll note that this is the first offence for my client. He has no other antecedents. In addition," I said, gesturing to the opposing Crown counsel, "I've already shown a copy of a job letter to my friend, which I can provide to you as well. The letter confirms that my client has secured employment and has a promising career as a skilled tradesman. Based on sentencing guidelines, I submit it's in his best interest as well as those of the community that he continue to be a productive member of society. An absolute discharge will protect his current as well as future employment."

The judge thought it over and looked over the exhibit I had submitted.

"What is the Crown looking for in this case?" the judge asked.

"A conditional discharge, your honour," the Crown counsel said.

"You're not that far off," said the judge. He considered the letter a moment longer and said, "Absolute discharge granted."

"Thank you, your honour," I said.

My client nodded appreciatively. I kept my cool, but inside I was glowing. I immediately raced back to Tom's office to tell him what happened.

"How'd you do that?" he asked when I delivered the news.

"I just listened to what other people were doing and thought, I might as well ask for something better."

"That's impressive."

"Seeing as how you think that," I said, "I'm looking for an articling position. What do you think?"

Tom hadn't budgeted for a student salary, but he agreed to take me on and cover my gas and parking. He even promised to let me keep the retainer for any new clients I picked up. For eight months, I skidded by with cases of summary offences—the less serious and non-indictable crimes—while I slowly picked up a few clients here and there.

Tom probably didn't think it was right to ask too much of someone he wasn't paying, so he never worked me too hard. As well as articling for Tom, in my spare time, I continued to spectate at Greater Toronto Area courts, furthering my informal education in different counsel styles and skills. I was quickly realizing that the minutes I spent in the courtroom were as valuable as every one I'd spent in class.

There was one such "teacher" who I followed more than anyone else. Whenever Reid Rusonik's name appeared on a courtroom docket, I made sure I was in the front row to watch him perform. A managing partner with Pinkofskys, Reid's intensity was theatrical. He'd go all out to defend his client's interests, leaving no stone unturned. He had a stare that bore into a witness's soul. Reid believed in taking legal aid certificates—helping those who couldn't afford legal representation—and Pinkofskys as a whole strongly believed in giving their clients the best legal defence, not just taking a guilty plea, to ensure that everyone received their right to trial. I admired that approach. It fit with my idealized view of law as a means of defending the interests of anyone—of everyone—around me, no matter how disenfranchised or dispossessed they might be.

I watched Reid so often that I eventually became noticeable as a regular at his trials. One afternoon, I saw him outside the courthouse by himself. *This is my chance*, I thought. I had no plan, no script, no professional approach. In hindsight, I probably could have benefitted from thinking things through a little more. Instead, I walked up to Reid and blurted out, "Hi, my name's Jagmeet. I'd like to work for you."

As the last word tumbled out of my mouth, I thought, *Did I really just walk up to Reid and ask him for a job? This was not a good idea.*

Reid looked at me with the same stare I'd seen him use against witnesses, officers, and experts to tear them apart. He wasn't just looking into my soul, but through it, into my soul's soul. He seemed to say without saying, *Did you just do that?* I stared right back, trying to seem confident. *Yup, I just did.*

He shook his head slowly. It was time for me to leave. I turned away, and then he said, "You know what? I'd like to hire you."

I didn't immediately process what he said. I was about to apologize when my mind played back his words and I finally got it.

"That's incredible," I said.

He gave me his card. "Send me your résumé, and we'll follow up with a meeting." We met up and Reid offered me a job to start with the firm as soon as I was called to the bar.

I told Tom the good news and he congratulated me. I finished up my articles and attended the ceremony where I was officially called to the bar. The following Monday, my dream came true when I walked into the downtown office of Pinkofskys for my first official day of work as a lawyer. I hit the ground running and realized that I still had so much to learn. It made for long days, but I didn't care—I knew that as long as I kept working hard, all of my family's financial worries would be taken care of. More important, I could help not just my own family but also others in similar circumstances.

—⁂—

I worked with Pinkofskys for just about a year before leaving and opening my own criminal law practice, Dhaliwal Law. I was glad for the change. With my new practice, I had the opportunity to make more money while working fewer hours, which freed up some time to volunteer my legal services for social justice causes.

Like a lot of people born in the late seventies and early eighties, I'd developed a taste for activism because of the Iraq War. I was still in university when the war began, and although Western University wasn't known for large campus protests, the injustice was too big to ignore. As hundreds of students formed in the university quad, I shouldered my way to the front of the marches, chanting slogans like "We want peace" and "Drop Bush, not bombs."

I'd continued my activist streak at York, where there was a more active student body. When we saw that tuition fees were going up unsustainably across Ontario, we took to the streets. I walked out of class in protest, along with thousands of other students. Later, I participated in anti-poverty and pro–human rights demonstrations. Often, the police approach to such protests was to use disproportionate force to manage the crowd. At more than one march, the police would barge in to physically push the protesters out of the way, cementing the feeling it was us against them.

Now, a few years later, I was entrenched in the buttoned-up world of the legal profession and yearning to get involved in social justice causes again. It happened that my brother, while at McMaster, had become involved with an anti-poverty group and another organization that was rallying for universal refugee and immigration rights.

"We could use your help," Gurratan told me. "The police often give protesters a hard time at rallies. We need someone who knows the law just to be there, keep an eye out, you know?"

I did know—what they needed was a legal observer—but I did him one better. "Put my name on your list of legal representation," I said. "If someone gets arrested, they can call me."

Most of the protesters were students in the beginning stages of discovering their ideals and political voices. Though they might be prone to mistakes, they deserved legal services, even if they couldn't afford them. In the end, I only ever received one call, from a young man charged with criminal mischief—damage to property. The charge could have stained his permanent record, but I spoke with the Crown and worked out an extrajudicial solution. The charges were dropped in exchange for the young man doing community service.

Around this time, my brother also started a group called the Sikh Activist Network. He co-founded it with his friend Amneet Singh, the bright kid from London who I'd known since he was fourteen. Amneet's brother and sister were close in age to me and his parents were like a second set of parents to me away from home. Gurratan and Amneet organized this collective of youth inspired by Sikhi's social justice roots. Their core mandate was that, as Sikhs, it was their duty to fight for the betterment of all people. And one major problem that all marginalized people faced, especially in the GTA, was random police checks.

Gurratan asked me to facilitate a series of "Know Your Rights" workshops at southern Ontario school campuses. As a lawyer, I could speak with expertise about civilians' general rights: when we're not obliged to speak to police, when it's better to walk away, and when it's safe or necessary to provide information. Basic dos and don'ts that I felt everyone should know.

I did seminars in lecture halls that were made up mostly of racialized folk. I'd start by quickly summarizing the importance and intention of the seminar before picking volunteers to act out a skit. I gave one a backpack and explained their role.

"You were at a party. There was a fight. Blood splattered

on your jacket, so you put it in your backpack and now you're on your way home." The other volunteer was a police officer. I told them, "You're investigating the disturbance, and you think he caused the fight. Your job is to be tough, be aggressive, be belligerent—whatever you think you need to be to search the civilian's pockets and bag, looking for grounds to press charges."

I was always impressed with how students might start off shy but would quickly get into character in compelling ways. I wanted young people facing the same problems as me to know how they could protect themselves against abuses of power. Nobody should feel coerced to give statements or hand over their identification or phones. We all have a Charter of Rights that guards us against potential injustice, but we have to know how to use it.

At the end of each presentation, I would open up the floor for questions. Arms shot up.

"I got stopped while walking through a park," said one, explaining what happened next.

"I got searched outside a 7-Eleven," said another.

"Police pull me over all the time!"

As they described to me each scenario, we peeled back the layers to expose what was happening in their communities. They were clearly targeted for the colour of their skin and their age. It was apparent, also, that carding and profiling were more widespread among black and Indigenous students than anyone else.

As disheartening as it was to see these prejudices that so many suffered, it filled me with pride to know that my little brother was fighting those very injustices and empowering people, and that he was succeeding in a concrete way. All my life, I'd tried to be a role model to Gurratan, but he'd become a role model to me, too. When I was looking after Gurratan in London, there were many times when I'd thought of him more like a son than as a little brother. Now it was clear he was neither: he was my equal. Soon, he'd become even more than that. Gurratan was about to become my mentor.

Chapter Sixteen

LOTTERY TICKET

Since moving into his apartment, my dad had developed serious heart and stomach issues. A few times, they got so bad that he needed to go to the hospital. Each time, he was so incapacitated that he couldn't even remember how he got there; we assumed he had his neighbours to thank for calling an ambulance. He would go into the hospital, where doctors would stabilize him and warn him that he was pushing his luck. After a couple of days in care, he'd be strong enough to be discharged. He would leave, only to end up drinking again. I couldn't understand what it was that made my dad swallow a bottle of vodka after hearing a doctor say, "You may die if you continue this."

My dad once told me that he drank to slow down his overactive mind. His thoughts had a habit of going into overdrive. Sometimes, that worked to his advantage; his obsessions made him a good study. I remember how, during better years, he'd spend hours in the corner of the living room with medical books, marking up and underlining the text as if he'd be quizzed on every single word. At first, he reached for a bottle to slow things down. Somewhere along the way, though, that easy outlet became a chemical dependency. Somewhere further along, it had started taking over his life. Now, it seemed that dependency claimed him almost completely.

For a stretch of time, my mom was the only one who visited him. After being called to the bar and getting my first job in my professional career, I was working long hours. At this point I was responsible for a mortgage on a house, all the bills, and most of the other expenses to support my mom, dad, and brother. My sister was established and pitched in regularly, too.

The morning I left Mississauga to pick Dad up for our court appearance, my mom warned me, "He's not doing too well."

I parked outside his apartment and looked for him in the lobby. He wasn't there, so I was about to head inside when I spotted him, alone on a bench in the park across the street. He didn't know what to do with his time. He probably didn't like being in his apartment because it was a reminder of things that were difficult to accept. Consequently, he spent a lot of time outdoors, sitting in nearby parks or bus stops, never far from his neighbourhood liquor store. Windsor was a small place, so I often wondered what it was like for former patients and colleagues to see him looking as rough as he did. The reality is they probably didn't recognize him. I barely recognized him myself.

My dad had lost thirty or forty pounds. His hair and beard were growing—not because he was returning to his faith, but because he had stopped seeing a barber. He wore layers and layers of stained clothes, and his pants were held up by a belt with new notches poked in it. To this day, whenever I see someone looking rough on the streets, there's often a split second when I think about my dad.

"Let's go inside," I said gently. "Maybe you can take a shower before we go."

He was slow to register, looking back at me with those glassy eyes I'd seen too many times, despite the fact that it was only late morning. It was hard to believe this was the same man who'd once taken so much pride in his appearance, who'd taught me that, as racialized folk, we couldn't afford not to look good.

And yet, there were remnants of my dad's former intellect in that body of his. On the highway to Toronto, I chatted about anything and everything, trying to keep him focused.

After what felt like a long drive, Dad and I finally arrived at the court. We waited outside the bankruptcy hearing room. The cubicle-laden office reminded me more of an office storage room than a courthouse. There were stacks of cardboard boxes piled in the corner between me and the brown door behind which our fate awaited.

The trustee in the bankruptcy court had challenged the full discharge that I'd filed for my father. The trustee argued that, given my dad's earning potential as a specialized doctor, he should be able to work and pay off his debts and interests in a relatively short period. I was there to convince the judge of a different view.

"My father has been out of work for almost seven years," I protested. "There's no guarantee he would be able to return any time soon. At his age and with his condition, he may never practise again." No doubt it was hard for my dad to sit there and hear my pessimistic defence, but truth hurts.

I pressed on. I told the judge that when debt is amassed as

a result of illness—and make no mistake, addiction is a serious illness—courts have ruled in favour of full discharges. I made the argument that having a massive debt weighing on people makes it even more difficult to recover. Financial stress is crippling, and I knew that until my father's debts were fully discharged, the odds were stacked against him.

The judge agreed with me and granted my parents a full discharge. I felt a wave of relief when he gave his ruling. It lifted a heavy burden from my parents, one that my mom could never carry alone. I hoped my dad would take this financial clean slate as a restart for his mind and body, too.

—⁓—

The last time I saw my father drunk is a memory I'd rather forget. My mom and I drove to see him in Windsor on a cold day in 2007. I was still building my new practice and was busier than ever, so it had been many months since my past visit. My mom was checking in on him semiregularly, however, and each time, she reported back that my dad was in worse and worse shape. I'd heard her warnings, but they couldn't prepare me for the man waiting in his apartment.

My dad's addiction had robbed him of his broad-shouldered, sturdy body and replaced it with the shell of an emaciated old man. He had dropped to 110 pounds, skin and bones, and he needed a walker just to move around. His hair was matted and clumpy, as though he hadn't combed it in years. He almost looked like he could be my grandfather rather than my father.

My dad had stopped being a regular father a while ago. But still, there's some part of us that sees our parents as parents no matter what. He was my dad, so somewhere in my mind, beneath the layers of dirty clothes, he was still a superhero. Seeing him so thin and frail disturbed me—it seemed far too real a reminder of our mortality.

"I'm sorry," my dad said, his words cracked and meek.

I put my arm around him. "We just want you to get help," I said.

I scanned the apartment. No recent pizza boxes, just what I'd seen the last time I'd visited—takeout containers, crinkled paper bags, and empty bottles. Cigarette butts and little wads of paper that I assumed were crumpled liquor receipts were sprinkled across every flat surface.

"We should probably help him take a shower," my mom suggested.

I took a deep breath and lifted my dad off the couch. I was shocked at how light he was. I carried him to the bathroom and sat him on the toilet to remove his clothes. I helped him into the shower, but his legs were too wobbly to stand, so I eased him to the floor of the tub, where he crumpled up over his crossed legs. Embarrassed, he tried to make small talk as a diversion.

"You're a lawyer now?" he asked.

"That's right, Dad," I said with a forced, awkward grin.

"You like it?" he asked, with red eyes and quivering lips.

"I really do," I said. "Now let's get you cleaned up. Give you some shampoo here, and you can scrub yourself down with some soap. Your nails are a little long—why don't we snip them?"

I dried him off, and as I carried him to his bedroom, I saw my mom filling a black garbage bag, making a futile effort to improve his conditions. I looked for some clean clothes in his drawers. There were wads of paper all over his bedroom, too. *Why is he keeping all these receipts?* I thought, as I picked one out of an open drawer and flattened the edges on his dresser. It was a lottery ticket. They all were. A hundred or more of them strewn about his home.

I had never seen my dad buy a lottery ticket in my life. His life had been a lottery ticket. From a humble farm in Panjab, he'd become a successful professional before his addiction had led him to lose it all. He'd been out of work for almost eight years, so I assumed the lottery tickets were his last-ditch efforts to support his family again. To be of use to us the only way he knew how: through economic means.

Deep down, I'd always known that my dad couldn't help himself, that this was an illness. But it had been hard to hold that perspective when we were dealing with the day-to-day realities and hurt caused by that illness. Washing my dad in the shower that day was the first time I believed the truth of what I'd intellectually understood. It was the first time I could start to forgive my dad's mistakes. There was no way anyone would wish to live in such horrible conditions, to deteriorate to the brink of death and try to regain their self-worth at a-hundred-million-to-one odds. No one would want this suffering. No healthy person would choose it. This was rock bottom. It had to be. I prayed it was. I had always been confused about how I could love my dad when we were so hurt by him. But in that moment, all of my confusion fell away. There was only love—the love of a son for a father who had tried his best but fallen sick with a disease.

Still, love alone wouldn't heal my dad's sickness—he had to want to help himself. I brought him back to the living room in cleaner clothes. It was impossible for the three of us to talk about normal things, but we were too defeated to confront the harsh reality: my dad was slowly killing himself. So we sat in silence.

"Do you want us to bring you to the hospital?" my mom finally asked. He shook his head no. "We can get a doctor over for a house call."

"No," he said. "I don't want anyone to see me like this."

There wasn't much more to do after that. On the way out, I grabbed a half-full bottle of vodka off the kitchen counter. I unscrewed the lid and was about to pour it down the sink, just like my ten-year-old self did in the basement of our Windsor home. But my mom took the bottle from my hand.

"Leave it," she said. "He'll just buy it again. He wants to drink, let him drink."

"He's going to die," I said.

"Either he will die, or he will go to a hospital to live. We can't force him—it's his choice."

Two days later, my dad called us from the Windsor hospital. He'd called the ambulance himself.

———

My dad had been to the best addiction rehab centres in North America and yet, after each discharge, he quickly abandoned every lesson and good habit for another drink. So when we visited him in the hospital, we were pretty skeptical when he said, "Take me to a treatment centre."

"You don't have insurance to cover the costs like before, so our options will be a little limited."

He nodded. "That's fine," he said. "Anything will do. I'm ready. I want to live."

Those four words gave me pause. For the first time, my dad appeared to understand that his addiction had reached a point of life and death. I squeezed his hand and said, "We'll see what we can find."

Windsor had a well-respected, publicly funded rehab centre called Brentwood Recovery, just a few blocks south of my dad's apartment. After my dad was discharged from the hospital, I helped him get into the passenger's seat of the car, loaded his walker in the trunk, and drove him directly to Brentwood. I'd gone by it many times and never noticed it until then. It just looked like another motel, tucked between a Superstore and a gas station. As I guided my dad up a ramp to the front doors, my doubts only intensified. If the best rehabs didn't save him, how would this?

"*Chardi kala*," I said as we entered the nondescript facility. I couldn't tell if I was speaking to him or myself or both of us. It didn't matter—we all needed a little rising spirits and courageous optimism, given the track record we were up against.

Eight weeks later, I returned to Brentwood and found a version of my dad that resembled the one I'd briefly met in the mid-nineties, after my grandfather died—the last time my dad had stayed sober for a prolonged period of time. In the past, whenever he'd tried to get sober, he'd projected a kind of exaggerated confidence about his recovery. Now, as he walked with me through the centre's hallways, he spoke humbly about his progress.

"I'm just trying my best," he said.

I put my arm around him. "You look better." It was true. He'd put some weight back on. He didn't need a walker anymore, and his hair was groomed.

He gave me a tour of the facility, showing me his dorm room

and his classroom for treatments sessions. He introduced me to an addictions counsellor.

"You must be really proud of your father," the counsellor said to me. "He's come a long way."

My dad blushed. "One day at a time," he said.

"One day at a time," the counsellor repeated with a smile.

As it turns out, my dad had a relationship with Brentwood that predated his becoming a patient there. He used to help out with psychiatric services and provided treatment to the people who needed it. One of Brentwood's founders, Father Paul, had sent a message to all the staff when he learned my father was in their care. The message was this: Dr. Dhaliwal looked after us when we needed him, now it's our turn to look after him.

As we settled into the cafeteria for a cup of tea, our conversation turned to what we'd do after he completed the program in another thirty days. We couldn't keep my dad in his apartment. It wasn't about the cost—living alone in that apartment was not a safe place for him. It was too isolating, too triggering, and too depressing.

My dad was less concerned about where he would live than about what he would do.

"I want to practise again," he told me. He was still suspended from practising by the Ontario College of Physicians and Surgeons.

"I'll help you with that," I said.

"And I need to get my driver's licence, too."

"I'll do anything I can to get you back on your feet."

My dad looked at his cup of tea. "I want my family back," he said quietly. I didn't respond. After a long pause, he said, "Will you help me with that?"

"Of course I'll try," I said.

"Let me live with you in Mississauga."

I shifted in my seat uncomfortably. Neither Manjot nor Gurratan were ready to see him yet. They'd lived apart from my dad for some time and had found a more peaceful existence with him outside their peripheries. The last thing I wanted to do was create another toxic environment that would reopen old wounds.

"I'm going to have to talk to everyone," I said.

This was a decision we had to make as a family, so I took my dad's request to my mom, Manjot, and Gurratan. My brother and sister were against it, but my mom was more open.

"I wouldn't be putting this idea forward unless I was sure Dad wasn't drinking anymore," I said. "It seems like he's really committed to the treatment."

I could see my siblings still had their doubts.

"If there's any sign that he starts drinking again, he's out," I said. "I know this isn't ideal, but I think we need to try it."

After my dad moved back in with us in Mississauga, I was nervous every day. I would constantly check for any signs or hints that he had relapsed. Despite my fears, it seemed he really was better. He dutifully kept clean. The hours he once dedicated to boozing in his bedroom he now spent studying medical journals and poring over newspapers, catching up on a world he'd checked out from for some time. He'd never done that before. I had cautious hope that this was the sign of a new start.

Not everything was so smooth, though. As soon as my dad showed his face to my siblings, they'd either leave the room or berate him. Gurratan was the harshest in the way he talked down to him.

"Leave. Get out of here," he said the moment my dad entered a room. He was angry, and understandably so. His anger grew from a lifetime of pain, but I tried to set a new example that would pave the way to forgiveness.

I knew that the anger was a dangerous force—something that could result in words or actions that I might regret. I remembered when I was a kid, I tried to take control over my anger. I decided that in any moments of frustration, when I felt the anger bubbling over, I would find a positive physical release. I used to go for a run. I threw on sneakers, ran out the door, and kept running until my lungs burned. If I got tired, I'd hear a voice in the back of my head pushing me: *That's all you got? I thought you were angry. Where's that anger now?* Sometimes, I would lose track of where I went, and only when I stopped would I take in my surroundings. I'd slowly jog home, exhausted and dripping with sweat, but calmer than when I left.

Still, the situation wasn't working with everyone under one roof again. There was too much friction and too much unresolved pain. My mom and I had forgiven my dad on our own terms, but my brother and sister weren't ready yet. I knew that, if it came down to it, I could probably find another place for my dad to live. But I felt strongly that he shouldn't live on his own. He was committed to reconnecting with his family, even if that was a long journey, and he wanted to get back to doing what he loved, which was healing people. He just needed a little more time to heal himself first.

Thankfully, my dad had gotten back in touch with his mom and siblings, from whom he'd grown distant. His mother was still in Panjab, but his nearest immediate family was a sister in New York. He needed more time to heal and the situation in

Mississauga wasn't working, so a plan was made to live in Panjab for a bit. I'm not exactly sure who suggested it, but we came up with the plan and it seemed to make sense. My grandmother was visiting in the States, so the plan was to drive to New York so that my grandmother and my dad could fly back to Panjab together.

I offered to drive my dad down, and Gurratan agreed to come along for the eight-hour drive. I was surprised, given he couldn't stand being in the same room as Dad. But I think he was slowly starting to believe that Dad had actually gotten better, and the fact that he was willing to live in Panjab to give himself more time to heal and to give the family more time to adjust to him built a lot of goodwill. It also helped that since neither of us had been to New York, we were excited to squeeze a little fun out of the unusual and uncertain circumstances. Why not? If life had taught us anything, it was that you couldn't wait until everything was stable to find joy, because life was never stable.

As we crossed the Peace Bridge over Lake Erie and onto the US interstate, my dad's good-natured personality came out of hiding. At one point, he asked me to pull over so he could relieve himself. He jumped out of the car and peed under the tire opposite Gurratan's side in the backseat, talking to my brother through the cracked window the entire time. The way he was positioned, Gurratan couldn't tell what was going on.

"You can't tell I'm peeing," he said conspiratorially to Gurratan. "Even if someone on the highway saw us, they would just think I'm having a conversation with you."

Normally, when my dad tried to be goofy like that, it wouldn't work. But it was such a genuine and bizarre moment that Gurratan couldn't keep a straight face. He started laughing uncontrollably, and I couldn't help but laugh along with him.

We arrived at my aunt's house that evening, and we spent the night catching up with our family. It was the first time I'd seen my aunt and grandmother in years, so there was plenty to talk about. The next day, we went sightseeing and shopping with my aunt and cousin. Considering the reason for our trip, the day off was surprisingly fun and carefree. The next day, my aunt and cousin had to be back at work, so Gurratan and I checked out the city on our own, while my dad spent time with his mom.

Finally, though, it was time to say goodbye to my dad and grandmother. They'd purchased one-way tickets, so we had no idea when our dad would return or in what condition.

Despite having had a relatively good time with my dad on the trip, Gurratan kept his distance at the airport. His lingering resentment was understandable. I hugged my dad near the departures gate and looked at his face for a long time. He looked healthier than he had been in a long time. I knew he still had a long way to go, and that his past track record would be hard to overcome. But still, I truly believed he was going to get better. It was something in his eyes. They shone with hope and determination, love and courage.

—⁊—

The specifics of what happened in Panjab during the next six months is still somewhat of a mystery to me. The way my dad describes it, he didn't just rediscover his faith, but the universal energy to which he belonged. Whatever it was, my dad was a changed person.

"I went inside my body and I realized there was a bigger world than the one I was looking for inside the bottle," he later told me. "It came out of me like water from a hand pump. The high feeling from alcohol was nothing in comparison to this. And as long as I pumped it, it poured from me."

What I do know is my dad set about rebuilding both his body and his mind. If I knew my father, he took to his new regimen with the same focus and obsessive nature he applied to studying medical literature. He began reading spiritual poetry and meditating regularly. He became a vegetarian and took up yoga. And he began each day by reflecting on *ek onkar*, the fundamental principle of the Sikh way of life. Or, as my mom put it, "We are all one."

The message gave him a sense of empowerment that addictions treatments didn't offer. My dad explained that in Canada, the focus was on accepting his illness. "They wanted me to say I was ill, that my addiction meant that I was unwell, and that I would always be an addict," he told me. "They wanted me to define myself by my illness. If I didn't want to define myself that way, they would say that meant I was even more unwell than I realized. What I learned was that yes, they were right. I am an addict, but I also have the infinite inside of me, as each of us does. With that, we are more powerful than addiction, and we can overcome any obstacle."

The day my dad returned to Canada, my mom and I met him in the arrivals terminal of Pearson Airport. I was excited to see him, but also nervous about how my brother and sister would take him coming back. The deal still remained that as long as he wasn't drinking, then he could be at home.

When my dad walked through the gate, I was relieved. He looked like a new man. His salt-and-pepper beard was growing again, and his hair was tied in a turban. When I wrapped my arms around him, I felt not bones, but the muscles of someone who could hold his 180-pound self in a handstand—and who eagerly showed us as much when we got home.

But not everyone was so eager to see it. Gurratan was still slow to trust my dad. When my dad tried to join Gurratan in the living room for the first time after coming back, my brother said to him, "Why are you here? Go upstairs."

"That's okay," my dad said as he walked back toward the stairs. "I understand you don't trust I can be better. I promise I will prove it to you."

My brother continued to tell my dad to leave the room whenever they were in the same place, and my dad continued to listen without complaint. I hoped that, with time, things would get better.

—⚜—

My father was healthy again, and he was putting in the effort to earn back his family's trust. What he didn't have much of, though, was purpose.

His conviction was strong. Every day he told me, "I want to get back to work." I knew that work was important to him—being a doctor and being able to practise was a defining part of who he was, and he wanted to return to it.

I figured now that he was sober, we could start by getting his driver's licence back. We went to the ministry of transportation's licensing centre to see what we needed to do. The service agent pulled up my dad's records.

"Mr. Dhaliwal," she said, "the records show that you have a medical suspension. Do you have any idea why?"

He thought about it long and hard but couldn't come up with a reason.

"Do you have a history of seizures or epilepsy?"

"No," he said.

"Acute diabetes?" He shook his head. "Uncontrolled sleep apnea? Any past psychiatric disorders with symptoms of suicidal thoughts?"

"Never," he said.

She frowned. "Whatever it is, you'll have to get a doctor to lift your suspension. I'm sorry."

We left empty-handed, and the next week, my dad saw his doctor. The reason for the mysterious suspension quickly became clear. A couple of years prior, when my dad had hit rock bottom, he had been hospitalized. As a result of his drinking, he had become prone to fainting and losing consciousness. Doctors are obligated to flag those types of concerns to the ministry of transportation, and the attending physician at the time had noted the medical condition on my dad's driving record.

My dad had been living healthy for over a year by this point, so we were confident the tests would confirm he was able to drive. Sure enough, the test results showed a clean bill of health and my dad's record was cleared. My dad's new licence arrived in the mail a few weeks later, marking his first steps back to independence.

Of course, all of that was a walk in the park compared to lifting the suspension on my dad's licence to practise medicine. He'd been suspended since 2000, so the process would require several rounds of negotiations and a series of steps as my dad slowly proved himself capable and trustworthy.

"I'll support you every step of the way," I told my dad as we went through the paperwork.

I went with my dad for his first official meeting with the College of Physicians and Surgeons of Ontario. I was there for emotional support, yes, but I had taken a page out of our bankruptcy court claim and was also serving as my dad's legal representation. It was unusual for a lawyer to be present in a physicians' meeting like that, but I wasn't concerned with precedent: my focus was finding a pathway for my dad to practise again. We'd had some preliminary conversations with the College that hadn't provided any definitive takeaways, and I wanted to make sure we came out of this meeting with something concrete. So, as we exchanged pleasantries with the committee, I took the opportunity to mention that I was a lawyer and to clearly state what our goal was.

"We're here to discuss a pathway for my father to return to practising medicine."

"There's nothing more we'd like to see than Dr. Dhaliwal practising and healthy again," said one of the College's council members.

"Great, then let's discuss what the path to lifting the suspension on his licence looks like."

The College staff were a little taken aback with the directness of my approach. Out of the corner of my eye, I could see my dad almost smiling. The irony of the situation wasn't lost on me, either. My father hadn't always been there for me, but there's no doubt he laid some of the foundation for me to have achieved what I had so far. The work that my dad had done as a doctor had opened up doors for me. I had walked through those doors, become a lawyer, and was now using my skills to help him get his licence back. There was an interesting symmetry to the whole thing.

I let the awkward silence run its course. Finally, one of the College representatives created the opening I was waiting for.

"We would need to be convinced that Dr. Dhaliwal was managing his addiction and would be able to return to practise to standards set by the College," the council member said.

"I absolutely understand," I replied. "What steps could my father take to demonstrate that he is fit to practise?"

The council member turned to my father. "We would need you to see a specialist on addiction and attend regular meetings before we could consider even a probationary return to practise," he said.

"Deal," I said before he could veer off to another topic. "We'll set up a follow-up meeting in three months to discuss the terms of a probationary return to practise."

My father began seeing the specialist suggested by the College and regularly attended the meetings for physicians recovering from addictions. My dad took to the meetings and specialist visits with an energy I hadn't seen before. Three months passed successfully, and before we knew it, we were back in a meeting with the College.

The council members had an impressive report from the specialist indicating my dad's perfect attendance at the meetings and meaningful contributions, as well as a positive prognosis regarding his recovery. With all of that, the College was prepared to consider a return to work.

The sticking point, though, was how many hours a week my dad would be allowed to practise. I was stunned when the Council offered five hours.

"How does that make sense?" I asked. "You expect him to rent an office, buy equipment, and pay staff while only being able to work one half day a week?"

"Your dad had many chances before we suspended his licence, and after every opportunity, he broke critical policy," one of the council members reminded us.

"I never received one patient complaint," my father protested. "Not one report of maltreatment or misconduct."

"That's correct, but it doesn't change the seriousness of the situation or the number of times you failed your monitoring," the council member said. "We're approving you for five hours a week. We'll try that for three months before we can consider the next step."

Though it was far less than we had hoped for, it was a start. My dad was going to practise again.

There was one final condition. Until the end of his probation, my dad needed to find a supervising doctor to voluntarily check in on him and monitor his practice. *That shouldn't be a problem*, I thought. There were plenty of psychiatrists in the Toronto area to choose from. But when we got in the car, my dad told me the only potential supervisors he trusted lived in Windsor.

"There's no way you can go back to Windsor on your own," I said, surprised my dad had even suggested the idea. "You're doing well here in Mississauga. It's not a good idea to go back to the same place where things went so wrong."

"Jagmeet, I don't know any psychiatrists here."

"It's Toronto—there are probably thousands of doctors to choose from."

"And how could I ask one of them out of the blue to supervise me? That's a big responsibility, and they would be putting their name on the line, too. I can't just ask anyone. I have colleagues in Windsor who I've worked with for almost two decades; I can explain to them that I'm committed to staying healthy."

He paused, trying to see if I was convinced. "Besides," he

continued, "Windsor is where my patients were. I won't have to start from scratch."

"It's not just that," I said. "It's one thing to set you up here with an office and staff on a part-time salary. But in Windsor, we'd need to get you an apartment again, furniture, your own car."

"I'll get a loan," he said.

"You can't get a loan. Bankruptcy, remember?"

I weighed the options as we drove home to Mississauga. My law practice was going well, so I had a decent enough salary to support one household, but not two. I had a line of credit that I carefully managed, and I was only just beginning to feel financially secure. Could I take another risk without jeopardizing the entire family?

"Fine," I said with a sigh. "If this is important to you, then let's do it. But if this is just about making money, don't worry about that. I can support us. We just want you to stay well."

"I want to practise again," he said.

My mom decided she would stay with my dad on the days that he was in Windsor. Her willingness to sacrifice so much for our family amazed me to no end.

We found a small office in Windsor and a part-time secretary. His five-hour weeks didn't even finance the overhead, so I covered all the expenses. I signed a lease for a decent apartment nearby at a reasonable rate. When it came to furnishing it, I knew just who to call.

The day we moved in, a box truck pulled into the moving zone at the back of the apartment. The words painted on the sign read MANSOUR'S FURNITURE. I watched from the balcony as the truck came to a stop, and I waved at Walid as he hopped out of the driver's side. My mom, dad, and I went downstairs to meet him.

Walid and I hadn't done the best job of staying in touch. But whenever we did reach out to each other, whether we were speaking on the phone or meeting up in person, we picked up right where we left off.

We slapped a hearty handshake that turned into a bear hug. Walid turned to my dad and shook his hand. "Welcome back to Windsor, Dr. Dhaliwal," he said. "Now let's get you set up."

Walid threw open the roll-up door on the back of the truck and the four of us started unloading new matching tables and chairs; couches and a bed set—pieces that my dad could take pride in.

"Thanks for the furniture hookup," I told Walid as we each grabbed a corner of a bed frame to carry down the ramp.

"Of course," Walid said. "We're brothers."

After furnishing my dad's apartment, I said my goodbyes and headed back to Mississauga. I left Windsor with mixed emotions. I was worried that the gamble we were taking would put our family back into the same precarious situation we had just climbed out of. I was worried that my dad would relapse, or that taking care of my dad would demand too much of my mom. There could be any number of things that might cause him to fall into a downward spiral.

Even with those reservations, though, I accepted that it re- quires courage to take risks on the people you love. Despite it all, I had never given up on my dad. And this time felt differ- ent. I was older now and able to take care of myself. I didn't need my dad to get better for me. I needed him to do it for himself.

After a couple of months of working without incident, my dad was given permission to practise for ten hours per week. A little while after that, it was fifteen. Bit by bit, the College lowered the terms of his probation.

In the spring of 2008, about a year since our first negotiation with the counsellors, we met one last time in the College's red office in Toronto's medical district. He'd done everything the College had asked, and when the meeting ended, my dad's probation was officially lifted. He still had to continue attending meetings in London, visiting the specialist, and being supervised by his sponsor for another year, but he was free to practise as many hours as he wanted. He was doing what he loved, healthy and relapse-free. Dr. Jagtaran Singh Dhaliwal was back.

"Thank you for supporting me," he told me as we left the building. "And for supporting the family." He stopped at the bottom of the steps, patted the shoulder of my winter jacket, and looked at me kindly. "You've taken care of the family for so long and you kept me alive. You have a big soul."

"I got it from mom," I said.

"She is a special woman," he said, smiling.

"Yes," I said with a laugh. "She definitely is."

He glanced about his surroundings on College Street, taking in the snow-dusted sidewalks between an old gothic church and various towers for rehab centres, blood clinics, and hospitals. Dozens of health professionals milled about on their lunch breaks, cocooned inside their dark parkas.

"I lost a lot of time," he finally said. "I'm lucky to still have any left. I want you to make the most of your time now. Go live your life. I'll take it from here."

I took his advice to heart, and a couple of months later, I went on my first solo vacation. The sheer luxury of travelling alone was a little overwhelming. Most trips I had ever taken were either with family or friends. The idea of going by myself felt so indulgent that it took me some time to get over the guilt of it. I went to the Caribbean and immersed myself in reggae music and delicious Rastafarian vegan food. I made friends and simply enjoyed the weather and the ocean. The trip wasn't anything life-changing. I didn't find myself or learn a specific life lesson. A lifetime of struggles had forced me to take account of myself and figure out who I was. The trip was pure fun—a carefree summer like nothing I'd had a chance to enjoy in a long time.

When I got home, I received more good news when my sister told us she was going to get married. She had met an amazing guy from overseas, and they were going to start their life together. I was sad to see my sister move so far away, but that couldn't dull my happiness for her. Though our family would be geographically fractured again, between two continents and different cities, I couldn't remember a time when we were so happy.

Loving someone is neither easy nor simple. It's complicated in the best circumstances, let alone when you're trying to figure out how to care for someone who causes you and your family harm. But love is an incredible force, and at its core lies the courage to forgive.

My father wasn't the one I grew up with, and I was no longer the insecure teenager unable to voice his fears, as I once was. We'd become new people. That's why I believe in reincarnation; I've seen it with my own eyes.

Chapter Seventeen

FOR THE BETTERMENT OF ALL PEOPLE

Throughout the rest of 2008 and into the next year, my family continued to mend the bonds that had been broken between us. My brother and I were living in the house in Mississauga, while my mom and dad remained in Windsor. Things were slowly but steadily getting better. Each time I visited my parents, I could see a bit more stress lifting from my mother's shoulders. My dad seemed to be healthy and was enjoying a busy practice.

I was grateful for the new peace that our family was building, especially as 2009 marked a challenging time for our community: the twenty-fifth anniversary of the November 1984 Sikh genocide.

Gurratan and Amneet had continued their work over the past couple of years developing a safe, positive space for the Sikh community to discuss the trauma and pain they'd suffered. They often consulted me for advice, and I did my best to guide them on a positive path. As a result of their organizing, Gurratan and Amneet had built up a massive network of progressive-minded youth, and had put on incredible events.

For the twenty-fifth anniversary, Gurratan and Amneet planned a big event called Tears and Ashes, referring to the Sikhs burned alive during the genocide and the many more who were secretly arrested and cremated until the midnineties. They planned to pack a thousand people into Brampton's Rose Theatre for an evening in which people could learn what really happened during the genocide and share their own stories of trauma.

Nothing like it had ever been done before. Until then, our community's coping mechanism was silence. So many of our parents shied away from activism because of fear, whether it was fear of being branded extremists, of being banned from India, or of the memory of the state hurting their family members back home. As a result, they raised us in a way that rewarded silence. But silence didn't help the mental health and addictions issues that trauma causes. Aside from creating a safe space for healing, the event was intended to reignite the spirit of activism in the community, especially its youth, and assure them it was okay to talk through their problems.

Leading up to the event, Amneet and Gurratan turned our house into their headquarters, with volunteers in and out of the house every evening. They lined up theatre groups who used tableaux to capture what had happened and to act out scenes that had been reported in official inquiries. They contacted survivors from the Greater Toronto Area who shared their vivid lived experiences. And they invited a genocide scholar to provide an academic perspective on everything.

Gurratan and Amneet were bringing legitimacy, credibility, and critical analysis to a historical event fraught with misinformation. I was happy providing support as an unofficial advisor, but I was surprised when Gurratan asked me to give a speech at the event.

"Why me?" I asked. "Why not a refugee or academic? Someone directly affected."

"We have both lined up, but we also need you. You *are* directly affected," Gurratan corrected. "Affected the way the majority of our community has been. You've been called a terrorist just for having a beard and a turban. And how many years has it been since Air India?" Everyone we knew had unequivocally condemned the bombing, but we still faced baseless suspicion because of the way we looked.

He was right. I'd seen it throughout my life—like so many marginalized groups, we Sikhs were expected to speak for the reprehensible crimes committed by a few bad people in our community, but we were never asked about the racism we faced or the crimes committed against us.

"Still," I said, "I seem like a random choice."

"We need a strong, young voice who knows the history and can talk about it passionately," Gurratan said.

"This is more than running civil rights seminars at universities," I said. "I've never done this before."

"Sure you have," Gurratan said with a smile. "You do it every day, in front of a judge."

I eventually relented and agreed to give the speech. On the night of the event, I waited backstage as the lights dimmed. I thought I would be nervous, but in the moment, I was in a positive state of mind, ready to try to provide a healing perspective.

I walked to the podium and spoke from the heart about my concerns for our community. I spoke about the need to recognize the massacre of Sikhs in November 1984 as a genocide. I stated that recognition would end the false notion that violence was communal in nature and instead clarify that it was planned and organized by the state. This action would officially recognize the pain suffered by the community. I said that recognizing a genocide denounces the actions against the target community and also works toward the prevention of any similar acts of violence in the future. It would be a first step toward healing. In closing, I said that the daily meditation of a Sikh is not to ensure justice and betterment for Sikhs alone. I explained that our mission is to ensure the betterment of all people, and that's what we would continue to do.

As the night drew to a close and I saw how many people came up to thank Gurratan, I'd never felt more proud of him. He and Amneet had managed to break the silence that plagued our community for twenty-five years. They organized more events about social justice and cultural issues affecting Canadians, as well as a massive Sikh arts festival, and throughout it all, Gurratan kept wrangling me to speak to crowds. Most times, I agreed to speak—at the time, it felt like a duty to my community and I couldn't say no to my brother. But I also saw how these events were making a difference. We were charting a new course forward, one that replaced the silence with activism. We were providing the language to express the frustrations and trauma of the community in a positive and productive way. More and more, I felt not obliged, but compelled, to speak. I might not have been able to put that in words at the time, but

Gurratan could see it—years later, he confessed to me, "I was trying to activate you."

—⚬—

The first steps of reconciling trauma are to speak about it and acknowledge the harm suffered. I learned that academically from research, and from discussions I had with experts. But I also knew it from personal experience. Much of the trauma I had endured only started to fully heal when I acknowledged the pain I've suffered.

So despite our best efforts to chart a positive path for our community's healing—relying on the language of justice and reconciliation, and tearing down divisive myths to build bridges between communities—it hurt when people claimed there was a rise in Sikh extremism in Canada; even when challenged, they were unable to provide an iota of evidence to substantiate those claims. Without any rhyme or reason the entire Sikh community was being cast as extremists, and none of our voices were given the space to respond.

More insults followed. In March 2010, my friend Harbaljit Singh Kahlon, a community organizer and political insider, called me with a scoop.

"You know Kamal Nath?" he asked.

I knew the name well. Kamal Nath was one of the members of the Indian National Congress Party who, some believed, had been involved in leading a mob of thousands that attacked a *Gurdwara* during the November 1984 Sikh genocide. Kamal Nath admitted he was present during the violence but denied that he led any mob. He was never charged. Quite the opposite, in fact—he'd risen to become minister of urban development.

"I got word Nath is coming to Ontario for some trade talks," Harbaljit said. "Meeting with the Ontario Liberals, invited here by Premier McGuinty himself."

"Are you serious?" As much as I understood the importance of having solid foreign relations, Nath remained a very divisive figure. How could someone with such a controversial history get invited on an official trade mission? I tried to imagine what would happen if a modern Canadian politician remained in some eyes the subject of similar serious allegations. It seemed unfathomable that they would retain their position, let alone rise.

"They're meeting next week at the King Edward Hotel in Toronto," he said. "Let's get the word out. We don't have much time."

The first people I called were Gurratan and Amneet. Amneet, though only twenty-five at the time, was one of the most politically astute people I knew. He and a group of young Sikh professionals started organizing meetings with representatives of the Ontario government to explain to them the disrespectful nature of inviting Nath.

"This is not something that happened generations ago," one of our group said to the politicians. "The violence is recent. Sikhs were targeted for just being Sikh, they were burned alive, shops and homes of Sikhs were destroyed, thousands were killed and thousands more displaced. That's what Kamal Nath represents in their minds."

Still, the Ontario government refused to disinvite him. On

the day of their meetings with Nath, we reached out to media and mobilized a couple of hundred protesters outside the King Edward Hotel. The crowd chanted "Go back, Kamal Nath!" and "Kamal Nath: human rights violator!" from behind a police-guarded barricade. Emotions were high. I played the role of legal observer, ready to provide assistance for any legal issues that could arise and to make sure nobody's safety was compromised.

The protest ended without a single issue. We ran a peaceful protest, flexing our democratic right to free speech. Sadly, it fell on uncaring political ears.

Nath also met with federal leaders from the Conservative Party of Canada. That disappointed us, too, but it didn't shock us. The Ontario Liberals and federal Liberals, on the other hand, were, for many Sikh Canadians, the default party. The party and the community had a solid relationship. That the party would so suddenly turn their backs on the community puzzled us. It felt to me as though they'd just taken the community for granted, assuming we'd never leave them.

Not all the Liberal politicians were so feckless, though. In June 2010, Sukh Dhaliwal, a Liberal MP for Surrey-Newton in BC, and Andrew Kania, representing Brampton West, prepared to read a petition in the House of Commons calling for the government to formally recognize the November 1984 massacres as "an organized campaign of genocide." More important, it asked Canada to call upon the Indian government to bring those responsible to justice.

Reading petitions in the House isn't a big deal. Members of Parliament are technically obligated to read a petition if they're presented with one. It's not anything binding. It just shows that there are people—in this case, thousands of them—who believe in the issue.

I was shocked to discover, then, that the Liberal Party's leader, Michael Ignatieff, was pressuring Kania to withdraw from reading the petition. Dhaliwal, to his credit, wouldn't capitulate.

Still, before Dhaliwal stood up in the House to read it, Ignatieff released a statement that threw the two MPs under the bus. The statement called the term "genocide" both inaccurate and inappropriate. "It is used here to provoke a charged, visceral response which will not bring Canadians closer to mutual understanding and closure in regard to these tragic events," Ignatieff wrote, adding that the Liberal Party "will never stand with those who seek to polarize communities, or aggravate the tensions around long-standing conflicts that divided us in other lands."

It was an absurd claim. The accepted description of the event was a riot between Hindus and Sikhs. The word "riot" suggested that there was communal, spontaneous violence between the two groups. But the biggest inquiry into the violence agreed that it was a planned and organized massacre. The petition sought to heal old wounds by replacing the concept of communal violence by more accurately calling it what it was. In light of that, Ignatieff's comments were offensive and seriously damaging.

I was still giving "Know Your Rights" seminars at universities, and after Ignatieff's statement, I also started running sessions to raise awareness about the Sikh genocide and refuting Ignatieff's claims. I printed copies of Ignatieff's statement and brought them to one such talk at the University of Waterloo.

I began by handing out excerpts of findings taken directly from the 2000 Nanavati Commission, an independent investigation into the Sikh genocide by a former Indian Supreme Court justice. Then I provided copies of the United Nations' definition of genocide.

"Genocide means any of the following acts committed with intent to destroy, in whole or in part, a national, ethnic, racial or religious group," I said, reading from the UN pamphlet. "One: killing members of the group. Two: causing serious bodily or mental harm to members of the group. Three: deliberately inflicting on the group conditions of life calculated to bring about its physical destruction in whole or in part. Four: imposing measures intended to prevent births within the group. And five: forcibly transferring children of the group to another group."

I looked out at the sea of faces. "You now have the definition of genocide. I've also given you some findings from an inquiry into an event that took place in November 1984. Take some time to read through everything," I said. I waited a couple of minutes before calling their attention again. "Can you find any evidence from the inquiry that would satisfy the definition as laid out by the United Nations?"

"Easily," said one of the students. A chorus of agreement echoed around her.

"Which act?" I asked.

"The first one. Based on the report there were at least two thousand seven hundred people killed in three days. I've read reports that put the numbers far higher, in the tens of thousands." *Somebody's done their homework*, I thought.

"But does the definition require a certain number?" I asked.

She looked quickly at the definition again and responded slowly, "No . . ."

"What if we're talking about an ethnic community of just one tribe made up of less than a hundred people, and that entire tribe was killed?" I asked.

I could see the example had worked. "So the UN definition purposefully doesn't include a threshold number of deaths," she said.

"I can't speak to how they came up with the wording," I said. "But yes, it's not a question of how many people were killed."

Another student jumped in. "Based on the Nanavati Commission, many women were raped, so there's both bodily and mental harm to thousands more. And obviously that was deliberate."

"Okay, so that's two of the five points," I said. "Now I'm going to give you something else to read."

I circulated the statement by Ignatieff and gave them a couple of minutes to go over it.

"How does that make you feel?" I asked.

"It's kind of outlandish, given that the evidence is pretty persuasive," said one student.

"Yeah," added another. "At a minimum, maybe you can say you're not a hundred per cent convinced, but what's Ignatieff's justification for saying he opposes it forever?"

"Seems unfair to characterize it as so black and white," added a student.

One of the students in the front row hemmed and hawed, her mental gears clearly grinding down this knowledge. "You seem to be on the fence," I said.

"No," she said. "It's the other two points in the definition of genocide." She looked down at one of the first handouts. "Trying to prevent births from that minority and moving their children from one group to another?"

"The definition doesn't say it has to be all five acts," I said. "It can be any one act."

"Exactly. Those last two sound like Canada," she said. "Our country has a history of sterilizing Indigenous people. And then there are residential schools. Does that mean the Canadian government committed genocide?"

"What do you think?" I asked.

"By the UN's definition, yes," she said.

"What do the rest of you think?" I asked the room.

There was a little surprise at the connection, followed by murmurs of agreement and head nods.

"I absolutely agree as well," I said. "Beyond the residential schools, which were a clear attempt to destroy Indigenous language and culture, the history of Canadian colonialism is rife with examples of attempts to wipe the land of the first inhabitants. And moving the conversation from Sikh genocide to the genocide of Indigenous people in Canada raises a very important point. Why does all of this matter? Why do we care to define genocide and then determine whether or not it has occurred?"

"It gives the survivor communities a sense of closure," one student said.

"Definitely. What else?"

"It can help bring those responsible to justice?"

"It can, and that's important, but why?"

I could see the light bulb go off over one student's head as his hand shot up.

"In order to prevent it from happening ever again," he said.

"Exactly. Acknowledging the harm suffered helps survivor communities on their pathway to healing, and to reconciling the harm suffered. Bringing the responsible parties to justice can also help in the healing process. But all of this plays a role in the broader goal of preventing these injustices from ever happening again. Every time we recognize a genocide, we are effectively denouncing what happened and affirming that we won't let it happen again."

I had versions of that same conversation at every seminar I ran. Each time I saw the understanding dawn in the students' eyes, I was given hope. The thought that a new generation could begin to see the world in a new way made me optimistic that we could find a more positive way forward. I felt I was making a difference.

—⚌—

After the controversy caused by the Liberal Party's official position, many Sikhs felt betrayed. But given their historical connection to the party, they didn't know where else to turn—it didn't feel as though there were any other options. The only political leaders who supported the Sikh community's concerns about Kamal Nath were Andrea Horwath, the leader of Ontario's New Democratic Party; and Jack Layton, the leader of Canada's NDP.

I was cynical about politics. Having come from an activist background and having worked with anti-poverty and immigration policy groups, my school of thought was that people get things done by forcing the hands of elected officials, not by getting themselves elected. Jack was a good example of someone who proved my cynicism wrong.

The first time my brother saw Jack was in Parliament during

the genocide petition. Gurratan and Amneet had remarked how supportive he had been to the Sikh community, particularly concerning human rights issues. They both approached him to offer their support. They were anti-poverty activists, so they were already supportive of many of the policies Jack Layton and the team were proposing to improve the lives of people.

"I'm a community activist," Gurratan said to Jack. "I like what you're doing."

What followed was kept secret from me for weeks.

Amneet was finishing his master's thesis in Ottawa. One evening, he called Gurratan with a proposition.

"We can't just work against things. We need to work *for* something."

"What do you have in mind?" Gurratan asked.

"We need to run someone in the next election," said Amneet.

"That's not what we do. We've never been involved in supporting a political party," my brother said.

"Hear me out," said Amneet. "The system is messed up. We need someone who can push back against these arrogant politicians who take us all for granted. We need someone who wants to go there just to fight for people."

My brother shared Amneet's vision—we needed not only a human rights champion, but a social justice champion, one who could serve the entire community, people of all backgrounds.

"Who do you have in mind?" asked Gurratan.

"The only person I can think of is Jagmeet. That's what he'd do."

My brother laughed. "Jagmeet doesn't want to be a politician."

"Exactly. That's why it has to be him. Can you think of anyone else who has goodwill in the community and who would take a consistent, principled stance on the issues that are affecting so many people every day?"

"There's got to be someone else," said Gurratan.

"Tell me who. If you can find me someone, I'll hang up right now and call them."

"Let me think about it."

Gurratan slept on it a couple of nights. We were living under the same roof, eating at the same dinner table, sleeping in bedrooms across a hall. But if he was dropping hints, I was oblivious.

Finally, Gurratan called Amneet back. "You're right," he said. "It has to be Jagmeet."

Good cop, bad cop happened naturally. Gurratan, the bad cop, bided his time. He waited until I got home after a late night in the office. He cornered me as I scoured the fridge.

"I think it's time you started to think a little bigger. In terms of your career, I mean."

"Really," I said as I retrieved cold lentils and Brussels sprouts and set them on the counter. "What do you mean?" I asked.

"I think you should consider running in the upcoming federal election."

I laughed as I poured my food into a cast-iron skillet and turned on the stove. I turned around and saw my brother wasn't laughing with me. "No way," I said.

Gurratan continued. "You're good with people, you're popular with the community. Young people listen when you talk."

"That doesn't mean I should run," I said. "Lots of people are good at those things. And I really don't see myself in electoral politics." My food started bubbling, so I quickly took the skillet off the heat and transferred my dinner to a plate. "Look, I just don't want to."

"Why not?"

"Because we have some stability right now. I don't want to actively choose a life of struggles after we've finally found some peace."

"The fact that you've struggled is *why* we need you," he said. "You know what it's like to feel powerless, but you've kept it together. More than that, you've pulled through it. And I know your nature—when you're motivated, you don't let challenges hold you back."

There was a long beat while we faced each other through the steam clouds emanating off my plate. I finally broke the silence. "Okay," I said. "I hear you, brother."

He let things go, at least for a while. But my brother is one of the most persistent human beings I know. A few days later, I saw Amneet's name appear on my buzzing phone. My intuition told me what he was calling about.

"I've already told Gurratan no," I said as soon as I picked up.

"I realize that," he said. "Hear me out, though. Five minutes."

Amneet avoided the guilt-tripping my brother had used and resorted to flattery instead. He flattered me with words like "charismatic," and he reminded me of the impact we'd had in teaching civil rights, fighting against poverty, addressing the trauma in our community, and protesting the stereotypes about us.

"You created space for marginalized people and made them

feel confident in who they are," he said. "I've watched you bring people together in a way I've never seen before. And it's all because you're genuine. You have no idea what a rarity that is in Ottawa. Believe me."

"I appreciate that. Thank you," I said. "But maybe you should consider someone else."

There was no way I was going to run, so I put the thought immediately out of my mind. That night, I headed home to have dinner with Gurratan and my parents, who had started visiting us each weekend. I knew how much they wanted to move back to Mississauga to be closer to us, so I'd pitched my dad the idea of moving his practice out of Windsor. He was experimenting by working one day a week in Brampton, and I was pretty sure we would get Mom and Dad to move back before long.

My mom prepared a small feast that evening. I thought our earlier conversation was done, so I wasn't prepared when Gurratan brought politics up again.

"So you talked to Amneet today?" he asked.

I tried to ignore him.

"And?" he pressed.

I let my silence speak for itself.

Gurratan put his fork down with a clang. "So that's it?" he asked. "You're not going to help the community? You don't care? All right, okay. I guess that's your goal."

My dad looked around the table, confused. "Why are they fighting?" he asked my mom.

"I don't know," she said with a shrug.

Gurratan was relentless. "You're letting your family down, you're letting your community down, and you're letting me down."

Neither of my parents had a political bone in their bodies, so I dismissed the first point. But it genuinely stung to hear the rest of it. All I wanted was, for once in my life, to be comfortable.

Survival had always been my mom's outlook, but it was never my dad's. My mom's mentality of focusing on getting by was very much rooted in common struggles of people who arrive to a new country. It's the goal for the first generation of immigrants: to survive. It's always the second generation that's given the luxury of thinking not just about surviving, but thriving. My dad skipped that step. He wanted more—for himself, for his family, for his children. His ambition is what brought him to Canada. A lot of what we had to be thankful for was inspired by his drive to never settle, even though that drive was part of what led to his undoing.

I'd always believed my brother was more like my dad, while I took after my mom, and our argument only made that clearer. But seeing how passionate Gurratan was, how unwilling he was to hear "no," I wondered if maybe I could benefit from being a bit more like him.

"It's not the life I want, brother," I said. I think he could sense I was starting to cave just a little. It wasn't much, maybe a slight crack in the armour. But it was all Gurratan needed to hear. He pulled his phone out of his pocket and fired off a text message to Amneet. He put his phone away and returned to eating, as if he hadn't just changed the course of our lives.

My brother and Amneet continued to apply pressure over the next four months. Finally, in mid-January 2011, I agreed to meet two NDP staffers from Ottawa, Rupinder Kaur and Linda MacAskill, at a vegetarian restaurant near our house. The two of them made another pitch for me to run. I knew Rupinder from back in the day. I had met her at the University of Guelph while I was studying at Western. She was press secretary to Jack Layton, and she knew how to argue persuasively. I hadn't met Linda before, but she was kind and gentle, while still remaining persistent and compelling.

I was flattered that so much effort was being made to convince me. They took a page out of Amneet's playbook and then explained the process to me. When they left, they gave me some paperwork that I would need to fill out if I made the decision to run. I took the envelope home and tossed it on the kitchen table. It sat there for weeks.

February rolled around. There wasn't a fixed date for the election, but all signs were pointing more and more to an early spring snap election, and I still hadn't opened the nomination paperwork. The NDP, thanks in no small part to Jack, was building huge momentum, especially in Quebec. Gurratan and Amneet saw the rising tide and kept pressing me to put my name in the mix.

My resistance was slowly wavering. I started to seriously consider what running would mean for me. I had gotten over the idea that it would take me down a less predictable path than my legal career. And I had been reflecting on my brother's argument that a life based on just trying to survive was a life robbed of its full potential. I needed to consider how I could thrive.

The question I kept grappling with was what I could offer, and the bigger question that came with it: Why me?

The answer didn't hit me all at once, but I started making connections. I thought about facing racism throughout my life, and how it taught me what it's like to feel as though you don't belong. Young Black men, Indigenous youth, new Canadians—

so many people were routinely made to feel they didn't belong, and although each person's experience was different, I could relate to some of that pain.

It takes courage to stand up to hate. It takes courage to love yourself when you've been told your whole life that you're ugly, or dirty, or a terrorist.

I thought about the sexual abuse and the shame and guilt that came with it. The fear of not being believed; or worse, the shame and guilt of believing the abuse was your own fault.

I thought about the trauma and pain of growing up with an alcoholic parent. That experience taught me that addiction isn't a choice. It also taught me never to give up. It helped me understand that anger can't heal pain; it only hurts you and the people around you. I learned to look at addiction as a treatable illness, an illness that lives off anger but that can be healed through love. Love is a powerful act of forgiveness.

I thought, too, about what it's like to live with fear. I recalled the warmth and kindness of friends and relatives who supported my family through difficult times. I remembered friends whose parents struggled after they lost work at the auto factories in Windsor, and who were made to feel they had no place in a modern economy. I remembered my own financial fears, not knowing if my family would have a home to live in, or if we would be able to pay the bills. And I knew it was a fear that far too many Canadians had faced and continue to face.

It's too easy for us all to think of ourselves as alone with our problems. As I reflected on my experiences, I started to see answers to the question, Why me? My mom's words came to me yet again: "We are all connected."

No matter how different we think we are, we share a common connection, to each other and to the world around us. Gradually it dawned on me that my brother was right. We did have a responsibility to help everyone thrive, whether they felt like they belonged or not; to fight for all those people who felt as though they didn't have anyone in their corner; to stand up for those who felt neglected and marginalized; or to embrace those who endured shame, guilt, financial hardship, persecution, or exclusion simply for being who they were.

Once I realized that, I never looked back. I had a team around me who offered support. Together, we began our work, and we've been at it ever since. We want to eradicate poverty and inequality. We want to encourage investment in affordable housing so everyone can find a place to call home. We want to defend the environment so everyone can have access to clean drinking water, breathe fresh air, and eat food free from toxins. We want to tear down barriers to education so that all of us can pursue our dreams. We want equality and justice for all. Most of all, we want to build a world where everyone belongs and no one is left behind.

Back then, once I finally became convinced that this was walking the right path, I knew what to do. Late one evening, I made my way to the kitchen. I picked up the envelope and slid out the documents I needed to complete to apply as a candidate for the riding of Bramalea-Gore-Malton.

The first field asked for my name. I paused. My full name is Jagmeet Singh Jimmy Dhaliwal. As a kid growing up in Newfoundland and Labrador, I was Jimmy Dhaliwal. When I moved to Windsor, I embraced who I was and went by Jagmeet Dhaliwal. I'd used that name for most of my youth. But now, I had a choice to make.

In South Asian traditions, your last name represents your clan, and your clan name represents your status in society. That traditional system of hierarchy was rejected by Sikh philosophy, which teaches that every human being is equal. In its place, the name "Singh" was used as a title of royalty given to uplift all people, regardless of their birth. It symbolizes the idea that all human beings, no matter who they are or where they're from, are equally noble.

If I wanted to fight for all people, I couldn't be Jagmeet Dhaliwal anymore.

I took a breath and signed my name: Jagmeet Singh.

Epilogue

LEADERSHIP CONVENTION—
OCTOBER 1, 2017

I pulled the blackout curtains aside and filled my hotel room with sunlight. The balcony opened to a sweeping view of Toronto from the harbourfront. I stepped outside wearing a pair of navy-blue suit pants, a crisp white dress shirt, and a steel/iron *kara* bracelet. I filled my lungs with the crisp October air. It was the morning of the NDP leadership nomination. It was the climax to the leadership adventure, with more anticipation and uncertainty in store. For a moment, I simply savoured the calm.

My meditation was interrupted by a knock at the door.

"I'll let them in," said Gurkiran, my soon-to-be fiancée.

I heard Gurkiran bringing my parents into the living room, so I quickly finished dressing in the full-length mirror. I tightened my *kirpan* strap over my shoulder and ran my hands through my beard, appreciating how a little age had created a path of grey in the middle. I bent forward, let my hair tumble past my chest, coiled it gently, and tied a topknot. I added a wooden-comb *kanga* to the base and wrapped a base turban with white cloth. Finally, I added a second layer of hot pink cloth, sculpting and shaping each fold as I wrapped it around my head.

I walked into the living room and gave my dad a big hug. He wore a matching hot pink turban.

"Did you ever think this day would come?" I asked.

"Never," he said. "It's too hard to imagine."

My mom, wearing a creamy, gold, flower-embroidered *salwar kameez*, hung up her jacket and embraced me.

"Isn't this amazing?" I asked her.

"Yes, it's okay," she said. I laughed. The answer was my mom in a nutshell. She wasn't fazed by any of the political achievements.

"How are you feeling?" she asked.

"Excited, nervous, but not too stressed," I said.

"Good," she said. "It's up to the will of the universe."

We were soon joined by my closest friends. I got a text message from Walid wishing me good luck. Amneet arrived not long after, and I thought about the first time I met him in London, my little brother's friend who asked me how high I could jump. Back then, I never would have guessed that I'd become a public servant, let alone run for leader of the New Democratic Party, and I certainly wouldn't have imagined being pushed there by a little fourteen-year-old challenging me on my ups.

Gurratan and his partner, Satvir, walked in. "This is awesome," he said with a grin. In many ways, this day was the realization of Gurratan pushing me to thrive, not just survive. To thrive was to use everything I had gone through in order to create the most positive change for people. Gurratan had always been my biggest supporter. His belief in my potential was stronger than anyone else's, including my own.

We sat around the living room telling jokes and stories, enjoying each other's company. I was surrounded by close friends and family, people with whom I'd gone through so much. We had all come a long way since our first forays into politics, so we were well accustomed to election night anxiety.

I didn't win my seat in the House of Commons in May 2011, the first time I ran, but I came within one percentage point and about five hundred votes, proving just how much our campaign meant to people. I knew that we'd built an incredible team. So later that year we picked ourselves up, shook off the loss, and made a historic victory in the same riding's provincial legislature. We unseated a fifteen-year incumbent and won the NDP its first-ever seat in Brampton East.

We didn't stop there. We held our seat in the next provincial general election, and over the course of six years, voters pushed me to fight against exorbitant car insurance premiums and the government's coziness with corporations. Together, we put an end to the Ontario police's carding practices, which so clearly targeted Indigenous people and people of colour. And we fought to finally call the Sikh genocide what it was. That push for justice got me banned from India, and when I put forward a bill for formal recognition of the genocide, it was rejected. But a month before I began my campaign for the federal party's leadership, a Liberal MPP put the bill back on the table. It passed, and the process of reconciliation for half a million Canadians took a bold step forward.

Compared to our past campaign, I personally didn't have as

much to lose this time. I was running with great leaders in our movement, so no matter what, the party of the people would be in good hands. The feeling inside the hotel living room was less stressful and more excited, buzzing with possibility. I'd continued to try to live by my promise—to represent all people—in the provincial legislature. I could feel the hair on the back of my neck stand up at the thought that I might have the chance to fight for all Canadians.

"It's just about time," said one of my friends. "Should we do a meditation first?"

All of us stood up and faced one of our friends, who led us in the meditation. My friend led the *Ardas*, a practice in which you reflect on those who came before and ask for the strength and wisdom to handle what will come next. She added her own powerful and moving words that brought almost all of us to tears. She asked that we find the courage and love to accept whatever happened that day. Then she ended with the final words of the *Ardas*, a reminder to connect with the one force, the universal energy to lift us with courageous optimism (*chardi kala*), and a request for universal well-being and the betterment of all (*sarbat da bhalla*).

We heard a knock on the door. It was my campaign manager, Michal Hay. "It's time to head down," she said. I put on my suit jacket, and we followed her into the elevator to the ballroom. The place was filled with a thousand party delegates and staff and volunteers.

I wished my fellow candidates good luck, greeted some friends and colleagues, and finally took my place in a seat between Michal and my parents. My brother and Gurkiran sat behind me.

Marit Stiles and Hans Marotte, the president and vice-president of Canada's NDP, approached the podium onstage to announce the results of the first round of voting. To win, a candidate had to receive more than 50 per cent of the 65,782 votes that had been cast. Marit and Hans proceeded in alphabetical order. Charlie Angus received a little over 12,000 votes. Niki Ashton was next, with just a little less than Charlie. I was too numb with excitement to understand what each number meant. Guy Caron was third, and his number of votes was read out.

I could sense the ripple of anticipation in the crowd. I reached back and grabbed Gurkiran's hand. At this point, my brother, father, and a number of others had figured it out. I still couldn't wrap my head around what was happening.

"Jagmeet Singh, number of votes," said Marit Stiles. "Thirty-five thousand—"

Before she finished, Gurratan and my dad jumped up in celebration. People in the audience screamed with joy, but my mother and I sat for an impossibly long moment, still processing that number—35,266—until it clicked. That was more than half of the total votes cast.

We'd won! I was now the leader of the NDP, following in the footsteps of Tom Mulcair, Tommy Douglas, David Lewis, Ed Broadbent, Audrey McLaughlin, Alexa McDonough, and Jack Layton. I suddenly remembered the day, during my first campaign, when Jack took me aside and said, "Never let them tell you it can't be done. It can be done." Those words echoed in my memory in that moment when, against the odds, we'd won.

I was flooded with hugs from friends, family, and supporters. As I climbed the stage steps, overwhelmed by love, I had to clear my eyes of tears. My squad crowded around me at the podium, and the purest feeling of gratitude rushed through me.

My brother grabbed my shoulder and leaned into my ear. "We did it," he said.

We had won, but our journey was far from over. On the road ahead, we would face many difficulties, but we would face them knowing one thing for certain: we are all in this together, because no matter what happens, we are all one.

ACKNOWLEDGEMENTS

I have to thank so many people. Of course, I will start with my family. I want to thank my mom and dad for having the courage to let me tell our story. Words alone cannot adequately thank them for the sacrifices and love they've bestowed on me over a lifetime.

I want to thank my brother, who went from being my student to my teacher. I raised him like a son, only to have him become my mentor. Thank you, Brother.

To my sister, thank you for a lifetime of support and for your limitless empathy and compassion.

To my life partner and wife, the writing of this book took me away a lot. You were a rock through it all. You supported me and helped me along the journey. Thank you.

I hope this came through clearly in the book, but I literally would not be here without the support of so many people, many of whom probably don't even know how much they helped. Thank you to my oldest friend—a teacher forced us to become friends but you chose to remain so. Thanks to the families who cooked for both my brother and me, and who probably didn't realize how much we depended on their help. Thank you to the friend to whom I first opened up a little about what I had gone through early in my life. In law school, a dear friend was there for me when I opened up in more detail about what I was going through, and that dear friend was the first to tell me it wasn't my fault. That friend witnessed some of my worst pain as it was happening. Thank you for being there.

Thank you to my uncle, who let my family stay with him when we didn't have anywhere else to go. Thank you to my other uncle who co-signed my mortgage when I didn't have anyone else who would. Thank you to my friend who helped me find a mortgage broker when I most needed one. Thanks to the mortgage broker who went above and beyond to help out a kid who he probably didn't know was almost down and out.

Thank you to Brentwood Rehabilitation, a publicly funded rehabilitation center that, in many ways, helped to save my family.

Thank you to Canada's health care system. When I blew out my ACL several years ago in a martial arts competition, a whole team of specialists and health care providers put me back together. My friends and family cared for me when I couldn't care for myself—thank you.

Thank you to my New Democratic family for your ongoing support and guidance.

Thank you to my publisher, Simon & Schuster Canada, for having faith in my story and for those people behind the scenes who guided me with editorial support and encouraged me to keep going.

Thank you to my friend at Skyrocket for coming up with the

Acknowledgements

concept of love and courage, and thank you to my friends at The Archery Club, for creating an amazing book cover.

This book is my small act of love and courage. Beyond sharing my experiences, I hope it helps those who have experienced challenges similar to the ones I've faced. You are not alone. You can ask for help. We are all one.

Thank you for giving me the honour of sharing my story with you.